J.0¢

ꙮPRAISE FOR COMING FORGIVENESSꙮ
A DAUGHTER'S STORY OF RACE, RAGE, AND RELIGION

Ronita Johnson's *Coming To Forgiveness* tells about growing up before and during the civil rights movement in Louisiana. She was a preacher's daughter held up as an example to the congregation by her charismatic father, who was an important man in his community. This is a poignant personal narrative, told with the painful truth of a girl that was thoughtful and observant, who didn't fit comfortably into any of the many worlds of color, culture, and class she had to bridge. But most of all, this is a story of a daughter failing the expectations of her father, and of herself, and going through a dark night of the soul, before finding her way back. *Coming To Forgiveness*, like Kathryn Stockett's *The Help*, brings to life the experiences of black people in the South during the civil rights movement and what it takes to heal with compassion and forgiveness.

> —Jean Shinoda Bolen, M.D, author of *Goddesses in Everywoman* and *Like a Tree*

At first glance you'll think this is a tale of an African American daughter of a southern preacher growing up, initially, in the south, and later in Northern California as the 60s were breaking out. This, in itself, makes for an absorbing read. However, it is more than that; this is a tale of deep healing and the power of forgiveness. It is told with fierce honesty, and courage, and is a source of empowering insight.

> —Justine Willis Toms, Co-founder, Managing Producer *New Dimensions Radio/Media*, author of *Small Pleasures: Finding Grace in a Chaotic World*, Inductee: Broadcaster's Hall of Fame, 2011

A humble portrayal of a life that dignifies the inherent wisdom of the human spirit. A must read for anyone doubting the transforming power of forgiveness.

> —Ruth King, emotional wisdom expert and author of *Healing Rage—Women Making Inner Peace Possible*

Coming to Forgiveness is an honest portrayal of Ronita Johnson's 50 year journey from victim to victor. Her humor, joyfulness and unquenchable spirit is a powerful testament to the potential we all have to heal from the woundings in our lives.

—MJ Ryan, author of *Attitude of Gratitude and Adaptability: How to Survive Change You Didn't Ask For*

The moment you open *Coming to Forgiveness*, its wisdom is clear. This is the wisdom of unconditional forgiveness, love and self-respect. Ultimately, Johnson has written a truly inspiring story of moving beyond the shame and fear that can hold us hostage, and of reclaiming one's life, one day at a time.

—L. Booth Sweeney, author of *Connected Wisdom*

Ronita Johnson's book is a great reckoning of the personal, political, and spiritual life. Nearly sisters in our age, her story breaks my heart over the different realities the accident of race and place can deal to little girls, and yet her search for self-hood is similar and universal. This story is a model and a map for growth, awareness, forgiveness, and purpose. Read it!

—Christina Baldwin is the author of *Life's Companion, Journal Writing as a Spiritual Practice, and Storycatcher, Making Sense of our Lives through the Power and Practice of Story*

A captivating description of what it was like to be a young African American girl growing up and living among the people and faces of racism in different regions of the United States in the 50's and 60's. Add to this, Ronita's experience as the daughter of a man whose love for her was distorted by his zealous passion for God and the church he serviced. The gift in it all? Many, but most amazing to me, the loving and talented woman that these experiences shaped and helped to create. You will feel pain, shock, respect, and admiration. Enjoy the read.

—Glenna Gerard, author of *Dialogue: Rediscover The Transforming Power Of Conversation*

We can be grateful that Ronita Johnson bravely nurtured her innate seeds of forgiveness into healing, living, leading, and writing, as we read her exceptional book, *Coming To Forgiveness – A Daughter's Story of Race, Rage and Religion*. She skillfully weaves the stark prose of her life struggles into the poetry of her transformation, lifting us into joy – both for her personal journey and for those who will be inspired by her courageous words.

—Joan Kenley, PhD, author of *Whose Body Is It Anyway? – Smart Alternative and Traditional Health Choices for Your Total Well-Being* and *Voice Power – A Breakthrough Method to Enhance Your Speaking Voice*

Ronita Johnson has written a book that is raw and revealing in its honesty. Betrayed and abused as a child, Ronita's story is that of a seeker who searches for love and ultimately finds it in her relationship with God. Ronita is a woman who has come through the fire and left behind a trail to help others find their own way. Her's is the quintessential archetypal journey where the seeker becomes the heroine. This is the story of Ronita Johnson's Heroine's Journey."

—Dr. Judith Rich, Transformational Therapist and Life Coach

Fifty years ago, after a painful family incident, Ronita Johnson vowed she would one day share her story with the world. This passionate, moving, beautifully crafted memoir is the tale it took her a lifetime of learning to tell. She describes her righteous anger as well as her journey to acceptance and forgiveness in a way that will enlighten and inspire readers.

—Elizabeth Fishel, author of *Sisters and Reunion*

This marvelous book is a wonder window that enables you to see the world through the eyes of a true keeper of the possible.

—Dawna Markova, Ph.D., author of *I Will Not Die an Unlived Life*, Co-Editor, *Random Acts of Kindness*

In this passionate and moving memoir, Ronita shares her journey to the farthest reaches of the human spirit....into the depths of despair and into the heart of healing and redemption. Her story is not only personal......it reaches into the essence of the societal questions around race and religion that shape our wounded world. I was deeply touched by this book and hope it finds a wide readership throughout our nation and the world.

—Juanita Brown Ph.D.
Co-Founder, The World Café.

COMING
TO
FORGIVENESS

A DAUGHTER'S STORY OF RACE, RAGE, AND RELIGION

Your guidance inspires me to dig deeper within. ♥ *Ronita*

RONITA JOHNSON

RJA

Ronita Johnson & Assoc.
Pleasant Hill, CA

Copyright © 2012 by Ronita Johnson
Coming To Forgiveness
A Daughter's Story of Race, Race and Religion

All names and many locations have been changed to protect the innocent, with
the exception of my immediate family, and: Brenda, Momretta, Miss Kennedy,
Mrs. Miles, Mrs. O'Neal, Dr. Gray, DOC, and Mrs. Wilson.

Printed in the United States
Cover and text design by Suzanne Nason, Twist Studio
Cover Photography by Jim Karogeorge

Printed in the United States

10 9 8 7 6 5 4 3 2 1

First Edition
ISBN 978-0-9848109-4-9

Coming To Forgiveness: a memoir/Ronita Johnson. — 1st ed.
1. Johnson, Ronita. 2. Johnson, Ronita — Family. 3. African American — women.
4. African American — Civil Rights. 5. Women. 6. Forgiveness — Self-Help. 7.
Forgiveness — Spirituality

Ronita Johnson & Associates
Publishing Company
Pleasanthill, CA 94523

If you are unable to order this book from your local bookseller, you may order
directly from the author by visiting www.comingtoforgiveness.com

Johnson, Ronita

DEDICATED TO MY FATHER

"In telling our truth we find forgiveness,
which leads to the freedom of our soul."

CONTENTS

PREFACE

I was fifteen and a half, but my body ached like I was ninety. I kept playing the day's horrid unfolding over and over in my mind as I looked up at the sky, searching for God. Where had he been? Why had he let this happen to me? I was a good girl.

My heart thumped with an intensity that made it difficult to breathe. Ice filled my veins but was no contest for the fire that pained my body. Tears flowed freely down my cheeks.

Suddenly, a thousand stars bumped against each other forming a jeweled crown on the night with one message:

One day I will tell my story.

ᚼTHE BLUE CURTAINᚼ

Four seasons of Spring had passed with few memories. Until that morning. The sound of sizzling bacon, synchronized with Dad's humming, filled the air. Rubbing my eyes, I squinted as the morning light burst through the tiny window in a spectrum of color. My crib stood in the open, tucked snugly between the kitchen counter and narrow wall of the single-bedroom apartment. Something was different!

The blue burlap fabric painted with red, yellow, and green flowers had appeared like a magician's dove, wrapping me in a cocoon. Yawning, I reached up and touched a red flower, believing it could fly away like dandelion fluff. Turning my head, I felt the blond curly hair and alabaster plastic skin next to my arm and greeted my closest companion, whose brown pupils were still.

"Good morning, Doris. Do you know who put this curtain here?"

Suddenly, Mom appeared. "Surprise! Now you've got your own privacy. Do you like it?" Mom asked.

"Uh-huh."

"Ronita, speak correct grammar. Look, I made a dress for Doris using the same fabric. Aren't you happy? Doris is happy."

"Uh-huh," I responded, as if a string had been pulled in the back of my head that released a set script. I looked at Doris. *I'm four; what's 'privacy'?*

Truth was, I had long outgrown the need for the protection of a baby bed. But our Hunters Point quarters in San Francisco left little choice. Where else would I sleep?

While contemplating Mom's surprise, Dad appeared, lifting me over the railing. "Time for breakfast."

From that day on, I was lifted over the railing and placed behind the blue curtain at the oddest times—right in the middle of tea parties, playing hopscotch, drawing pictures or watching "Woody Woodpecker." At night, I'd beg Mom, "Please leave the curtains open," suspicious of the strange sounds that came through the darkness. But it was the same answer every night as she pulled them shut.

"Be a good girl. Say your prayers. See you in the morning. Nighty night."

Sleep never came quickly because of the leaky faucet, Dad rustling through papers, and the humming of television. Plus, I hated sleep, certain I was missing the most important happenings of any day: being with people. The clock ticked loudly as I thrashed back and forth. So I'd whisper the alphabet in Doris's ears until the lights went out or my imaginary friends showed up. The horses would prance with gold tassels and the clowns would juggle bubbles that popped, then multiplied, as I muffled the laughter coming out of my mouth.

Bedtime always came too early when I heard a knock at the front door. Mom would say, "We're having company. Let's tuck in Doris and you both go right to sleep." Light drained too quickly when the curtain dropped, as she walked the few steps to the door. "Coming," and I would think, *Company; I love company.*

Leaning against the railing, I'd open one eye and then the other listening to the voices, but with the curtain, all I could make out were shadows. Seeing fat and thin silhouettes, I'd draw portraits, sure if I had the opportunity to be introduced like I was before the blue curtain, all the people would want to play with me. But Mom had warned me several times.

"When I close this curtain, do not open it."

"What if I have to pee?" I'd ask.

"Urinate; it's called urinate," she'd tell me.

Sometimes, I'd drink too much water and even though I called out in the night, nobody would answer. So I learned quickly. *Better hold my bladder and don't ever peek.*

I'd listen and listen, struggling to stay awake, determined to hear the last "Goodnight" out the front door. Instead, I'd conk out, my voice trailing off in Doris's ear.

"We must have done something to be hidden behind this curtain. We're like the animals at the zoo. But don't worry, Doris, one day we'll be free. I hate this blue curtain too."

Years later I would look back on how dominant a role the curtain would play in my life long after it disappeared. Most often, it held me hostage when I wanted freedom, but it also pushed me forward impulsively when I was afraid. Those years behind the curtain were ones when I just wanted to know the mechanics of life—how things worked and how they fit together. Behind the curtain I would constantly wonder, what would happen IF...?

Like the time I spontaneously placed green olive pits in both my nostrils. Or the time I stuck Mom's crochet needles in my ears. Somehow, whatever IF I wondered about either landed me in the emergency room or a huge scolding from my parents. I blamed the curtain for the mischief that followed when I was set free of it—the mischief that seemed to follow me wherever I went. On top of that, I never learned from my mistakes like most children my age did... never heard warning bells to tell me I was about to make another huge error in my ways. And yet, no matter the punishment, surprise, or hurt that my actions would earn me, my will would not be denied and would spring forth like a weed.

It seemed from my early days my destiny had been set. It spelled T-R-O-U-B-L-E.

ℭ FAMILY MIGRATION ℑ

The only reason we were in California in the first place was because our skin was the wrong color. Dad's family gave refuge and pumped hope into my parents' veins. Great Aunt Tea had gotten the fever first when a big oil tank exploded and destroyed her rental property outside of Houston, Texas. She and her husband took it as an omen, collected the insurance money, and headed straight for San Francisco, believing in the milk and honey stories for coloreds that had become legend. She set up house in Hunters Point and a week later was working on the assembly line at Maxwell House Coffee. The pay was decent and, most importantly, she was free of harassment. Once a month, she'd write home to her sister. As the family gathered around the kitchen table, it was so quiet, you could hear a pin drop; California was like a foreign country.

> Dear Orea,
>
> Herman and I are fine, but we miss all of the family back home. Can't get used to these tall buildings, the big park with wild geese and a wishing well right in the middle of town. The ocean reminds me of the times we spent in Galveston at the beach. Most days, it is cold and windy.
>
> We had a tremor the other day and I got on my knees and prayed real hard to Jesus hoping it wouldn't ever come back.
>
> These are some nice white folks. They talk with you like you got sense. I can sit anywhere I want on the bus and eat anywhere too. Y'all need to come on out here. You can stay with me as long as you want.
>
> God keep you safe and bless you.
>
> Your Sister, Tea

Six months later, hypnotized by the hope that stirred in her heart, Dad's older sister Lily Bell and husband Claude took off. His youngest sister Zemma Mae followed and within a year the five adults filled Tea's two-bedroom apartment. By the time Dad and Mom made the transition, Great Aunt Tea had sent for her kids, bought a Victorian home on Broderick Street, and signed over the apartment to Lily and Claude. It was May of 1948, and I was six months old.

Driven by promises of milk and honey, Mom and Dad got up early, stood in crowded lines, and filled out applications for jobs requiring college degrees. Their feet were blistered red and often they would go all day without eating. "We're going to make it," they kept saying to each other as days turned into weeks, then months, and applications were denied or never reviewed. Professional jobs existed all right, but so did discrimination. Worried about their dwindling savings and their pride, Mom finally took a job as a teacher's aide at the children's center where Aunt Zemma worked. It wasn't Mom's vision, but as she cashed her first check and placed the twenty-five dollars on the table, gratitude filled her heart.

Dad's search for a job ended two weeks later, when he became a coordinator for the city's recreational department. It wasn't white collar, but it fit his passion for stimulating the creative minds of young people. In no time, he lost himself developing the curriculum, managing basketball tournaments, checker matches, mask making, puppet shows, kite-flying contests, finger-painting exhibits, and excursions to the museum. Children of all ages flocked to the center, and Dad flourished.

ᏬHUNTERS POINTᏬ

W e lived in an all-colored community set on a parcel of hills made up of military barracks left over from the war. The gray, dormitory-style buildings were converted to one and two-bedroom living quarters to accommodate the migration of colored people. The air was clean and on Saturday mornings you would find men tipping their hats, women sweeping the sidewalks, babies napping in strollers, and children jumping rope or playing hide-and-go-seek. The landscape was filled with cement, except for patchy parcels of grassy hills sprouting wildflowers. You could look out on the bay and see the seagulls swooping down and ships with big letters on their sides floating on the water. Evenings were of blinding orange, yellow, and magenta or thick fog that made you shiver.

Mom would spend time with me working on my alphabet, correcting my grammar, sentence structure, and my counting. Dad read to me at night before I recited my prayers, "Now I lay me down to sleep..." and then lifted me over the railing.

It was a time of sweetness where Doris and I rolled down hills, I sat glued to television, Dad scared the neighborhood kids at Halloween with papier-mâché monsters lighting up the doorway, and Mom unbuttoned my wool coat on a cold day before making homemade soup.

Once a month on Saturday afternoon my extended family of about twenty would gather for picnics at Golden Gate Park, trips to the zoo, and the flower garden. Blankets were spread over green grass as tasty tuna sandwiches, fried chicken, potato salad, red soda pop, and pound cake were emptied from tins and wicker baskets.

Conversation started light and a sense of ease permeated the air. "This is a good life, hey Shaa," my aunt Lily would say. "Shaa" was a

Creole term, which replaced one's name and was used often in my family. Before I finished playing in the sandbox, my family would be slapping each other on the shoulder, kidding and joking about community and family affairs. Dad would stir up the hornet's nest, create controversy and then fold over laughing. But as the sun moved and the ants trailed across the blanket, a tense reality would form, reminding my family of a South they knew still existed.

"You hear the latest news about cousin Boone? He spoke up at work about the conditions, got beat up and fired. Can't even feed his family 'cause nobody will hire him."

"Ought to be glad they didn't kill him for speaking up," my uncle would say. "Why those white people make it so hard for us to love them like the good book says?" someone else would say. Silence would fill the air for a few moments as thoughts of down home fluttered like wings of a bird. I didn't know what to make of how the mood had shifted and grabbed Doris as someone would say again, "This is a good life, hey Shaa?"

MOM'S WAY OF LOVING

Mom appeared each morning, spreading the blue curtain wide open. "Wake up, sleepyhead, time to get up." My overalls lay neatly folded on the kitchen chair with my favorite pink sweater. Grabbing Mom's hand, we would walk the few steps to the bathroom. Hot steam filled the morning air, and I would giggle from the tickle under my arms as Mom wiped. She trained me well.

"Never, ever wear dirty underwear or socks, so if a car hits you, they will see how clean you are." I became obsessed with soap and water. I'd almost fall over, spreading my legs way too wide before looking up at the finger that wagged back and forth like a ticking clock with the warning that always came next.

"Don't ever let anybody touch your hot spot except Mommy."

After dressing she'd brush my hair one hundred times and part it right down the middle with pastel hair ribbons and barrettes, completing my preparation for looking pretty.

I learned from Mom it's better to have one good pair of shoes and three good dresses than lots of anything that is cheap. She purchased the most beautiful fabrics, carefully cutting out the pattern and pressing her foot to the pedal on the Singer as the thread looped through the hooks, "nun-nun-nun-nun" into the wee hours of the night. I couldn't sleep, but I knew something special was coming with tiny pearl buttons or lace appliqué sprinkled around the collar and down the front. I loved looking pretty!

I'm not sure where Mom learned about loving me. All I know is she took pride in everything—the direction of the forks and knives, the exact level of how the towels were hung, where the milk was placed on the left and the butter on the right. Her day began early with precision and she stopped only to gift herself with one pleasure—a cup of coffee. She knew just what spices and herbs were necessary to turn the most ordinary meal into something that made my lips go "Smack." "Putting the big pot in the little pot," my family called it. One thing was certain; she lived up to the motto passed forward by her mother: "Keep your house orderly and clean. Mind your child and be a good wife."

There were times, though, when I would have gone dirty, hastily eaten crackers all over me and dressed in shabby clothes just to have her touch. Just to have her place my little head in her lap while stroking my locks with her soft hands. I imagined the warmth of her body next to mine in an embrace for no other reason than I was her baby. Something I never figured out was what held her back from hugging, cuddling, and caressing me the way I did with Doris. I guess she just wasn't made that way.

As I grew up, a longing in me intensified and wouldn't go away, especially as I noticed other mommies. She and I formed an uneasy bond as a result and I came to lean on Dad for hugs and kisses. He'd pick me up with his large pink hands, rubbing his unshaved face all over mine, whispering "I love you" and squeezing me so tight, I could hardly breathe. Sometimes, I'd fall asleep listening to the beat of his heart, knowing the two of us were forever intertwined. My heart lingered right there; taking root and sprouting, growing deeper and stronger with each thump until I was completely captivated by Dad's love, knowing for the rest of my life, that's where my heart would stay.

SPOTLIGHT

I paid attention as people pinched my cheeks, patted my head, and stood back with silly grins on their faces. "Aren't you adorable." It was acknowledgment enough to fuel Mom's enthusiasm for keeping me dressed like a porcelain doll. Feeling special came easy as the only child on both sides of the family, especially with the closet stuffed with patent-leather shoes, pedal pushers, hair ribbons, clothes for Doris, furry animals, puzzles and books. I passed from one lap to another, my relatives eagerly offering ice cream, rides across the Bay Bridge, trips to the park, or my favorite homemade chili.

At family gatherings, conversations would cause my head to oscillate like a fan as I listened to every opinion, every joke. I noticed how hands flapped up, then down, and voices got loud, then soft. Sometimes, it was hard to follow with everybody talking over everybody else. But I would try my best to keep up, as my favorite aunt

Lily Bell, whom we called Bea, would hug me in her lap. "What say you, Shaa?"

I'd attempt to express myself, putting my hands on my hips and causing everybody to break out with laughter. Aunt Bea would look at her brother with admiration. "She's just like you. Not afraid of anything. Got something to say about everything."

Dad would laugh too, then throw me over his broad shoulders and push me up high until I got dizzy. I never complained. Then, after Dad felt I'd had enough attention, he'd deepen his voice, playfully scolding my relatives.

"Don't encourage her to be a clown."

I would land on my feet as Dad invited me to recite something. It was a game, a sort of test I learned early about not being thrown off-guard. "Stand up straight now, and look at me," he urged. I would repeat a nursery rhyme and Dad would applaud and lift me again to the heavens.

There was just something about his *way*, while holding his hand, sitting on his lap or simply glancing at his face, that made me feel safe and certain there was nothing I couldn't do. And at night behind the curtain, sure he was right about everything, I would shake my finger at Doris and imitate him. "Stand up straight and look me in the eyes."

WHAT'S CUSH?

I was the only colored girl in my kindergarten class when the local television station selected our school for a series on young homemakers.

Mom said, "You can wear your Sunday dress, but don't get it

dirty." I wanted to look pretty too, but wondered, *How will I keep clean? We're making bread.* Before we started, the teacher gave us instructions. "Now look at me and follow whatever I do, children." I proudly put on my little red apron, filled with images of becoming the next Princess Summerfall Winterspring on "Howdy Doody." I'd never made bread before, but had watched Mom mixing and stirring and figured, *It can't be that hard.* The reporter walked in briskly. His navy-blue suit, starched white shirt, and black tie were immaculate.

There were two rows of parallel tables with spaces for the six of us. Newspaper covered the floor. The reporter pulled out a notepad as the teacher cleared her voice.

"Get behind the table and get your bowls, children." I tried to remember all Mom's instructions: "Speak clearly, don't slump, and look straight at the reporter."

"Place the water in the bowl and sprinkle the yeast over the water," the teacher said.

"Combine the flour and sugar and mix everything together."

I poured out too much flour and the mixture got all bubbly and started to form hard lumps, causing me to grunt as I put all my strength into mixing with the wooden spoon. The reporter leaned down and started talking real slow, like we were all retarded.

"What's your name? How old are you? What did you have for breakfast? What do you want to be when you grow up?"

Alice covered her face with her hands, "I ate eggs, bacon, toast, and milk," and "Huh, I dunno," she said.

"And how old are you," he repeated, as Alice hid her face in her apron before saying, "Five."

The reporter moved on to Sarah. "I'm over five and I'm going to be a doctor and we had pancakes with butter and syrup and a big glass of Hershey's chocolate milk," she spoke up, sticking her tongue through the big gap where her tooth used to be.

Suddenly Jimmy, the only boy, interrupted her loudly and pointed at his chest. "I'm five, going to get me a horse, be a cowboy and I had a big bowl of cornflakes and milk," and then he pulled out his imaginary gun and shot the reporter.

By this time I was covered in dough, propping my arm up at the elbow with my other hand, continuing to shake it high in the air, wondering, *Doesn't he see me?* He looked slightly in my direction and my mouth took off.

"My name's Ronita and we had cush. I'm going to be an actress when I grow up and I'm almost five," looking right in his face. The reporter was about to turn and then he stopped. "What's cush?" And just then, I looked up to see Mom standing at the door.

I never knew where the name "cush" came from. All I knew was it was my favorite breakfast.

"You get a bowl and fill it with yellow stuff and white stuff. Then you put in an egg, some milk, some sugar and salt." I was talking fast, enjoying the spotlight and knowing Mom and Dad would be so proud. The reporter's expression didn't change as he scribbled.

"Then you get a big black pot and put this much grease." I showed him the amount with my hands. "When the grease is hot, you pour everything in the pot and stir it up."

Dad did this with his eyes closed, as the mixture would crackle and pop, and bubbles rose all around the edges like the hot sun fired by a black night. It created the most wonderful smell in my nostrils.

"Then you take a big spoon and turn it over until it's black," I continued, looking straight at the reporter. The oil would soak into the mixture and then break into hundreds of little pieces.

"And then I get a big bowl of the cush with milk and sugar." The oil would just float in the milk. "I always ask for more and lick the bowl to the very last drop." The reporter turned up his mouth, as the other kids went "Ewww."

"It's good; really, really good," I shared, but I could see by the look on everybody's face that nobody believed me.

"Now knead the bread," the teacher said, trying to refocus our attention, because everyone was distracted by my old family recipe. I looked over expecting to see Mom beaming with pride. I had done everything she said. But she wasn't smiling.

Mom held my hand a lot tighter and stared at me sternly as we walked to the bus stop, alerting me before she spoke that she wasn't proud of me at all. In fact, quite the contrary.

"Sometimes people don't understand our ways and have judgments about how we live. You have to learn when to talk and when to be quiet. We live in a world that isn't always kind or fair. We're different."

I didn't know what she was talking about, but I wondered if it had anything to do with not being picked to hold the pink ribbon to go around the Maypole with the other kids at school.

That night on the black-and-white television screen the report came on and there I was, smiling. The phone jingled and Mom said "Ssssh" to Aunt Bea, trying to listen as Sarah and Jimmy got to say "doctor" and "cowboy." And then it was over! I pulled on Dad's sleeve. "Why didn't they let me talk?"

There was really no answer. Except that it was 1952.

⚞SHATTERED INNOCENCE⚟

I t was months into my fifth year, while rolling in the tall grass be-hind our complex, that Mom called out to me.

"Aunt Bea's sick. You're staying with Mrs. Daniels today. Now you be a good girl and take your nap."

Mrs. Daniels was our upstairs neighbor and took in laundry for a living. On the few occasions that Mom left me with her, I always napped in her bed, while her younger son took a nap in his own bed that he shared with his fourteen-year-old brother, Horace. I'd lay there in my undershirt and panties, with Doris under my arm until I fell asleep. I dreamed a lot about making friends with cloud people and rainbows and would wake up wondering, *Was that real?*

That day, the dream was different. I smelled PineSol and felt an oppressive weight on my tiny body. I couldn't move and I didn't see Doris. My panties were missing too. I slept on my side or my stomach, but in the dream I was looking up at the ceiling. I felt a pain and heard Mom's words,

"Never let anyone touch your hot spot."

It was drilled in my brain as an absolute no-no and I wanted to wake up, confused about what was going on. This dream felt too real.

Drowsy, I opened my eyes and saw Horace on top of me. He looked funny, panting with his mouth open and his tongue hanging out. As soon as he noticed me looking at him, he covered my mouth with his hand. I tried to move again. I started squirming and kicking, but his weight kept me pinned down. Tears streamed from my eyes as I struggled, trying to get free. The more I struggled, the more he dug in, causing the pain to intensify. I tried to scream, but his hand was firmly planted. *This is wrong*, I kept saying to myself. *It hurts!* But I was helpless.

"Now I lay me down to sleep, I pray the Lord my soul to keep," I kept repeating to myself. Then Horace moved once more. He looked down at me and said, "You'd better not tell or I'll do it to you again."

Tears stained my face; I didn't know what to do. After Horace left, I laid there quietly, hoping he wouldn't come back. *What just happened?* "Never let anyone touch your hot spot" echoed like a scratched record in my ear. An unrecognizable feeling swept over me that said, *You just did something very bad.* I kept blinking and placing my hands over my ears, wanting to blot out the words and still hoping that it was all a bad dream as my eyes searched for the comfort of Doris. My hot spot burned, but I was too afraid to touch myself. I fumbled with my panties, as if dressing for the first time. The voice kept whispering, *You just did something very bad.*

I slowly dressed and came out, just in time to find Mrs. Daniels walking through the front door with groceries. "I was just coming to wake you up, child," she said. Horace stared at me with piercing dark eyes. "You'd better not tell," they said. I didn't.

By the time Mom appeared at the door I had fallen into silence, shaken and searching within myself to understand. *Why did Horace do that?*

I knew the bad thing that had just taken place could happen again; Horace lived upstairs. It was one of the few times I found peace behind the blue curtain as I prayed. "I'm sorry, Jesus, for being a naughty girl." I wasn't exactly sure what I had done wrong, but I couldn't shake the nagging feeling. *You—Are—Bad!* I tossed and turned, placing my hands over my ears—unable to get the words out of my head until a voice spoke to me: *Secret; you must keep this a secret.* And just like that, something new and insidious split me in half through my center. It would become the place where I stood divided—one foot in guilt and shame, trapped in pain and keeping secrets to survive. The other foot in wonder and play, exploring adventure and trusting my own instincts. My existence hung in this delicate balance. But because I had lost the ability to rely solely on my instincts, I found myself always off-balance.

⟨BEING CALLED⟩

In the early Summer of 1953, when I was almost six, I finally asked Mom, "What does 'being called' mean?" Those were the words I kept hearing, over and over through the blue curtain. Mom looked as if she had been silently asking herself the same question.

"You know your teacher at school? Your father will be like her, except he will teach about Jesus so we will all go to heaven. You know all about heaven?" I bobbed my head up and down, hoping Jesus would still let me go to heaven after what Horace had done to me.

We always went to church and sometimes I'd get to play hide-and-seek or find the treasure with the other children in the tall bushes. I liked games with playmates and thought Dad's being called sounded like fun. The only thing was Dad had gotten quieter and looked more serious, thumbing through a maroon leather book with red trim that said HOLY BIBLE. Plus, we weren't giggling as much. I missed our visits to Playland-at-the-Beach to see Laffing Sal chuckling, playing in the bumper cars, and licking chocolate ice cream cones. I missed picnics at Golden Gate Park and piggyback rides. Now, on Friday nights, I hardly ever heard the jingle talking about Pabst Blue Ribbon beer or the referee say, "Break it up."

Dad was gone a lot more, too. "Church meetings," Mom always said. I'd hear him when he returned home, dropping one shoe and then the other before getting a glass of water. I'd lie real still listening to the drip-drip and my heartbeat before Mom would call out, "Turn off the faucet." They didn't know how many nights I lay there listening to that sound.

That night, I was wide awake, talking with Doris about Dad's being called, when whoosh, the curtain flew open. Doris and I played dead. We could feel Dad's breath as he bent down and smoothed the hair off my face and kissed me on the cheek. I wanted to grab his neck, but I was supposed to be asleep long ago. After he closed the curtain, I whispered to Doris, "Fooled Dad again!"

He started talking out loud, "Lord, I am ready to do your will and be your humble servant." I wondered, *Who is Dad talking to?*

A month before I was to begin first grade, a strange man showed up one evening at our apartment. He kept looking at Dad, then Mom, then me, as he sipped his coffee and munched on Mom's sugar cookies. All the while they were talking, I stared at the strange man's hand, noticing his index and middle finger were missing. I wanted to ask him, "Does that hurt?" but didn't dare, still trying to figure out why Mom hadn't sent me behind the curtain.

Suddenly, like old times, Dad patted his lap. "Come and sit with me," and I jumped up, balancing myself on his knee. I just wanted to stay up late, have another cookie, and see the man's fingers up close. At the first pause, I asked the man, "Do you want to meet Doris?" I jumped up to get her and stepped over the man's feet.

Dad's hand grabbed my tiny arm, shook me back and forth, and came down hard on my rear end.

"How dare you not say excuse me! You never walk over some-one's feet. Now apologize, and don't you cry."

My lips quivered as the words tumbled forward. "Excuse me, sir, I'm sorry."

Dad's eyes softened, like nothing had happened. "Forgive my daughter, she's just excited. My wife and I have talked it over and the answer is yes."

The man stood. "God bless you," he said. "You'll never regret this decision." I slumped against the sofa. *What just happened?*

That night, lying behind the blue curtain, I struggled with my tender sense of who I was. It was as hard to understand as that inci-dent with Horace. *What did I do?* Dad's hand had struck with such a precise sting that I couldn't stop sniffling and my face felt hot. Not saying "excuse me" hardly seemed a reason for such a shift in Dad's behavior. And when the strange man left, all that was said was "Go to bed." Bruised by Dad's gruffness, I started a bad habit of biting my fingernails and twirling my hair. It calmed me, and I looked Doris right in the face. "I don't like Daddy being called." It turned out the man was a presiding elder and had recruited Dad to pastor his first church in Minden, Louisiana. "It's an honor," Mom kept saying. Dad had driven us down South before, but I didn't remember it. All I knew was Louisiana sounded a long way from home. The only good thing was I'd never be threatened by Horace again.

My right front tooth fell out just before we left for Minden. In addition to the quarter left under my pillow, I got one wish to go anywhere I wanted. Hands-down for my favorite place in the world, Playland-at-the Beach, where foghorns sounded in the distance, seals hunted for fish, and I made sandcastles and ran after tiny waves in the ocean.

Red candy apples and pink popcorn stuck to my fingers as I rode the twister, the merry-go-round, and the Ferris wheel. Dad stood close by as we moved in the mirror maze and squeezed through the spin dryers of the fun house. Then we stopped and stared into the second-floor window where Laffing Sal towered forty feet over me with her red hair, freckles, and a floppy black hat while I peeked out between Dad's legs. Little did I know she would reinforce the symbolism of the blue curtain, my journey of straddling the fence of life—horrifying fear and abandoned joy wrapped up in my world as Dad's daughter.

A few days later, steam blurred my vision as Mom, Doris, and I waved goodbye to Dad through the big window of the choo-choo train. I kept asking Mom, "Why can't we drive with Dad?" But she just said, "We're going to see your grandparents first. We'll meet up with your father in Minden."

Gusts from the train doors blew excitement into my face each time the conductor announced, "All aboard." I squeezed Doris, and continued to pester the good-looking man in a soldier's uniform who had gotten on the train in Los Angeles and sat across from us. I kept pulling on his sleeve and informed him, "We're going to live in Loosanna."

MOTHER DEAR AND BUD

When it came to my grandparents, sketchy stories abounded about my father's African heritage. My great-great-great-grandmothers had been handpicked to give pleasure and bear children by the white English masters. Ensuing generations were so fair-skinned that noticeable signs of African genes had almost disappeared, except for the broad nostrils on my grandmother's side.

Folks in the city of Abbeville called her Miss Orea, but in family circles she was called Mother Dear. She stood five feet tall with a tiny waist, shapely legs, and size 52HHH bosoms. She combed her thinning hair into a bun, wore a chignon and very little makeup except for white powder that she applied with a red sponge puff. She had the first and last words to say about most things and would strut around town like a seven-foot gazelle. A teacher by trade, she taught music and occasionally played hymns at Sunday morning service.

Mother Dear was obsessed by appearances and on Saturdays would prance down the sidewalk until she arrived at her favorite shoe store. She'd waltz through the door smelling like freshly bloomed honeysuckle.

"Mr. Petty, I love the new selection of shoes in your display. Got them in red?" Next thing you know she'd be slipping her size-six foot into every pair, adding to her collection of shoes in every style and color.

She loved bright, shiny, exquisite things she couldn't afford—braided mahogany furniture, crystal chandeliers, dainty porcelain figurines, gold-plated cups and saucers, silver tea sets, lace spreads and frilly drapes. She was the queen of layaway, caught in a cycle of paying off one item and placing another item on hold. Nobody knew for sure what went through her head, but one thing was certain—money was always tight, because any that could have been saved for a rainy day was used up well in advance. "God will make a way" became her slogan.

My grandfather, Bud, was a good-looking, kind soul. He never spoke a harsh word and was too soft-spoken to even think about going toe to toe with his wife's mouth or her temper. His daily existence was to come home after a hard day pressing clothes in the back room of the cleaner's, sit down and take off his black shoes. They looked funny because he would take a razor blade and cut tiny slits in the front part where his toes rested, in order to let them breathe in the stifling hot air of the pressing room. Each day when he returned home, he would place them neatly under the rocking chair on the back porch, then take out two cigarettes and smoke them in solitude until he was called to dinner.

Bud would eat in silence, while his wife and children chatted on and on about whatever was on their minds. Every now and then, he would grunt or say "yep" to acknowledge a question. And then after dinner, he would go back to the rocking chair, take out two more cigarettes and smoke them while the day turned into night. He would go to bed early and start his day all over again with the same routine, never missing work.

His only indulgence occurred on Saturday evenings after he got home from work. He'd put on a clean white shirt and a freshly pressed pair of pants, grab a short bottle of homemade whiskey he kept under the porch, and walk two blocks down to the corner store. This is where all the guys hung out, playing checkers and dominoes, and some of those single party ladies were there too. But Bud knew better than to even look in their direction, as Mother Dear had spies all over the place who'd just love to whip up a good story. With his droopy eyes, he took his time concentrating on the checkerboard as if his fortune were wrapped up in making the right move. You couldn't tell by looking what Bud was thinking, because he neither smiled nor frowned. He had the same look on his face day after day, as if reconciled to believing the cards life had dealt were neither good nor bad.

ᏊᎡOBERT᠑

Dad was sandwiched two years apart between Lily Bell and Zemma Mae. Tall and lanky as a kid, he ate anything you put in front of him and spent his time devouring books, chasing jackrabbits, frogs, and possums or sitting by the fire listening to stories his mother made up on the spot. By age ten, he had become famous for scaring his sisters and anybody else who cared to listen to ghost stories while walking with him in the woods. He was raised with Mother Dear's schoolhouse motto, "Spare the rod and spoil the child," and after a few samples of her switch, got frightened at the very thought of disobedience.

In 1932, at age eleven, his childhood days ended without notice when his grandmother suffered a severe stroke and moved in with the family. Gradually, Mother Dear passed the daily responsibility of bathing, feeding, washing bedsores, and cleaning dirty linen to her son. He kept up his grades, but hurrying home every day cut deep into time for developing boyhood friendships. He suffered within, but knew better than to complain, choosing instead to pull harmless pranks on his sisters. It became his way of coping with life.

Mother Dear's spending habits eventually forced her to take up sewing. She would pull apart Lily Bell and Zemma's pantaloons, blouses, and skirts and make floral-print shirts and pants for her son. The kids at school would call him "sissy," but he never retaliated. Instead, he would repeat the Bible verses he learned from his grandmother about turning the other cheek. The words brought him such comfort that reading the Bible became a favorite pastime, even after his grandmother had long fallen asleep.

Dad had memorized all sixty-six books of the Bible by the time he stood at his grandmother's gravesite. Throwing red dirt over the lowered casket, he remembered her words. "Never forget the passages; especially the words spoken by Jesus. When you're in trouble get on your knees. Ask Him to help you and He will."

Accepted into Leland, a reputable religious Negro college in Southern Louisiana, Dad left home in September 1937, with one suitcase. He had turned sixteen on July 2. He carried a toothbrush, comb, baking soda, hair grease, a sweater, two homemade pairs of pants, a shirt, two sets of underwear, a pair of shoes and socks, and his grandmother's Bible in his secondhand suitcase. In later years, he would crack jokes about himself.

"I looked like a scared bird standing on the corner, waiting for the bus. My legs were so bony sticking out of those trousers. And Lord have mercy, that pink shirt." Turned out Mother Dear had unintentionally washed his best shirt with something red.

That day his biggest flood of warmth had come from Bud, who surprised him with a package wrapped in brown paper.

"Don't open this up, boy, till you get where you're going. I love you, Son, you take care."

As the bus turned the corner to his final stop, he carefully unwrapped the brown paper. His heart soared as he glanced down at the trousers, one black, the other brown, two white linen shirts, a multicolored bowtie, and a stylish, light-brown wool jacket, all practically new. It strengthened his faith in the power of prayer as he had asked God, "Please make a way for me to receive some real college clothes."

Burning the midnight oil, he plunged into his studies with vigor, never forgetting his mother's words: "A degree is your only ticket to success." He was hungry for peer conversation and joined the glee club where his smooth tenor voice made him popular with the girls. He was unaccustomed to being with anybody but his sisters, but his confidence grew with each new choir rendition. He joined the orator's club and excelled at reciting poetry and the words of famous authors.

One day he drifted into the auditorium where students were auditioning for the annual spring musical. Dad got the lead part. However, fate had other plans. Costumes were required and extra activities cost money. Having to decline playing the part only deepened his conviction: "There is nothing standing in the way of my dreams. All I have to do is make up my mind because with Jesus by my side, I can do anything!"

By the Winter of his sophomore year, he had decided to major in education and eagerly tore into the letter from his mother when it arrived—tuition was due. "There have been some unexpected circumstances and the money has run out. You must come home."

Fearful someone was ill and knowing firsthand the expense of doctors' bills, he packed his bag and hurried home. Fear turned to resentment as his eyes settled on the shiny new Buick parked on the lawn. He knew his mother's logic all too well as he braced himself for her explanation of the deal too good to pass up.

"Son, people see you on the outside before they know you on the inside. It's our job to make people comfortable with what they see, so they believe and accept we're good colored people, good as everybody else. And sometimes we have to sacrifice our own desires for others."

The translation was that Mother Dear bought a new car every two years and sending Lily Bell to college had cut into her purchasing powers. Dad's college fund was the sacrifice and although he loved his mother, all he could think of was how he had been betrayed.

Articulate, clean-cut, and handsome, he had no trouble getting employment at the local movie theater selling snacks and performing odd jobs. For the next year he saved every dime, determined to tuck away his dreams of making a difference in the world until he had enough to return to college. He marched across the stage clutching his college diploma in 1942. He had accomplished his goal and owed no one but God.

By July, he was on his way to boot camp and two years in the United States Army. His last request before waving goodbye to his sister Zemma, a sophomore in college, was "Find me a wife."

WALTER AND MARY LOU

Mom's roots could be traced to eight generations of Footes beginning in the late 1700s. Her father's descendants came from Canada and England and her mother's from France, Canada, and Native Atakapas Indians. Both were mixed with slaves.

My grandfather, Walter, lived on a three-block stretch of houses that belonged to his ten brothers and sisters, some of the first contractors, educators, and entrepreneurs in Lafayette, Louisiana. Walter wasn't a college man, but found his way as a trustworthy supply clerk for Southern Pacific Railroad. With no debt and a good salary, he invested in real estate, building shotgun houses in response to the demand of rural colored people moving to the city. It made him a shrewd, street-smart businessman who didn't have to ask anybody for anything—a value he cherished like a rare stamp. He was a stern, solitary man, prone to keeping information behind lock and key; a man dominated by his own opinion and unaffected by human frailties.

Walter's wife, Mary Lou, went about her existence as a meek homemaker, her only goal, seemingly, to make everybody else happy. Life was a routine of being available for her husband's simplest wish, cooking fresh hot meals, cleaning, sewing, and tending to their five offspring.

JUANITA

Mom was the second of four girls. Brown-skinned with long, thick hair, she was born with a strong will and sense of possessing whatever she felt rightfully belonged to her. She'd rival with her older sister Dorothy for their father's attention and approval, competing for grades and accomplishing acts of charity around the community.

In a family of five kids, recognition didn't come easy, and Mom was always trying to figure out how she could shine. Joining the new high-school band with her cousins seemed like an excellent option, and so she didn't think anything of it to ask her father for uniform money. He snapped, "That's plain foolishness." Next thing he knew, she was working for his older sister, Ida.

Aunt Ida was a woman before her time—flying to New York as the buyer of her own dress shop, restaurant and jazz club owner, and one of the city's first colored health inspectors. Ida liked Mom's spunk and offered her a job in her shop for as long as she wanted.

Receiving a salary at such a young age gave Mom the freedom to do as she pleased and instilled in her the value of hard work and saving money. As she marched past her father in her new band uniform with her new trombone, she held her head up high, swearing she'd never ask him for anything other than her college tuition. That was pretty much how her life moved forward from then on.

Mom learned the cues of dating as a third wheel with her older sister and girl cousins. However, no matter how much fun she had dancing at her Aunt Ida's juke joint, Sunday morning was always reserved for Sunday school. She eventually decided working with children was what she wanted to do with her life.

With excellent grades and glowing letters of recommendation, Mom prepared to enter Southern University in Baton Rouge in 1940. Her father had promised to support her financially, as he had her older sister Dorothy. But during the first week of August, all her dreams came crashing down. She arrived home to find Walter in bed with a fever. The news was grave. The years of long, cold nights on the railroad had compromised his lungs; an acute form of pneumonia had developed. The only cure was extended bed rest and no work.

Walter broke the news harshly. "We need your college money to support the family." It was the only time Mom disrespected her dad, raising her voice, "It's not fair!" before fleeing to her room, tears overflowing.

Walter watched every dime and barely gave enough money to his wife to clothe and feed the family. Mary Lou never complained and even seemed to appreciate her husband's work ethic, but she spoke up that day and offered to get a job. Walter was sick, but he was firm. "No wife of mine is going to work. Who is going to stay home and take care of me?" Meanwhile, Mom wasted no time reconstructing her dream. She became a clerk at one of the department stores and by the end of one year had saved enough to attend weekend classes in town at Southern University extension.

It was a time of war, and schools were desperate for teachers. With one year of college and letters of recommendation from her professors, Mom was hired as an elementary substitute teacher in Vermillion Parish. Taking a cue from her dad, she spent only what was necessary, while she dreamed of attending college full-time, leading to a life of independence. By 1942 at age 20, Mom entered the summer session as a junior at Southern University. It would change her life.

EGGS IN ONE BASKET

Zemma had taken her job of wife-hunting seriously. The first few weeks of summer school, she observed Juanita always raising her hand in class and one day just walked up to her and said, "I want you to meet my brother." Juanita blushed. "I've already got a boy-friend," but Zemma insisted, "You can have two." The girls became instant friends and before long, Juanita had given Zemma permission to send her picture to Robert.

He placed her picture under his pillow. *My good luck charm*, he thought. He spent hours dreaming, looking at her face: large almond eyes, perfect teeth, high cheekbones, a charming smile, flawless caramel complexion, and hair falling down her back. *She's the most beautiful girl I've ever seen.* Letters began crossing the Atlantic immediately:

> Ma Cherie Juanita,
>
> You sure are pretty.
>
> I hope you can come to this city one day. It's filled with an air that is so different from America—blocks

of art galleries, smoke-filled sidewalk cafes, cheese and wine with every meal, hot summers and snowy winters, and melancholy love songs. I love looking at Notre Dame and the Eiffel Tower. The people don't seem to care what race I am and I've learned a little French.

It's a hard war we're fighting. Every day we come face to face with the enemy, bullets flying over my head, whistling through the air. I shoot back never knowing where they land or if I have taken a life. It bothers me, and I ask God to forgive me if I killed anybody, but it's war.

In a way I'm a hero; saved my buddy from a bullet, but got scrap metal in my left leg. With all that blood I thought something serious had happened to me. But the doctor fixed me right up and said there won't be any permanent damage. The segregation is as bad as the war—being called names, shivering on latrine duty and having to stay clear of loose bullets. We have eyes in the backs of our heads because every week a colored soldier gets shot.

You sure are pretty. When this war is over the first thing I'm going to do is march straight to your house. Affectionately, Robert

When the first letter arrived, Juanita tossed it aside casually—by the third, she found herself fascinated by his stories and the pretty stationery. She started watching for the postman, carefully tearing open the envelope the very last thing before she went to bed, dreaming about the adventures, and hoping that he would keep himself safe.

But Juanita hadn't been totally honest with Zemma. She had more than a boyfriend. Even though an engagement ring had not been exchanged, a medical student named Andrew was her fiancé. For three years, the two of them had spoken about making a life together and getting married upon his graduation in 1947. Andrew's grueling schedule had left Juanita idle time to innocently entertain having a friend like Robert in a faraway country. *It will help the time go by fast*, she thought. But as the letters continued over the months, she found herself having feelings for someone she'd never met.

One Sunday afternoon after the family had returned from church Juanita heard a knock on the door. She peeked out and saw Zemma standing next to a bright-eyed young man. "Surprise!" they both blurted out, as she opened the door in shock. Robert stepped forward with a warm handshake and then hugged her like they had known each other forever. Juanita felt weak in her knees as he embraced her and could hardly speak, as she stepped back to meet his stance: six feet tall, wavy hair, twinkle in his eye, and polished from head to toe. She quickly introduced Zemma and her brother to Mary Lou. It was the beginning of Robert driving the twenty-eight country miles from Abbeville to Lafayette every Saturday or Sunday, for he had made up his mind. *Juanita is the girl of my dreams. I'm going to make her my wife!*

Juanita had come to believe in the saying, "Don't put all your eggs in one basket" and thought nothing of saying "Yes" to Andrew when he came home for Christmas break. His second evening home, the situation got tense, as an unscheduled Robert knocked on the door to find Andrew sitting comfortably in Juanita's living room. There was no choice but to invite him in. At first the three of them sat eating pecan pie, listening to each other swallow, and staring awkwardly at the clock. As the last piece of pie was eaten the two young men began lavishing Juanita with small talk, trying to outdo each other with clever conversation. Andrew's focus on cutting open cadavers was no match for Robert. His war stories, sweetened with "permettez-moi de vous dire, vous devriez voir," and "Je tiens à vous tenir," curled

Juanita's toes. She wasn't sure what he was saying, but she was captivated. Andrew looked on in disbelief.

Neither of her callers budged that night and finally, after her father walked through the room for the fourth time, Juanita stood up.
"It's getting late," which was enough for both suitors to stand, almost
bumping into each other as they leaned over to kiss her goodnight
on the cheek. As she stood at the door waving goodbye, she thought
to herself, *This is crazy, I've got to make a decision.*

Juanita was left alone with her thoughts as Andrew returned to
medical school and Robert entered Denver University to begin work
on his Master's degree. Robert knew his competition was fierce. He
began writing every day, telling himself, *I can't lose her.* On March 1,
he made his move.

> Ma Cherie Juanita,
>
> > Je t'aime. I love you. I want to live life
> > with you by my side each day. Let us
> > dream together and be together. Je t'aime.
> > Veux-tu m'épouser? I love you. Will you
> > marry me?
> > Eternally, Robert

It was enough to cause a mighty disturbance in Juanita, who desperately wanted to make the best decision and knew she would be
well provided for as a doctor's wife. But she had to admit; there was
something alluring about Robert's way that made financial certainty
less important.

Mary Lou helped her daughter to decide. "Robert is kind and
thoughtful. He makes time to talk with your Dad and me and is a
good listener. I believe he will make you a good husband and be a
good father."

What Juanita didn't know was Robert had used a strategy he
learned in the military and from his own life—cover all your bases.

He had approached Walter and Mary Lou without Juanita's permission, asking right out for her hand in marriage. Walter was happy to have one less girl to worry about, and Mary Lou just plain liked Robert. Andrew never knew what he did wrong, and it was rumored that he never got over the news of Juanita's betrayal.

My parents became engaged by mail. The church wedding was set for August 31, 1946, Juanita's birthday.

They both plunged into action. Robert, eager to impress his wife-to-be, applied for every principal position in the state, hopeful he could support his bride in style. Finishing his Master's would have to wait!

The last touches of a large church wedding were nearly complete the day Robert received the letter. "You've been accepted as principal at the Rosen Wahl Elementary School. We need you by August 17." Juanita was disappointed that she had to rearrange her lavish wedding, but rearrange she did as sixty family members squeezed into the family home on August 14 to celebrate their union. As she kissed him for the first time as his wife, she hoped she had made the right choice.

⬧TILL DEATH DO US PART⬧

Dad and Mom settled in Madisonville, a small waterfront community north of New Orleans in St. Tammany Parish with a large population of light-skinned, colored people who passed for white. They rented a room for $38.00 in the home of an old couple who lived right outside of town. Mom would rise at 4:30 to heat the bath water, prepare breakfast and lay out her husband's clothes. Her mother had taught her this expression of love and it had been passed down for generations. Dad loved being cared for and spent his early morning hour reading his grandmother's tattered Bible as he prepared for the responsibility of molding and shaping innocent young lives.

In Dad's 1941 Chevrolet it was an eighteen-minute ride to the old wooden school. They passed fields of rice paddies and plump cotton bushes surrounded by red soil. Canopies of moss hung from trees and pecans were plentiful. Honeybees buzzed. Dad would shoo away the old hound dog that always found its way onto the front porch, then sweep. "Cleanliness is next to godliness," he would say. Mom would slap the seats with the dust cloth, pick yellow wildflowers from the pasture right behind the schoolhouse and arrange them artistically in a mayonnaise jar.

As principal, Dad did everything from serving as headmaster to cleaning the outhouse. His faculty consisted of one other female teacher and his new wife. Together, the trio alternated, teaching reading, writing, arithmetic, manners, and grooming to the town's thirty-nine colored children.

They hardly left each other's sides the first year, sinking deeper into the routine of preparing lesson plans, wiping runny noses, and making sure children got home safely. And when Mom woke earlier than usual one April morning, she nudged Dad once, then twice as he raised his sleepy head. She placed his large, smooth hand first on her face and then moved it slowly to her swollen tummy, as she leaned into his arms. He sprang up. "You're having a baby!" It had been unexpected, but they both gave thanks for the blessing. It was then Mom knew for sure she had picked the right husband. By the end of the school year, Mom and Dad had moved into a little house right next to the school.

ᎯREALITY᎒

Part of Dad's responsibility as principal was to feed the children. A couple times a week, he would drive to the only grocery store in town to buy vegetables, rice, flour, and powdered milk for the women to prepare lunch. Sometimes, Mom would tag along, until her pregnancy made car rides uncomfortable.

On one such trip, Dad decided to take an older boy and girl with him to expose them to purchasing and counting money. As he ordered the food, the white female clerk called him "boy." Dad hadn't been called that name in a long time. All the colored folks and even some of the white people called him "Professor." He showed the children the direction of the sweets and then returned to speak with the clerk.

"I'm trying to teach the children about respect and would appreciate not being called a boy," he said softly.

Her face contorted. "Boy, what did you say? Hey y'all, this boy is talking back to me. Who the hell do you think you are? Somebody, go fetch Rufus to put this boy in his place!"

Dad was immediately sorry for speaking up and just as quickly said, "I'm sorry, Ma'am," hoping it would just all go away. His movements quickened. "Let's go, children." They all kept their heads down and walked quickly outside. As he rolled down the road as fast as he could, he could see in his rearview mirror a crowd of angry white people shaking their fists and shouting, "Don't come back, Nigger!"

A bad feeling came over Mom when she heard what had happened. "Stay away from town for a while. We'll ask Mr. Johnny to get groceries. I don't want my baby growing up without a father," she said, as she soothed her swollen feet. The moon was nearly full the next night when a truck pulled up on the road in front of the house. Dusk had fallen and Dad could just make out the six men; three up front and three in back. All of a sudden, the truck came alive; the horn started to blare and cursing shattered the quiet of the evening. Mom peeked through the curtains and saw bats, pitchforks, and ropes dangling from the back of the open truck. "Where's that uppity boy?" someone shouted. Fear chilled every bone in her body as stories of lynching, rape, and being set on fire began to run a marathon in her mind. Threatening foul words continued pouring from the mouths of the men, piercing the night's silence. "You and your gal better come out of there, Nigger," they shouted.

Just then a sensation Mom had never felt before shot through her body. Startled, she bent over, grabbing her belly. "No, no, no, not now," she moaned. Dad's mind began to swim in a river of uncertainty. Sweat poured into his eyes, as Mom whispered, "Run, run, I will be all right." Dad's head pounded as he shook his head. "No, I can't leave you, I won't leave you!"

"Come out, Nigger, time to take your medicine. Come on out, or we'll come in there and drag you out!" someone yelled from the mob. Mom struggled to her feet and grabbed Dad's neck. "You don't have a choice now, run, run. I love you. God will take care of us, now go."

The heckling from the men increased as Mom loosened Dad's grip from around her waist. For a few seconds time stopped as he dropped his head and closed his eyes. "Jesus, what do I do?" Either way, the risk felt unbearable. In an instant he made his decision. He hunched over and bolted out the back door, the tall shrubs hitting him in his face, camouflaging his movements through the bushes. He ran with every breath, stumbling blindly as sweat began to pour down his temples, his mind filled with the ghosts of history past. *Why did I open my mouth? Turn around, beg for mercy. Go back, don't be afraid. Juanita can't protect herself. Got to get help, but who?*

Dad was winded when he stumbled onto one of the colored

church elders. Mr. Bars was a hunter who often roamed the woods early in the morning, shooting rabbits and wild turkeys. Breathless, Dad could hardly tell his story, "They've come to kill me. My wife's in labor, please help. Hurry! Hurry!"

Mr. Bars, familiar with stories of hatred, didn't hesitate. "Let me get my girls first." He returned with two rifles and a handgun. "You know how to use these, Son?" Dad nodded, and they both took off in the direction of the house.

The smell of wood burning filled the air before he could see the house. Mr. Bars, aged from years of hard work and arthritis, was lagging way behind, but Dad tore through the bushes—stumbling, walking, and running all at the same time. "Oh no, God, please don't let it be," he shouted. As he neared the back door, all he could hear was sobbing.

Mom was slumped over on the bedroom floor, trembling, rocking, and cradling herself. The truck was gone, but the house smelled of smoke and gasoline from the fire that had scorched the front porch and wood shed.

Mr. Bars had never been quick to react, but this incident of near catastrophe filled his veins with anger. "We'll get my wife to see about your Missus and go find out who did this." Mr. Bars rounded up his two brothers and an uncle and they headed off down the abandoned road. They didn't speak, and their rifles were loaded and ready. But bullfrogs were all they found that night, croaking loudly in the moonlight. The sun was about to rise by the time Dad walked through the door. Mom fell into his arms and wept, grateful he was safe and relieved the pains had been a false alarm.

Against Mom's advice, Dad decided he couldn't let the incident go without reporting what happened to the sheriff. He found him smoking a cigar at his automobile repair shop. As Dad stepped out of his car, the sheriff smirked.

"That's a mighty pretty gal you've got at home, when's she due? And Nigger, don't you ever tell a white woman what to call you. She can call you whatever she damn well please."

The sheriff's hate-filled spittle sprayed on Dad's face. He backed away slowly, still facing the sheriff, thankful that he could see colored people out of both corners of his eyes. He got into his car, quickly slipped the keys in the ignition, and took off for home.

Fear became a permanent houseguest after the incident. Every car backfiring, rifle shot, or smell of burning brush caused the fine hairs to rise on their arms. After weeks of tossing and turning, Dad spoke. "Honey, it's too dangerous. I'm worried sick about you and the baby. I can't concentrate. Go home and be safe with your parents." It was an excruciating decision, but the only answer. Mom returned to Lafayette for the next four weeks until I was born.

No one can know what trauma occurred to the fetus during those hours of terror in Madisonville, what emotions pumped through her veins and passed through her bloodstream to me. But finally, after thirty-five hours of panting, sweating, screaming, and repositioning my breeched body, I arrived at 3:55 a.m. on a Tuesday morning. It was November 4, 1947. I weighed eight-and-a-half pounds and was completely bald.

"What are we going to name her?" Mom asked, as Dad looked at me for the first time.

"I want her to know how much we love each other, so I'm naming her after the both of us—Ro and Nita...Ronita.

Smiling down on me, Mom agreed. "I like it too."

Pure joy filled his heart as he looked at me with amazement. "I promise to always keep you safe and love you with every piece of my heart."

If only the angels had told him what it meant to love me unconditionally.

Over the next months, Dad drove back and forth to see his family while we lived with Walter and Mary Lou. Keeping us safe preoccupied him as he struggled with his responsibilities—provider, husband, father, schoolmaster, and son. Promises to Mother Dear as the one child she could depend on to stay in Louisiana weighed against making a living and raising his family in a safe environment. Many nights he found himself walking the creaky floors or kneeling in prayer. *Lord, what do I do?* With Lily Bell's constant reminders of opportunity in California, Dad made his decision by the end of the school year.

Memorial Day weekend, Mother Dear and Mary Lou clutched the shoulders of their children as they pulled away in preparation for the dusty, three-day journey to a place where Dad would never be called "boy" again.

ᐊSOUTHERN WELCOMEᐅ

Living in California had pulled a shade down over those days of fear and terror. It had been almost six years, but thoughts of Madisonville and keeping us safe had occupied Dad's mind more than he wanted to admit on the lonely highway. Wanting to believe the South had changed, he put on a happy face when he picked us up at the train station on a Thursday afternoon in 1953. It was steamy hot. I felt sticky and couldn't sit still.

I noticed a wrinkled-up, dark-skinned lady in a dress three sizes too big for her sitting on the porch, fanning and rocking as we crept down the road, red dust flying everywhere. She waved, and my head turned around as far as it could go. *Does she know us?* The road had a sharp tilt downward like we were driving into a crater. Thick chinaberry trees lined the street and a spotted brown mangy dog barked. One-story shacks like I remembered from *Huckleberry Finn* were scattered among muted-colored houses of different sizes and shapes. Dad drove slowly, looking around until we came to a dead-end where a big white house in need of paint stood right smack in the middle of a yard big enough for four Maypoles. Cars were parked haphazardly on the grass, and I asked, "Who lives here?"

Dad smiled. "We do," as the screen door opened, and a stout woman with a lace apron stepped out of the doorway with a wide grin. "They here, they here."

"Welcome, welcome, come on in, did y'all have a safe trip? Make yourself at home. I'm Sister Turner, this here is Brother Turner, dat dere is Sister Hodges and Brother Hodges." Wide, grinning, brown-skinned faces of every shade huddled around us like we had just been saved from aliens.

The friendly lady looked straight in my face, as I wiggled up and down. "What's your name, little child?"

"May I go to the bathroom, please?" I asked.

"Oh surely, child," another lady said and led me down the hall.

The bathroom was nearly big as our whole apartment in San Francisco. I sat there mesmerized, staring at the big white tub and the sunshine coming through the window. Suddenly, I heard a knock on the door and a soft voice, "What y'all doing in there?" I quickly flushed. When I opened the door, a girl my same height stood staring at me. Her long hair was combed neatly in pigtails with plaid ribbons.

"Is this the first time you went to the bathroom?"

I tried to talk proper like Mom did sometimes when the phone rang and white people said "hello."

"No. We come from California."

Her name was Brenda, and she took my hand and led me back

to the living room, just as Dad paused. "And this is Ronita, our first-born. She's almost six. We're really looking forward to her brother or sister."

I turned with a puzzled look and had no idea what he meant. But the thought of someone else to play with Doris and me instantly made me giggle.

I caught on quick—church folks were like family, calling each other Sister this and Brother that, the same way we used "Shaa," like a surname. These sisters wasted no time inviting us to the dinner table. I felt every eye ogling me. My eyes ogled too as a steady stream of food filled the table. Cheese dripped down the side of a glass dish filled with macaroni. Big chunks of fried red tomatoes mixed with okra and onions were still bubbling. Butter-coated fat corn kernels, and there was fluffy rice, mashed potatoes, brown sugar over yams, snap beans, collard greens with ham, dark-colored gravy, golden fried chicken, juice running out of a pot roast, corn bread and a red checkered towel with hot biscuits. Streaks of cold sweat ran down the aluminum pitcher filled with lemonade.

"M'm, m'm, good," I said, echoing the slogan from the Campbell's soup commercial. I smiled at Mom. "I like this place," and everybody laughed.

"Would you bless the food, Reverend?" Sister Hodges asked.

I had never figured out why we bowed our heads. *Why wouldn't we look up? Wasn't Jesus in heaven?* I had asked Dad about this many times, but his explanations left my question unanswered.

"Thank you, Lord, for all you have done for us. Thank you for a safe journey from California. Bless these good people and the hands that prepared this food"... and he went on for a long time. I knew praying was serious and opening my eyes was forbidden. But I peeked with one eye anyway, curious to see if anybody else but me wanted Dad to hurry up so we could eat. A woman caught me, winked, and

I almost burst out laughing. Finally, Dad said, "Now rise, Peter, slay and eat." I had asked Dad what that meant too, but his explanation made no sense to me.

Dishes of food started coming faster than I could eat. I looked at Mom for her approval, unaccustomed to taking whatever I pleased. She nodded, "Go ahead, eat anything you want, but remember the poor little starving children in Africa." My mind switched momentarily to the television advertisement of skeleton children with flies in their eyes and bloated bellies. I always felt sorry for them. Mom was a terrific cook, except when she prepared droopy Brussels sprouts, rutabaga, and soggy broccoli. That was the only food I struggled to swallow. I hoped one day I could go to Africa and give all the starving children my soggy vegetables. But not today. All I hoped for now was that my stomach would stretch so I could eat more butter and biscuits.

My head swayed back and forth as the grown-ups yakked on and on about the town and the church until I knew, *I want to be outside, play, and see everything*.

"Can I be excused, Dad?"

Dad said, "It's always 'May I' not 'Can I' because you always can."

I wanted to believe him, but after watching him change over the last few months, deep down inside I was no longer confident I could do *anything* I wanted.

Brenda took me outside and I twirled around in the yard. "Wow, you could fit a couple of apartments here!"

"Come on," Brenda shouted and before me, I saw a huge forest just like the pictures in *Little Red Riding Hood*. The air was fresh with a fall breeze, and golden-yellow and maroon leaves blew across thick trees. A woodpecker crashed the sound of silence in the distance. A gray cat with white stripes purred by a dilapidated wood sandbox. I could see a trail leading into the foliage.

"What's back there?" I asked Brenda, breaking the silence.

"The woods," she responded quickly, "You can't never go back there."

"Why?" I asked, as my eyes grew round like moons.

"That's where the really bad people live."

A hard thumping began in my chest. Although the scar was carved in my consciousness, I had tried to blank out the one really bad person I knew, Horace.

Brenda said, "What's wrong?"

I wasn't about to share my secret with her but thought I should go inside right that minute and tell Dad, "We're not safe."

"Where does that go?" I asked, pointing to a narrow dirt path while trying to control my breathing. Thoughts of Horace were hard to push away.

"That's where I go to school," Brenda said.

"That's the way to school?" I asked again, thinking she didn't understand me.

"Uh-huh, that's J. L. Jones, that's where I go to school, and you will too."

I couldn't believe it; this great big house and school right next door. Except for the woods, I was falling more in love by the minute. Brenda and I walked back to the front porch. We plopped ourselves in the wooden swing and there we swung until we both fell asleep.

The sound of the screen slamming woke me up. "Goodbye, goodbye, y'all. Call if you need anything, and see you on Sunday."

Dad wrapped his arms around Mom and grabbed my hand as the last car pulled off and the dust settled. Little glimpses of orange pierced through the darkness and I heard a loud, strange sound that filled the night with music.

"What's that noise?" I asked Dad.

"Crickets. You'll hear them most nights."

Finding a cricket to examine moved to the top of my exploration list. *How do they make that loud sound?* I wondered.

I was not fully awake as Mom led me to a large room right next to the bathroom. I grabbed her tight around her big stomach and then jumped right on the clean sheets when she said, "This is your very own room." My head fell straight on the pillow but Mom scooted me off. "Bath first."

Dad poked his head in and found me tucked in bed. "Did you say your prayers?"

"Tired, Dad," I yawned.

"We're never too tired to pray," and he joined me on my knees as I laced my fingers together.

"Bless Mommy and Daddy. Thank you, Jesus, for my new friend Brenda, my big bathtub with lots of bubbles, chicken breast, and my own bed. Amen." As I drifted off I looked seriously at Doris. *Do you know where my little brother or sister is coming from?* But she was already asleep.

⟨⟨MY ASSIGNMENT⟩⟩

I wore myself out the next few days playing in the sandbox, chasing the cat through the blackberry bushes, jumping in and out of mud puddles in my new galoshes, running back and forth whenever the phone rang, and bugging Mom, "Can Brenda come over and play, p-l-e-a-s-e?"

Sunday morning, Dad shook me gently. "Good morning, does Doris like her new bed?" It felt natural to wake up in my new room, and I sat up quickly, moving right to his shoulder as his arms surrounded me.

"Today, we go to our new church. The grown-ups and all the children will be watching us. You have a responsibility as my daughter to show them how little girls act when they love Jesus. And you have a responsibility to show Jesus how much you love him too. You do love Jesus?"

I nodded.

"I know you aren't going to let me down and you aren't going to let Jesus down, either." He kissed my forehead and patted Doris. "Now hurry up, we don't want to be late on our first Sunday."

I sat there for a few moments, not entirely sure what I was supposed to do so that all the people would know how much I loved Jesus. All I knew was one thing, *I want Daddy to be proud of me, stay happy like he was before he was called so that his hands never hit me again.* I was sure I knew the meaning of Dad's pride—never step over adults' feet or interrupt without saying "Excuse me, please." Always say please and thank you. Never look solemn when adults are being friendly, even when I don't feel well. Share my food and toys. Smile. Keep my clothes clean. Say my prayers every night.

I thought, *If I do all those things, Dad will know I'm a good girl who loves Jesus.*

The sign on the red-brick building read "Mt. Zion C.M.E. Church." A man standing out by the sign marked "Pastor" quickly dropped and squashed his cigarette before waving as we drove up. My morning talk with Dad was fresh in my thoughts.

Dad looked handsome and smelled of Old Spice. Mom had starched and ironed his white shirt and placed his handkerchief squarely in the pocket of his black suit. He wore his favorite red Holy Spirit tie and you could see your face glow in his spit-shined Stacy Adam shoes. Mom was wearing a new big-stomach dress and I felt sorry for her, remembering how it felt when my stomach hurt. She looked at me, as if reading my mind. "You're going to be a big sister soon." I still hadn't guessed that Mom's poked-out stomach had something to do with that!

The burn on my neck hurt. Mom had insisted on Shirley Temple curls and we had spent early Saturday morning preparing for my ordeal. I had to lie on the kitchen counter looking at the paint chipped ceiling while she washed and parted my long, thick hair. The two hours of pressing and curling would begin after dinner. I'd get so sleepy until the red curling iron sizzled against my skin, waking me up.

I looked down at my green, polished-cotton dress and smoothed my petticoat before bouncing over to grab Dad's hand. The temperature had shot up for fall, but that didn't change Mom's idea of first impressions—hat, gloves, purse, and a sweater. I strained my neck looking for Brenda, as people started sticking out their hands: "Hello, I'm Sister Pearl; Hello, I'm Sister Ruby; Hello I'm Brother Jones," and so on, until we had shaken hands with everyone present. Dad let go of my hand, kissed Mom on the cheek, and then disappeared up some wrought-iron stairs on the side of the church, leaving Mom and me to keep on smiling.

We followed the crowd to the basement where people were sectioned off in small groups. Sunday school had started. Sister Rollins, the little children's teacher, grabbed Mom's hand. "Welcome, welcome, so glad y'all are here."

All eyes were on me and I waved at Brenda as Mom walked away. Sister Rollins talked about being good soldiers for Christ and asked me to read a scripture from our lesson book. Then it was time for collection. Mom had forgotten to give me a nickel, so when the tray got to me, I just passed it.

"You don't got no money?" the boy next to me said.

I felt ashamed because all the children put something in the tray, mostly pennies.

"My Daddy forgot to give me money, and it's you don't have any money." The little boy snickered, and I hoped I hadn't failed my first test already. I made a mental note. Never forget your Sunday school money again!

The sanctuary was plain with wooden floors and white, clear-pane windows. As we entered, I noticed a big sign that looked like an eye hanging on the wall that read, "In God We Trust."

You'd have thought we were getting married as Mom and I walked down the long aisle and sat down in the second pew. My petticoat scratched my legs and I wished Mom would stop starching it. The organ started to play as the choir marched in, "Holy, Holy, Holy, Lord God Almighty...." Everyone stood and applauded, as Dad strolled out purposefully and stood behind the plain wood podium.

Every moment was filled as we stood up and down between the affirmation of faith, prayers, choir songs, scriptures from the Old and New Testament, and the benevolent offering. Then finally Dad stood alone.

"I'm bursting from the Southern hospitality and want to thank you all for welcoming me and my family. We got here safe, even though I broke a few speeding laws on the highway. I had to make up time driving through some of those towns. You know the ones I'm talking about, where you get picked up for nothing at all." I heard chuckling from the audience. "And the leaves from those bushes sure make it rough when you stop for the bathroom." People started to laugh. "I think my daughter is going to turn into a chicken breast." More laughter, and then Dad cleared his throat. I could tell he was going to get serious.

"God called me and I questioned Him. Not me, God, I'm not worthy. Have you ever questioned God? I didn't feel worthy, but who am I to question God? I accept now and forever that God laid His hands on me and I'm His servant. I'm here to do His will. I'm so glad that Jesus picked me, because there are a lot of other things I could be doing." People started laughing again, and he knew his charm was working. He closed his eyes. "Let's bow our heads."

"Thank you, Jesus," echoed from the congregation.

"God, you said you would never leave us alone, that you know our burdens and will never give us too much to bear. We are your people, and we're trying to do your work. We have families to raise and crops to harvest. We need your strength for good health. We pray for the sick and the shut in. We pray that you keep us safe in these hard times, protect us Lord."

Dad was saying the things that were in their hearts, as if he had sat down personally with each family and knew their stories and their hardships. "Thank you, Jesus" got louder from the audience as Dad reached his conclusion and we all said, "Amen."

It took me a while before realizing that the scripture reading at the beginning of the service was the text of Dad's sermon. He read it again and gave a three-point overview. Then he began to elaborate on his first point, calmly and elegantly, using big words like "pontificate" and "repudiate" that meant nothing to me. By the time he was on his second point, his voice had gotten a half-octave higher and you could see little beads of sweat shining across his forehead. He'd wring his hands in deep contemplation as he looked at his sermon and then the congregation. I couldn't take my eyes off Dad, even though I didn't understand most of what he was saying.

By the third point, people were hopping and hollering as Dad said, "and as I close." Sweat dripped profusely and he loosened his tie before wiping his brow with Mom's starched handkerchief. He wrapped both hands around the edges of the podium and drummed his right forefinger in a steady cadence, then stomped his foot down hard. From the sound, it looked like it hurt. The three men sitting in the pulpit egged him on, "Come on, Preacher, make it plain," and then Dad beat up his Bible with his fist.

People started swaying in their seats, sweating and fanning, rocking and standing, humming and crying. "Amen, thank you, Jesus, yes God, hallelujah, glory, glory, good God Almighty." A lady took off running up and down the aisles, with her hands in the air. She'd stop, scream like a chimpanzee at the zoo, and take off again.

Unfamiliar with the "Holy Spirit," I drew closer to Mom and hoped Dad wasn't getting ill. Ushers were fanning folks and trying to hold somebody down as a pair of thick, gold-rimmed glasses flew across the aisle. The choir started singing and I sat, wide-eyed and frozen. One woman looked like she had been fighting—hair undone and a button popped off her blouse, showing way too much cleavage. Mom whispered, "Don't turn around," but I couldn't help it. *Where did all these hollering people come from*?

I looked at Dad's red face as he started singing, "We are our heavenly father's children, but there are times when we answer God's call. If we are willing, He will teach us, to obey, no matter where, for He knows just how much we can bear." Wow, Dad could really sing; his voice reached out and touched that part of me that cried when I watched sad movies where someone died. Dad spread his arms wide open, and the crowd was invited to salvation through the only living savior, Jesus. One, three, eight people came down front and grabbed Dad's outstretched right hand. "Welcome brother, welcome my sister."

Mom looked at me and said, "Come on, we're joining too." I was surprised. *Aren't we already saved?* but, I followed Mom quietly as she pulled me along. Dad read from a green book, not the one with the red edges, and everybody responded "Yes" when he asked, "Do you..." I said nothing, still confused about why we were standing before all these people.

The organ began to play as every person in church stood up and marched around to welcome the new members, especially us. It took forever. I shifted from one foot to the other saying "Hello" as more scratches tormented my thighs. After the last handshake, all I wanted to do was ease my fingers into a tub of warm soothing water. Collection came next, announcements, and finally benediction. I was exhausted, but Dad marched right down front, grabbed Mom and me by the hand, and paraded us right to the front door. We shook everybody's hand all over again, while people said, "Welcome, sho enjoyed the message. Loved yo singing too."

I had been poked, hugged, squeezed, shaken and patted by the time the last person said "Goodbye," and I couldn't wait to go home, tell Doris everything, and take a nap.

"Meet me around the back," Dad told Mom. "We're invited to dinner."

&UNTIL THE SUN GOES DOWN&

O ne of most faithful members lived about 150 steps behind the church. Folks called her "Momretta." When she saw us coming, she held the back door open with her arms stretched out wide.

"Come on in here, Pastor, I know you is hungry 'cause you sho did stir us up." She was one of the darkest-skinned people I'd ever seen. Her hair was tightly curled with lots of grease and her teeth were white as milk. As we entered, a lot of the same faces from our welcome party greeted us. Dad received pats on the back. "Come on in, Pastor, sit."

As soon as everybody patted Dad on the back, Momretta's husband Brother Adam invited him and all the other men to follow him to the backyard. It created quite a commotion as the women trotted off to the kitchen clinking glasses. One of the sisters hurried by with a big pitcher of grape Kool-Aid. That's what I followed. Plus, I was eager to get outside and play on the swing under the shaded oak tree, since I couldn't go home.

Momretta stopped me right in my tracks. "You stay inside with us, child; we're gonna eat soon," and I remembered Dad's instructions about minding my elders. No sooner had I picked up a fan that read "Benevolent Funeral Home" than a lady rang a bell. "Time to eat!"

The screen door kept slamming "bam!" until all the men were standing in the dining room, waiting on the blessing. A woman held out a basin with water and a fresh towel, while another woman swatted flies. I must have heard Dad pray over 15,000 times before I was eighteen, and never did I hear him say the same thing twice. It was as if he had an inner knowing of just the right words, intonations, and emotions like a direct pipeline to Jesus. My belief kept me from praying out loud for a long time, because I got tongue-tied talking to Jesus.

I got food-drunk on the aroma, waiting for the blessing to be over, and then everybody started jostling for a chair as soon as "Amen" was uttered. "Come on in here, child," Momretta said as I entered a little room off the kitchen. Assuming I didn't want to hear grown-up talk, she had created a reproduction of the dining table just for me—a tiny chair, linen table covering, plates, saucers, and silverware.

"Can I, no, *may* I have the breast, please?" I asked.

"Sure can," she smiled, as she waited on me hand and foot. I felt so special, not knowing that eating with the church members would become a Sunday tradition.

After dinner, I was sure the day was over. My tummy was full, and I needed a nap with Doris. But I was in for another surprise. Dad took Mom home then turned around and headed straight back to church with me in the back seat, red dust flying everywhere. The Christian Youth Fellowship met every Sunday at 5:00. It was sandwiched in perfectly, giving Dad just enough time to digest his food and perhaps catch a couple of winks. All the youth from junior high to high school would sit on wood benches formed in the shape of a U. Dad led the discussion, while they talked about going to heaven. I was the only five-year-old present, but Dad insisted, "You can never get enough of being in church." CYF finished at 6:30 and Dad prepared for the last service of the day—7:00 evening worship, an abbreviated replica of the morning service.

That first Sunday, I fell asleep on the short ride home and don't know who put on my pajamas. Next morning, I told Doris about people crying and shouting, our very own parking space, getting saved again, Momretta, and the older kids at CYF. I showed her the scratch marks on my legs and asked her to kiss my stiff hand. They both still hurt. She had one question, "Was it easy?" I knew what she meant and hugged her.

"Yes, showing the people how much I loved Jesus was easy. Except it takes all day. All I have to do now is smile at the old people, shake hands with the new people, and get lots of attention as Dad's daughter." I could tell from how well it had gone that I could stop worrying. Those good church folks thought Dad walked on water just like Jesus—and I knew it was going to be lots of fun for the rest of my life.

◖NO SENSE TO ME ◗

The school year had started three weeks earlier. Mom left me with my legs dangling in the big chair of the principal's office. Fresh from my new success of showing all the people how I loved Jesus, I stood in front of the class with my new book satchel under my arm as the teacher instructed the kids, "Say hello to Ronita." I noticed the different shades of black, brown, and beige, ponytails, bangs, missing front teeth, big ears, and fingers in noses looking right at me saying, "Good morning, Ronita." I strained my neck, looking for anybody white like the children from my old school. Then I remembered, *I haven't seen any white people since we arrived.*

"Where are the other children?" I asked Mom that night as she brushed my hair.

"What other children?" she asked.

"The children with the red hair, blue eyes, and freckles?"

"Oh," she replied. She cleared her throat then became silent, which had become a sign for me of something serious. "Colored children and white children don't go to school or play together here. White children live in another part of town."

"Why, Mom? Why can't we play together?"

"We live in Louisiana now, and the parents want to keep their children separated because that's what their parents did," she finished.

The words poured slowly from her mouth without making sense in my head.

"What, Mom? What's sa-pa-rated?"

"Don't think about it, God loves all children. Now say your prayers and go to sleep." Confused, I shook my head and figured I'd never see another white person again, except on television. That night, I had one wish saying my prayers—sleepovers and tea parties, like I heard the girls talking about at my old school.

Having a friend like Brenda made it easy to fit in and learn the names of my new classmates. Encouraged by my folks' attitude of education being the most important thing after being saved, I eagerly completed my homework every night and liked my first-grade teacher. After a week, it was as if I had never missed a day of school. Good thing too, because Mom was getting crankier as her stomach got bigger.

"Ronita, keep Doris off the floor. Get your elbows off the table. Eat your oatmeal. Quit that clicking noise. Stop rocking while I plait your hair. Come here! Go outside! Take your bath. Clean the ring out of the tub. Go to sleep. Wake up. Do your homework. Say your prayers. Brush your teeth. Move, N-O-W!"

I couldn't figure out why she was mad at me. I was still getting settled in our new house and trying to learn the names of my classmates. Dad busied himself organizing affairs at church and except for meals, our time together felt limited.

Eager to explore more of where we lived, I jumped at the chance to follow Dad one Saturday morning when Mom sent him out to the grocery store. Dad said, "Stay close by," as he pulled up to the A&P grocery market and unfolded Mom's list. I covered my mouth with surprise. *White and colored people together in the same place.* I wondered, *Are the white ladies sick?* because colored ladies dressed in white uniforms like nurses, held white babies in their arms, and watched the grocery basket. It was then that I figured Mom was wrong—white children and colored children played together; we just didn't know any of them.

I saw two porcelain water fountains by the bin with the vegetables. From a distance they looked the same, but as I got closer, I noticed that one sparkled with cleanliness. The other was covered with mildew and some kind of black crud covered the spout. The water struggled to trickle out. It wasn't much of a choice, and I got on my tippy toes and leaned over.

"What the hell are you doing, Nigger, don't you know you can't drink out of that water fountain? Can't you read that sign that says 'White Only'?"

The man was dressed in a dingy white uniform and towered over me. I wondered, *What's a nigger*? His face reddened, and I was getting really scared.

"You dirty little nigger, I ought to string you up," and he raised his arm like he was going to strike me. My mouth opened, but nothing came out and my legs wouldn't move, even though I told them to.

Dad came running over when he heard the commotion. He grabbed my hand. "My little girl didn't know, it won't happen again."

The store attendant started in again. "You'd better watch out if you bring that little nigger back into this store."

"Yes, Sir," Dad said as my feet hardly touched the floor. We headed to the line marked "colored," as the white and colored people stared and pointed at us, especially the colored ladies in white, who I found out later were "the help."

"What did I do wrong, Dad?" He didn't answer, and I got really quiet, sorry I had taken that ride with him in the first place. Years later, I realized how difficult it was for Dad to answer my innocent question. How do you explain prejudice to a child that just celebrated her sixth birthday? How the environment breeds a certain kind of hatred that becomes the very blood running through a person's veins? Where a boy or girl is vulnerable and dependent on a parent or guardian for survival and how prejudice is a learned expression fueled by fear, jealousy, inferiority, stupidity, and ignorance? What do you say about skin color, how it leads a person to swear, beat, rape, castrate, hang, torture, and humiliate another human being? How do you tell a child, especially a child like me who had sat next to white children that you are less, inferior, second-class…in danger? How do you tell her to be careful of her language, careful who to talk with, where to go, how to smile politely, and how not to shudder like a scared animal when somebody white speaks to you? These thoughts must have pounded against Dad's head as he slammed the car door. Tears were right at the surface as I kept wondering, *Why was that man so mad at me? I just wanted a drink of water. What did I do?*

We both sat in the car for a moment while I waited for an explanation. When Dad started to speak, his voice changed the way it did when he wanted me to understand something extra-important.

"I told you to stay close. You can't wander off by yourself anymore. You could get hurt. Remember, you've got to always do what I say; your life depends on it." He sounded upset with me, but I didn't know why.

I trembled on the ride home and tears streamed down my face. *I'm a nigger!* The very sight of me brought disgust to the faces of white people like I was a bug to be squashed.

I would come to believe the label of "nigger" was tattooed right between my eyes; nothing could remove it, nothing could save me—not being cute, obedient, well-mannered nor being studious. Not loving Jesus with all my heart or saying my prayers every night. And what I began to understand was how that label contained me, our family, and entire community in a one-mile bubble where survival was all that mattered.

Two kinds of bad people existed in my world. Horace, and the other kind living right behind my house that Brenda had told me about. That night, I asked for two things after feeling that deep fear—a light in my room and Jesus to keep the really bad people from ever hurting me again.

ᏣNAMESAKEᏧ

Mom looked like she had swallowed a couple of watermelons and I kept seeing cards with a bird holding a baby in his beak on the kitchen table. I guessed a bird was dropping off a baby real soon. The day after Thanksgiving, Mom put my hand on her stomach and explained.

"That's where your brother or sister is coming from." I pulled my hand away quickly, startled by something that moved.

"How will that happen?" I asked, bewildered.

"It just happens," Mom responded.

But she left me with no further explanation until December 4, 1953. Dad had dropped me off to stay overnight with Momretta. After school, we went straight to a one-story wood building where friendly nurses smiled and said, "Aren't you lucky." My senses sat up. It smelled like PineSol. Usually memories of Horace came during afternoon naps, causing me to cup my hands over my private parts to protect myself before falling asleep. Many times, I wished doom on Horace—hoped he was eaten by werewolves, killed by vampires, or shot by Edward G. Robinson like I saw on Saturday afternoon TV movies. The worst thing about the memory was the feeling of guilt. I just couldn't shake the image of Jesus looking down on me, telling me, "You're bad." I kept asking His forgiveness and even made promises I'd never let a boy touch me again. But the feeling of sin was never far away. I knew Dad was preaching right at me every Sunday morning when he talked about going to hell.

We stopped in front of the wide glass window where colored babies of every hue were sleeping or crying. The nurse picked up a light-skinned baby boy with curly hair. His eyes were open and he had his fist in his mouth. Dad tapped on the thick window, trying to get his attention. "That's your brother, Robert Jerome." He was cuter than Doris, cuter than any baby I'd ever seen and I couldn't wait to pick him up, feed him, and teach him how to jump rope!

"Shh" became the rule after Mom brought him home. I'd tiptoe to his cradle, stand with my chin in my hand watching him breathe, yawn, grunt, and sleep. He liked to sleep. He liked to eat, too, and suck on a fat nipple Mom was always boiling in water along with his bottles. He had long eyelashes and large round eyes, and the most beautiful skin tone like he had been lying in the sun on the Mediterranean. I'd pinch my nose when Mom took off his diaper, hanging around curiously.

"What's that thing between his legs?" I asked her.

"Boys have privates too," she told me. I thought again of Horace.

I loved him from the beginning, even though I noticed right away how attention began to shift. I noticed his new clothes and toys from church members, but for some reason I wasn't jealous. He made Mom and Dad smile. Anyway, I figured we wouldn't compete for dolls or tea sets. Dad was so proud and would lift him way up in the air until his baby formula would come drooling down his shirt.

The first Sunday Mom brought my brother to church, Dad cleared his throat right before announcements and we all waited. "I'd like to introduce you to my namesake, Robert Jerome Thomas." The congregation stood and clapped, while I wondered, *I'm the oldest. Shouldn't I have been introduced as the namesake*? I knew namesake must be a good thing because Dad kept repeating it over and over again. At home I waited patiently for Mom to cover his baby bed with a blue curtain. It never arrived!

I don't know why I didn't pinch my brother hard for lying snuggled in Mom's arms or sitting on Dad's knee, the knee where I used to sit. Maybe it was because he was just too good-natured, chuckling with his deep dimples and contented brown eyes.

Dad must have sensed I felt neglected because over the Easter break, he bought a slab of lumber and thick rope and then asked me, "Which one of these trees would hold a big girl like you?" I pointed to the tree closest to the trail where the property line ended and the schoolyard began. I imagined I could see clear across the yard, past the marching band and track field, right into the midst of all the action. But too many times I found myself thinking about my predicament of being a nigger.

Over the next few years, I would come to realize a thing or two about segregation. It was like the story moms oldest sister, Aunt

Dorothy told me about the live crayfish for her étoufée recipe.

"You place the crayfish in a pot of cold water and sit it on the stove under a slow flame. The water gets warmer and warmer, but the crayfish don't feel it, 'cause it happens gradually. Before you know it, they all cooked and dead."

I guessed colored people were being cooked every day, dead to our own human rights and sense of dignity.

Swinging in my tree I realized my life was marked by school, church, babysitting at Momretta's, occasional visits to Brenda and the grocery store. I never left home thirsty. The only other time the radius expanded were trips to town for supplies or Sunday dinners with church members. I missed running back and forth from the ocean waves, feeding peanuts to the elephants at the zoo, and the wind blowing through my hair in Uncle Claude's convertible. Gone was the freedom to explore and speak to anyone I pleased.

I was taking in everything I'd see around our house—shapes and colors of leaves dancing to the beat of howling wind, garter snakes slithering through the grass, the black dog with a chain healed into his neck, lightning bugs flying in the night, worms tickling the psalm of my hands, *Woody Woodpecker, Bugs Bunny* and *Daffy Duck*. Some Saturdays, Doris and I would spend the afternoon watching sky scrapers in the blue sky and talking to God. "Why do the nice people in the cartoons always get hurt? Who am I? What will I be when I grow up? It was just about the same time my brother began to stand up, my appetite for make-believe grew even larger. I brought fantasy home each day!"

"Dad, can I be a mouse or a friendly ghoul in the school play? A ballerina? Can I dive out of the sky? Be a tap dancer? Can I watch the school band practice; become a majorette, twirl a baton? Can I go take swimming lessons? Go to the beach in Houston with Momretta? Please can I stay at Patty's house overnight with the other girls? Can

I take pictures of butterflies with your camera? Can I be a Brownie? Can I, can I, can I?"

Dad would remind me over and over again. "It's 'may I'" and then contradict himself.

I'd ask, "Why not?" even though I knew better.

"Remember, you must be an example for others. You're special and represent Jesus. Except for being a Brownie, those things are off-limits for you and your brother and stop asking why. Children are to be seen and not heard."

I didn't understand what fantasy had to do with being a good soldier for Christ, but as the world expanded around me like a string of colored balloons, my ability to float up to the sky shrank each time Dad stuck in a pin with "no."

I felt delicate, struggling to balance myself on a slippery slope of two sides pushing against each other. It was clear even at six—Dad had an image cut perfectly in his mind of who I was to be, and I had no choice but to accept his vision.

"Push me harder, Dad," I kept saying, knowing one day when I was bigger I'd swing right up to see Jesus myself.

❧ OLD MACDONALD ❧

Brother Hodges showed up one Saturday morning, tapping on the back screen. "Time to plant." I went with Dad to help till the soil and pull weeds, while worms and other critters scurried for shelter. It was fun at first until I tired of the sun beaming down on my neck, bending down, getting rocks out of my shoes, scraping my hands and feet on the dirt, and carrying heavy water pails after breaking up the hard earth. I'd be a muddy mess by the end of the day and would look at Mom rocking Robert on the porch swing. I couldn't wait until he was big enough to help.

Sometimes Dad let me watch him slop the hog he kept at a white man's pen. That hog ate anything! We had chickens, too, and eggs with golden yellow yolks, sometimes two. A few times, Mom cracked an egg and a red streak poured right out the shell. I'd ask her, "What's that?" but she never explained until one morning there were dozens of tiny yellow furry chicks running around the coop. I tried to name them, but they all looked alike. That's when she told me only this: "That's the red streak." I was more confused than ever, but had learned questioning too much got me bopped in the mouth.

Dad planted corn, sweet potatoes, cabbage, collards, mustard greens, string beans, tomatoes, squash, and watermelon. Once in a while when we ate Sunday dinner at home, Mom would fry chicken and cook a yummy meal right out of our vegetable garden, but she could only cook on Saturday, 'cause Sunday was "The Lord's Day"! I always felt sorry for the hen. Dad caught her by the legs, turning her quickly upside down. He'd place his hand around her neck and swing her like a rope until her head came off. She looked real funny, body flopping all over the yard, staining the green grass with red. I'd gaze at her closed eyes a long time, because she looked so peaceful, not at all like somebody had just died. Finally one day I had to ask Dad, "Did she go to heaven?" He looked at me and said, "God made everything. When you're good and do what you're told, you always go to heaven." But I wondered, *What bad thing did the hen do because Dad sure did wring her neck.*

ᑲ BAD DADDY ᑐ

As the school year ended, I looked forward to picking wild black-berries, daydreaming in my tree swing, catching honeybees in Mom's mayonnaise jar, and playing school with my dolls. It was May 1954. Brown vs. The Board of Education had just passed and Dad preached until his wet shirt stuck to his skin about how mistreated we were as colored people. I might have forgotten all about it except it was the summer the Dad who scared me showed up, right after I finished reciting a scripture in Sunday school.

I was always prepared to recite the lesson, because Dad didn't want us to be hypocrites, even though I didn't know what that was. I had just put my hands up to Vanessa's ears, and asked her real low, "Your mommy let you bring your baby doll to church?" My whispering had been too quiet, so I asked her again. My father's big hands lifted me right off the bench, my legs losing all signs of muscle. He marched me straight to the ladies' room, holding my arm hard and repeating himself. "You'd better learn how to keep your mouth shut and pay attention." I hoped some lady was sitting on the toilet and would let Dad have it, "You're not supposed to be in here."

He pulled his belt from around his waist and I was stunned.

Since my brother was born, there had been swats on the rear end or bops in my face when I didn't move fast enough, repeated something I had heard from school, or tore one of my *good* dresses. But this was different. Dad's face looked like the gangsters and angry cowboys from the movies. A knot began to rise in my stomach.

The bathroom became my prison of "No Daddy, Yes Daddy," as the strap whipped through the air like rope. It hurt something awful, stinging my legs, arms, and bottom.

I tried to speak through the choking tears. "All I did was…" but he interrupted me with, "Don't you dare talk back!"

I had no idea what I had done, but Dad had worked himself into a fury that scared me so. I wondered, *Who is this person?* I didn't want to come out of the bathroom, but Dad had been explicit after he tired of hitting me.

"Dry those tears, get yourself together, and get back to Sunday school." I wanted to sink into the ground, as I emerged sniffling with my head down, feeling every eye looking right at me, hoping Mom wasn't off in the nursery attending to Robert.

When Sunday school was over, Brenda hugged me and Mom-retta picked me up. "My little baby child, don't be sad. You know your daddy loves you," as the tears started falling again, even harder this time. But it wasn't all right. All I wished for was to vanish!

Now let me tell you the difference between a whipping and a whooping. Any time Dad put all his weight into the downward motion of his belt—he always used a belt—and hit me so hard I couldn't think straight, with fifteen or twenty licks until snot clogged my nose and gave a sermon before and after hitting me, it was considered a whooping. The goal was to crystallize the lesson so I wouldn't do it again. But for some reason I just never understood, I kept learning lessons over and over again. Whippings were brief, four or five licks, sometimes seven—I always counted—and no sermons. Anyway, I got a whooping that morning. The news must have traveled through the congregation fast because people started to whisper as Mom, Robert, and I passed down the aisle. During prayer, I bowed my head and asked Jesus, *Why did Dad whoop me in front of all the church?* Jesus didn't answer, but that whooping seemed to set Dad on fire during his sermon, because more people than usual joined church that day.

I came to understand that disciplining me in front of everyone was one of the ways Dad showed the congregation what he stood for—how obedience and correct behavior are essential requirements of Jesus, even though it may be painful for those you love and yourself. A new boundary was set that day and the members didn't dare cross it. I had become the sacrificial lamb and the scar was etched in me forever. That week, I sank a little deeper into the part of me where secrets rested. When Dad wasn't looking, I tried to run over the gray cat with my blue tricycle. Lucky for her, she got away.

I jumped at unexpected noises and became nervous, exaggerating every action as I tried hard to be the perfect daughter in hopes of avoiding Dad's wrath. Half the time, I didn't know what I had done to get him so upset, other than be convenient for his frustrations. Maybe he got tired of being a nigger too. It was these times that began to overshadow the good times and cloud over my soul for days. My heart longed for California, free to be me without obligation or responsibility. I wanted my old dad back. But it was too late. I had to forget the past, almost like it didn't happen, remembering people and places as specks of light across the horizon. All that mattered now was making sense of what was in front of me: Dad's lungs filled with the oxygen of being the servant of Jesus. He breathed Jesus 24–7.

He'd come home tired every night, chronicling the day's events of visiting members, family crises, church finances, deaths and run-ins with white people. He was doctor, lawyer, marriage counselor, and chief. Folks trusted him, believing the holy man could fix every problem. Don't get me wrong; I felt special knowing people had so much confidence and faith, but he was a human being, not GOD. And he was my Daddy, with his own family. I came to believe taking care of all those people made him happy and made him sad. But the good church folks didn't seem to care about that much.

More than a few times my cloudy days seemed to set me up for colds. Getting a whooping was the number one thing I hated and getting a cold was number two. I'd pray at night when I got a tickle in my throat, hoping Jesus would spare me Dad's old-fashioned remedy. He'd warm a bottle of castor oil, pour half of it in a glass with a spoonful of baking soda and two tablespoons of orange juice. The liquid would take on a life of its own, foaming and sizzling like it was fuel for a rocket ship. I'd hide under the sheets as Mom tried to convince me, "Swallow it."

"Mom, it's nasty," I kept saying, turning away.

Dad would get fed up, march in my room and say, "Drink it. Drink it now." I'd nearly choke as he brought the glass up to my mouth. And I'd better not spit it up or spill any of it, because he'd fix me another fresh glass. I never understood why my brother didn't have to drink castor oil, and he got colds all the time.

UNPREDICTABLE

My godmother in Louisiana had sent me a play piano for my fourth birthday. I began banging away, teaching myself "Twinkle, Twinkle, Little Star" right away. By six, I could play all the nursery rhymes and couldn't wait to perform on a grown-up piano like the director at our church. Joy was too soft a word to describe what I felt as we drove up to my first piano teacher's house. The first thing I saw when Mrs. Anderson opened the door was the darkwood upright piano in the corner.

She greeted Dad. "You can wait for her if you like. We'll be about thirty minutes." But he bowed politely. "I'll come back when she's finished." I was relieved.

"So, you want to play the piano, Ronita?" she asked.

"Yes Ma'am, more than anything in the whole wide world."

"Let me see your hands."

I held them out as she turned them over back and forth. *What is she looking for?* I wondered. She hit every C from bass to treble clef, telling me how the keys were organized. The acoustics ran through me like a chime. All I wanted to do was touch it with my little fingers.

Before I knew it, Dad was knocking on the door. "See you next week," she said, and I was sorry it was over. Time moved slowly between my lessons, but time moved too fast when I was sitting on her piano stool, my legs dangling, playing short melodies that touched me in places I didn't know existed inside of me. I listened intently, placing my fingers exactly where she told me, feeling there was nothing better than hearing the sound I made. Now, every night when I got on my knees, I thanked God for Mrs. Anderson and Dad's sensitivity.

Over the years, I came to know him as someone who could turn himself on or off like a faucet. Problem was, I never knew when his temperature gauge would switch from hot to cold or what might set him off. During the week he seemed neutral, lighter, delighting us with silly clown skits, funny face pantomimes, or root beer floats from Frosty Freeze. I loved his relaxed times and wished I knew how to make them multiply, but that was Dad's own secret. I loved listening to his crazy stories about growing up—eating possum sandwiches, hunting squirrels and frogs, and scaring his sisters with stories of the bogeyman. He'd wrap his burgundy paisley bathrobe around his body, fluff up his hair, plop Mom's hat on his head, and become Red Skelton or Milton Berle. He'd roll his eyes like Rochester from *The Jack Benny Show*, paint his eyebrows dark black, put on glasses and place a carrot in his mouth, pretending to be Groucho Marx. Robert and I would laugh so hard we'd almost pee our pants.

Every now and then I suggested to Dad, "You should be a comedian." He said, "Laughter is the key to people's hearts and a long life." I cherished these silly times as they drew me closer to the memory I kept tucked in my heart—an image constructed from yesterday of a loving father who threw me over his shoulder as I went "wheeeee!" And I struggled to figure out what came over him as the weekend drew closer and laughter took a holiday.

⚬SKIN COLOR⚬

I don't know who started it, but it was a game we played at school— holding up our arms and looking at the color of our skin. "You're black, you're brown, you're almost white, you're tar black." And then we'd giggle, putting our hands over our mouths. At Momretta's, there was always conversation about skin color. "That baby is so black, it's purple. Pity, going to have a rough time in life." I would look at my light skin, hoping it never turned brown.

One morning after we turned off the dirt road headed to church, a red siren came out of nowhere. A policeman pulled right up to Dad on a big silver-and-black motorcycle. He yelled, "PULL OVER, NOW!"

Dad wasn't a slow driver, mind you. Most of the time he drove like a madman. The height of it was a few months earlier when Mom and I had to hold on to our hats swaying left to right as Dad drove 100 mph on winding roads to keep his commitment to speak at three commencement ceremonies in one day. But that morning, I was sure he wasn't going faster than the 15 mph speed limit. I watched the policemen cock the brake, rise up off the seat like a giant, and slowly move his mouth.

"What y'all doing riding around with those niggers in your car?"

I knew that word now and instinct told me to sit down, don't move, and keep my brother quiet.

"Who that gal in the car?" he asked again looking straight at Mom. "Them your half-breeds? Gimme your license."

The laughter that had filled our car moments before was now replaced with dead silence.

When he stepped back up to the window, Dad addressed him. "Officer, Sir, I'm not a white man; I'm a colored man and this is my wife and children."

The policemen studied Dad's face for a long time and then went around to the passenger's side and stuck his head into the window, glaring at Mom and then at us. I didn't get it. His arm and my arm were nearly the same color. I couldn't understand why he hated us so, and nearly asked him, but I knew I'd best keep my mouth shut. I remembered the angry man in the grocery store and the way white people crossed the street as we walked down the sidewalk whenever we went to the supply store. They acted like we smelled bad. I had seen policemen on television and just hoped he wasn't going to shoot us. He kept looking at us like we were going to change colors right before him and then he said, "Get out of here and don't let me stop you again."

I got a big lump in my chest that day and could hardly sit still in church without thinking about the big stick the policeman kept banging in his hand. But Dad brought our experience right into the sermon as we all bowed our heads and prayed to God, thankful another colored person had escaped once more. I mumbled words of appreciation and prayed again, "God, please keep my skin from turning dark brown."

❦FIRST DEATH❧

When my grandma Mary Lou got sick, I saw Mom show emotion for the first time. When Robert was sick or Dad preached until he wept or I got a whooping, she was always calm and cool—nothing seemed to shake my Mom. But that day, as Dad and I walked to the bedroom of my grandparents' home, Mom had tissues in her lap and a few tears on her face.

"It's just a matter of time," she whispered.

Someone said to me, "Would you sing?" It was a strange request, but Dad said, "Go ahead, sing 'Jesus Loves Me This I Know.'" I walked up to my grandma's bedside and stared. She was smaller than I had remembered from our Christmas holiday visit, but I wasn't afraid. I touched her hand as the melody poured from my mouth. I sang over and over until my throat was as dry as a potato chip. While the family closed in around me, I felt something touch my heart with tenderness. I knew these moments were precious and special. Quietness filled the room until Mom's sobs grew louder while Dad wrapped his arms around her and prayed, "She's now with Jesus."

My first dead person. I leaned over more, almost touching Grandma's face. People were always dying on television and I was always wiping my face, going through tissue after tissue. I wondered, *Will Grandma look like the hen after Dad wrung its neck?* But when I looked at her, she looked asleep with a little smile on her face. I figured she must be happy, but nobody saw that but me because they were all crying.

Grandma's passing gave me an opportunity to have Aunt Dorothy all to myself. She grieved Grandma's passing by cooking a big pot of okra gumbo and taking me to shop. I loved getting new clothes. As we walked into this dress shop, two white ladies spoke to us real friendly. I had become wary of white people, but when they saw us coming they were so pleasant.

"Howdy, Miss Dorothy. We sorry to hear about your ma." Those ladies knew all about Grandma passing and gave both of us condolences, as my eyes devoured the fine clothing. The white lady said, "I've got something really special for you to wear to the funeral." I guessed nobody told them we are segregated and they are supposed to be mean to us.

Those white ladies made a big fuss over me, lifting my arms in the air and pulling the dress over my head. It was white organza with an overlay of lace in a fancy zigzag design with a three-inch satin belt and a lace collar. I looked like one of those wedding dolls I'd seen at the department store—the ones that never landed under our Christmas tree.

Aunt Dorothy looked at the price tag and screamed, "Thirty-eight dollars!"

"It's Eye-ta-li-an," the clerk pointed out. "Look at the workmanship, the quality of fabric. You won't see this again and it's got a big hem."

I waited, thinking *I'm going to die if I don't get this dress*, while Aunt Dorothy shut the dressing-room curtain.

I was the best-dressed person at the funeral in my new white patent-leather shoes and lace-trimmed socks. I wasn't scared at all as I passed Grandma's coffin lined with pink chiffon. I stood tall on the podium to sing "Jesus Loves Me." When I sang, though, people started crying, some really loud. I just hoped they weren't crying because I sounded bad; I hoped Grandma wouldn't get too cold, either, as they laid her on the stone slab above the ground and my relatives cried "Goodbye." That's when Grandma's passing chiseled through my emotions. I was familiar with the scriptures about living and dying, and heard Dad's eulogies when old people died at our church. But I had never thought about death as something that would happen to Mom or Dad. They couldn't be included, could they? Only then, did the tears begin to fall.

HEAVEN AND HELL

Robert and I had been tucked away at Momretta's for the day. She had become his babysitter while Mom took courses at Grambling College and, sometimes, he would spend the night. Returning home, I found our house turned into a sort of museum. Several white sheets hung on a string dividing the living and dining room. One side sparkled with white Christmas lights and soft choir music played on the phonograph. Bibles were spread all over and tiny angels were pinned to the sheet. A big bowl of white punch with pineapple sherbet, tiny Spam finger sandwiches, and a white cake sat on the table with real silverware, dishes, and cloth napkins. One of the church elders was leading a game, "Finish the verse from the Bible."

Dark-red bulbs illuminated the other side and there were red candles and strange-looking devil heads. A pot of hot chili, crackers, chocolate cake with red icing, and hot cider sat on the table with plastic spoons, bowls, paper napkins, and cups. Honky-tonk played, which confused me. Dad never allowed "devil worship" music in our house. He'd rant whenever I heard someone's car radio blasting. "Close your ears. The words will make you a very bad child." A group of people were sitting in a circle whispering in each other's ears, playing a game called "Gossip" and laughing. I wondered, *What's going on?*

The party was one of Dad's brainstorm fundraisers. A punch bowl with folded slips of paper that said "Heaven" or "Hell" was on the table where you paid your entry fee. I watched the faces of people coming through the door, and noticed their lips turn up or down depending on which they picked. It was a mixture. Some folks didn't seem to mind being in hell at all and some were really disappointed, like they were going to cry. But the reaction of those going to heaven was also mixed. Did they want to be in hell? I was confused. I didn't talk to anybody, though, as it was an event for the adults, and Dad had said, "Look, don't touch, and stay out of the way."

One thing was clear. I told myself I had to be in heaven, only heaven, because I didn't want Satan's pitchfork sticking me in a fiery lake, burning my skin for the rest of my life like it said in Revelations. The only thing was the chili. It smelled so good and reminded me of Aunt Bea. Why couldn't they have chili in heaven? I only got to see the hell room once. After that Dad shook his finger. "Stay on the heaven side." All I could hear was laughter as I swallowed that boring white cake.

As the evening wore on, the hell side got so much more crowded and noisier than the heaven side that it spilled over into the yard. It caused me to wonder, *Are people telling the truth? If hell is all Dad makes it out to be, why is everybody in the hell side having such a good time?*

I was learning that people aren't always who they appear to be!

ᕲ DUSTING MYSELF OFF ᕲ

A red-and-white two-wheel bicycle sparkled under the Christmas tree right after my eighth birthday. I could hardly hold it up, but Dad steadied the bike and ran alongside me as I pedaled. Every day, I finished my homework early and begged him, "Please, steady me again so I can practice."

I hadn't gotten to practice nearly enough when Dad said, "You're going down the big hill this weekend."

My brother waved goodbye from my old blue-and-white tricycle as we climbed the steep gravel up to the top of the hill.

"Be careful," Mom yelled from the yard. Even though the hill was steep, I prepared to pedal anyway, hoping Dad would see me being fearless like the disciples in the Bible.

"This isn't so bad," I told Dad, as he released me.

Concentration was important—pedal, brake, coast, pedal, brake, coast I said to myself, attempting to avoid the bumps. Then my speed picked up, and up, and up until my feet couldn't keep up with the pedals. I hit a hole and toppled over with a grunt. Gravel stuck to my knee and it hurt. I was having trouble breathing as Dad examined me closely for broken bones. "Okay, Dad, I'm through practicing today."

"Hold on," Dad said. "Dust yourself off. Your practice isn't over. "

"But Daddy, I'm bleeding."

"Dust yourself off, I said, a little blood never killed anybody. Now get right back up that hill. And if you fall, you'll go again until you succeed."

Blood was dripping in my socks and spilling onto the gravel, but I walked my bike up the hill and rode it straight down, even though I was frightened out of my wits.

In his sermon the next day, Dad couldn't stop talking about having faith and how life will give you some scrapes, but you have to dust yourself off and keep your eye on the prize. He often used real episodes of trauma from my life to humanize the Bible's teachings, which left me with a mixed reaction. I disliked the hurt as the real story unfolded, but I loved being the central figure each Sunday as he made parables of my growing up. One thing became clearer to me after that incident. Failure was not an option when showing Jesus how much I loved Him.

❧I GOT THE SPIRIT❧

A s Dad's reputation for being a fire-spitting preacher spread, he got invitation after invitation to preach at church revivals. There was a long list of why I didn't like church revivals. The outhouse smelled so bad. I couldn't sit on the seat, so I'd hover as best I could, trying not to tinkle on my panties. I didn't like it when creepy insects slithered across the floor. I didn't like flying cockroaches, being bitten by mosquitoes, cobwebs, and giant spiders that sat right over the big hole and stared at me while I tried to pee. I didn't like dark roads with no lights where roaming cows, abandoned dogs, and wild foxes jumped in front of headlights while Dad swerved to the right or left, nearly running off the road. I didn't like conversations about colored people driving around after dark in the woods, because you never knew if a policeman or a group of white people would pull you over. And you didn't have to be doing anything wrong, either. All you had to do was show up at the wrong time and place and you'd be dead. I was too young to die!

I didn't like being squished between three adults in the back seat of our car getting home after midnight or looking at the yellow and red matter of dead moths, butterflies, crickets, and flies on the car bumper. I didn't like being the oldest without a choice—Robert got to stay with Momretta. Even worse than all those things, I didn't like the routine—driving back and forth from our house to the country, wood-framed church house for five nights straight, sometimes ten— back and forth. I'd be too sleepy the next morning to talk with Doris, who was getting very old.

It was August 1956, our fourth day of five, and I was fanning myself with hot air as the sun began to recede. Dad had gone inside to prepare himself and begin the praise portion with the early comers.

As Mom and I walked in, we noticed the little church was packed and we had to sit toward the back. I had on a blue two-piece taffeta dress with a full bodice, and a yellow can-can with heavy starch. It was the country and I didn't know why I had to look so fancy and polished, but Mom insisted, "Image is important."

We entered as the prayer group was finishing, the church already in full swing with "Amen" and "Hallelujah." An old man led the moaning, like he was going up and down musical scales but missing every other note. The whole congregation would respond back. Every now and then the leader would speak, "I love the Lord, He heard my cry," and the people would say, "I love the Lord, He heard my cry." They would go on and on like this for thirty minutes, taking turns until the people were all stirred up. I sat looking all around at the rocking bodies, closed eyes and shaking heads—the shape of faces, funny hats, flour-sack dresses, bald heads, bushy eyebrows, rusty ankles, feet with bunions, big bosoms and big bottoms that spread across hard folding chairs with slits. A few children with runny noses and bare feet sat on the floor. Nobody had on taffeta!

Dad was seated in the pulpit with all the other preachers around him, twitching in their seats, sitting on the edges and tapping their shoes against each other in anticipation of what was to come. Each night had gotten better. More people, more souls saved and the little wicker baskets overflowing with dollar bills.

The senior pastor chuckled as he introduced Dad. "He's got a fire burning in his soul, a man of God, anointed. Been tearing up this place for three nights. If you never heard him before, you're in for a treat." The people responded, "Amen, yes Sir." All I knew was it was hotter than the night before, and not a fan with Benevolent Funeral Home printed on it in sight!

Dad closed his eyes in deep meditation, preparing himself, while the pastor finished his introduction. He stood, studied the congre-

gation for a minute and started singing, getting the folks back on
their feet, continuing to stir up their emotions. As he finished his
last stanza, we all bowed our heads in prayer. I usually closed my eyes
tight, but tonight I looked up at dozens of bugs swarming the lightbulbs hanging sparsely from the ceiling. I hoped they stayed there!

Dad plowed into his remarks, purposely forgetting his usual sto-
rytelling and jokes. People started standing and getting in a frenzy.
Dad was the ultimate storyteller; he would make scriptures come
alive with his voice and body movements. "Moses parted the sea
with his staff," and I'd visualize the ocean opening up as Dad raised
his arms.

Sometimes, Dad would bring props, like the time he brought a
pillowcase of feathers when his text was from Deuteronomy. "Like
an eagle that stirs up its nest, that flutters over its young, spreading
out its wings, catching them on its pinions." By the time he was finished preaching, there were feathers all over the front of the church.
The janitor threatened to quit and Dad had to give him a raise!

Dad used any antic he could to get people to repent and come
to Jesus. Over time, I noticed every message was the same. Different
titles and scriptures all leading to the same conclusion. "If you don't
do right, you're going to hell." I paid attention to that, even though
I would drift off into my own little world, wishing I were at home,
running my fingers across the piano keys or playing with my dolls. I
couldn't drift too far, though, because Dad would drill me after every
sermon, and I'd better have the correct answer or he'd raise his voice
at me and send me to my room.

The heat felt like it shot up ten degrees as Dad ended his second point, building, always building toward the crescendo when the
people would fall out all over the floor. I prepared myself for the
entertainment—people yelling, screaming, and running around the
church like they were on fire.

All of a sudden, a large, dark-brown beetle headed straight down from the ceiling like it was a Kamikaze bomber pilot and flew into the bosom of my dress. I hated those bugs; they made a fierce buzzing noise, and stuck to whatever they attached themselves to. I let out a loud, deafening "AHHHHHHHHH!" and started beating my chest with both hands. I knocked over my chair, then Mom's, as people quickly moved out of my way. I continued kicking, screaming "AHHHHHHHHH!" and beating my chest, while Mom tried to calm me down. Dad kept on preaching, in competition with my shrieking "AHHHHHHHHH," sure he had struck a nerve within me. I fell to the floor beating myself and rolling over back and forth, hoping to kill the buzzing noise. Mom was beside herself, wondering, What's gotten into her? Dad's voice grew louder and other people now joined me, starting to scream and holler, as I knocked over more chairs.

The floor of the wooden church started to shake as if it were going to collapse. I thought I was going to pass out from exhaustion, as Mom let me be and the ushers stood there, paralyzed. I beat my chest like a gorilla until the sound stopped and the bug was crushed on the floor. I collapsed, exhausted—my taffeta dirty from head to toe. As I stood looking for my purse with a sense of accomplishment, all I could hear was the good country folk whispering, "That's the preacher's kid; she's got the spirit."

It was Dad's finest hour. He said, "And a little child shall lead them," as he stretched out his hands for invitation to discipleship. Twenty people joined that night.

⚬THE SYSTEM⚭

Our church affiliation worked like a family, with a bloodline from the White Methodists that went back to the late 1800s. We were called Christian Methodist. There were nine regions across the United Stated with individual bishops. Everybody bowed to them and their decision was final. Once a year the bishops came together for convocation where they shared stories, fellowshipped, and stuck their chests out about how their region was the best. All the potential new leadership was first identified here. It was a process that was taken very seriously. Each bishop would brag about the rising stars in their region, and from there the talk about them grew like strawberry vines.

Whatever happened at convocation eventually trickled down to the annual conference held every year in a big city church in mid-September. It was like a regional family reunion for pastors, congregations, and families, with lots of preaching, singing, back-slapping, eating, and making new friends. There were lots of long meetings, too, where gavels slammed on dark wooden tables and people grumbled or applauded while they voted. If you missed any of the week's activities, you were sure to be present for the climax on Sunday. That's when the bishop's appointment of pastors was read off, while everybody held their breath.

As a little girl, I knew none of what was going on in terms of the politics. But over the years I came to understand the meaning of showing up and showing off for this form of hierarchy. From time to time, Dad would say to Mom, "The presiding elder is coming." In those early days, I never remembered the bishop coming. I both loved and hated when the presiding elder or any company associated with the church from out of town showed up because Mom wanted the whole house squeaky-clean. Robert was too young to do housework and I was expected to help Mom wash, wax, and polish. Little time was left to swing, daydream, or read. But the good news was Mom would make a special meal—seafood okra and crab gumbo with French bread or stuffed prawns with jambalaya and homemade rolls. She'd bake a four-layer German chocolate cake, make custard for homemade ice cream and vanilla fudge with pecans for dessert. Robert and I would stand next to the kitchen counter, waiting to lick the bowl of anything sweet. Sometimes, I thought the presiding elder came to town just to eat Mom's good cooking, because when it came time for his preaching, the holy ghost sat on the pews cold and limp.

The sanctuary was packed that year in 1956. The pastors sat together and much of the church was segregated based on gender. Ladies with wide-brimmed hats came late and squeezed their big fat behinds in tiny pew spaces, causing everybody to sit up and look stuffed. When the bishop's secretary stood, cleared her voice, and began to speak, a crackling sound burst through the microphone.

"Rev. Joseph Taylor appointed to Mitchell C.M.E in Opelousas." Applause broke out.

"Rev. C. C. Odom appointed to Jackson Temple C.M.E. in Monroe." More applause.

"Rev. J. D. Sims retained as pastor, Jones Memorial in New Iberia." I heard nothing except "Amen."

"Rev. Benjamin Smith, Sr. moved to Bossier City." "Oh no, not my pastor," some woman shouted.

I looked at Mom, sitting like a statue with Robert on her lap. *Hope this will be over soon.*

"Rev. R. C. Thomas appointed to Williams Memorial C.M.E. Temple, Shreveport."

"What?" I just heard my daddy's name, as groans and cheers broke out. I glanced over at Momretta and saw tears streaming down her chocolate face.

᠙TRANSITION᠙

Shreveport was twenty-eight miles away. As far as I was concerned, it was like moving to China and I didn't want to go, but
Dad was full of promises.

"You'll see Momretta, make new friends, and Brenda can come
and visit."

"But what about my piano teacher and my tree swing, and my big
bed, the chickens and..." I persisted.

"Remember, you are my big girl and this is what Jesus wants us to
do," Dad reminded me.

I didn't want to move and had a little talk with Jesus that night,
but next morning nothing had changed. I tried to steady myself as
the conflict inside me took hold—I was supposed to be Dad's obedient daughter, while simultaneously dismissing all meaningful feelings that had begun to bud inside me. What was I supposed to do
with that?

I knew a little of Shreveport. Mom took me there twice to purchase my taffeta and polished-cotton dress. Each time we went to a
store called Selber Brothers where she bought me the most beautiful
Twinkle Toe shoes of metallic gold and black patent leather. The day
we left Minden, I just focused all my attention on getting more new
shoes and pretty dresses.

When we stopped at a beautiful red-brick house with white trim,
a large bay window, and a front porch, I blinked. White and pink
caladiums bloomed all around the entryway and the grass was the
greenest I had ever seen. I figured, *Dad is lost*, but after fiddling with
the lock the door flew open. I walked backwards through the front
door, and couldn't help thinking, *This looks like a rich man's house*.
When I turned around, freshly waxed hardwood floors, beautiful up-

holstered furniture, and mahogany wood sparkled before me. The kitchen was large and modern with a big white refrigerator, maple cabinets, and a stainless-steel sink. A window and side door accentuated the brightness of the house, and the glow from the sun seemed to radiate all over the room. There was a long hall with three spacious bedrooms on one side and a larger master bedroom on the other, and one-and-a-half baths.

Dad acted as our guide. "This first bedroom will be my study, the second bedroom is yours, Ronita, the third is Robert's, and the master suite is ours." I couldn't believe it; we had moved into a house like Mom's doctor.

"Happy now?" Dad asked, as I bounced on the bed.

"Yes," I smiled and had to admit, aside from thoughts of Brenda, rustic Minden was disappearing faster than I expected.

ᙚTHE TEMPLE᙭

Our first Sunday duplicated all I had remembered from before, except we sat in the third row. The night before, Dad recited his "You're the preacher's daughter" speech, which I had come to despise. I had learned to look Dad straight in the eye, hear everything he said, and run my own sarcastic conversation in my head. *Yes, I know. All the adults, young people, and children are looking at you. You've got to show them and Jesus how you're an example of what it means to love him.* I wanted to say out loud, *And when I don't you'll kick my butt and embarrass me in front of all the people, won't you?* At almost ten years old, I didn't want to be the model for anything except myself.

"What about Robert, doesn't he have to be an example too?" Dad thought for a few minutes, and then called Robert into my room and gave him the same talk before answering me.

"You don't worry about Robert, you just do what you're supposed to do."

My brother just nodded his head to everything Dad said. His personality was totally opposite mine—accepting without question, easygoing, quiet as a mouse, and always shadowing Mom.

Williams Memorial C.M.E. church was affectionately called "The Temple." It held twice as many people, but the people were just as nice. A large part of the congregation was comprised of young professional people who looked about the same age as my parents, in their mid-thirties and early forties; more "sophisticated," I overheard Mom say. Right from the beginning I noticed the fashionable clothes, fancy hairstyles, stylish hats and shoes on the adults and the children my age. It was like walking through a Selber Brothers fashion show. Shabby-looking people were scattered among the crowd too, but I didn't pay much attention to them. People at the new church talked proper with less drawn-out verbs, like they were practicing for a speech competition. There were more old people too, especially the ladies in the white uniforms with the doilies on their heads serving communion.

The anthem from the choir was so on pitch that Dad stood up and clapped for five minutes. After church, children my age gathered around me, while I pondered, *Which one of these girls is going to be my best friend?* No sooner did I think it, I looked down and saw a girl with Twinkle Toe shoes. I smiled. Her name was Ann. Dinner followed church, but this time I had lots of kids to play with and didn't mind going to CYF.

My only sadness was coming home to an empty room. Doris was gone. She knew all my secrets, had dried my tears and shared my laughter. I guessed carrying all my highs and lows took a toll on her. She died two days after we arrived in Shreveport; just fell apart, even though I tried to patch her back together. I had another doll named Rebecca, but she was too bourgeois to dry my tears and kept telling me it was time to "Grow up."

WHO NEEDS NUMBERS?

It took twenty-five minutes to walk to my new school, but Dad dropped me off the first week to make sure I knew the way. A warning came the second week. "Don't talk to anybody," so I crossed over on the other side when I saw anybody walking toward me, especially boys. In Minden, boys were always pulling on my hair and pushing me on the slide. And I hadn't forgotten about Horace. So any time I saw a boy, I put my head down and walked really fast.

My new teacher, Mrs. Moore, placed me in the second row and this time, I didn't know anybody. I guess she felt sorry for me beginning school late and all, because right away I got to go over to her house. "Tutoring," she told Mom and Dad, even though we never studied my homework. She'd fix my favorite hamburgers and French fries in her ranch-style house on Milam Street, where colored professional people like doctors, lawyers, dentists, school principals, and businessmen lived. I got to walk around her house and even pick up the pretty figurines or play her piano anytime I wanted. Her husband wasn't there much, but when he was, he never raised his voice, so I asked, "Where's your children?" She looked at me without her usual smile and said, "I couldn't have children. But you can be my little girl, if you like." Every chance I got, you'd find me at her house.

At school, I gobbled up reading and writing, but not arithmetic. My head wouldn't work right even though Dad made me practice over and over every night for my test. Next morning, my mind would act like an eraser with everything wiped clean. Mrs. Moore would pass over me, so I wasn't embarrassed when we had to recite our multiplication tables. Over time, I figured arithmetic must not be that important in life, because she gave me a B anyway.

❦MRS. O'NEAL❧

Right after school began, Mom started wearing those puffy stomach dresses again. But this time I knew I was having another brother or sister. I wished for a little sister so I'd have another doll to play with because Robert only liked hobby horses and shooting his tin gun. Meanwhile, I'd become obsessed with playing the piano. Dad would knock on our neighbor's door where I practiced. "Tell Ronita it's time to come home." I never wanted to leave, fascinated by the intricacies of every composition in my premier book, staying focused on the complicated measure I practiced over and over until it was perfect. I was taking lessons from the best piano teacher in town, Mrs. O'Neal, who was the organist at our church. I wasn't sure of her age, but the bags under her eyes and her thinning gray hair tied in a bun with a hairpin assured me she had lived a very long time.

The first time I saw her sitting at the organ I wondered if she had fallen asleep. And then the most immense sound filled every crevice of the sanctuary. I was unable to take my eyes off her; it seemed she had chosen just this moment to play a serenade to me. And while I felt an awakening in my chest, there was sadness, as if we shared a special place of pain. Maybe she had secrets too. I fell under the spell of her music, as she lowered her head, closed her eyes, and finished. The sound from the pipes lingered in the air until the chord became no sound, and I was left with the memory of what had been, floating in my heart. This was the musical overture that began each Sunday morning.

Mrs. O'Neal didn't fool around when it came to knowing your lessons. She sat in her overstuffed embroidered chair, counting... "And one, and two, and three," while the metronome clicked back and forth, and her black-and-white Chihuahua slept peacefully in her lap. She kept a fourteen-inch peach switch right by her side. I'd seen her bony fingers use it the very first time I waited for my lesson when a girl hit a wrong note. She struck quickly, "whoop" right across her knuckles. That girl sniffled through the rest of her lesson. I guess the parents condoned it because week after week somebody got that switch. But I wasn't going to give her a chance to make me cry like Dad did and made a mental note, *You will practice your lessons until you get it right.* Mrs. O'Neal never hit me once!

KNEE BABY

On the last Sunday in March 1957 in the late afternoon, my sister was born. I nearly bumped my head from jumping up and down. Dad gave her the funniest name I'd ever heard, Kelesha Lei. She was so fair-skinned, the nurses couldn't keep from gossiping.

"Either there's a cradle mix-up or this colored lady had a white baby."

She had fat arms and thighs, red curly hair, and a strong set of lungs. I couldn't wait to dress her up like my dolls and serve her at tea parties. Dad stood admiringly as she napped, while Mom bustled about the house sterilizing bottles and diapers and folding sheets. Robert and I watched all the commotion before scooting off to our own worlds to play on the gym set Dad bought us for Christmas.

There were dresses of pink, yellow, blue, and green with matching booties, ribbons, sweaters, blankets, and toy animals. I had never seen so much stuff for one little baby; so much stuff that at night during my prayers I started asking Jesus to send me godparents like the Jacksons.

Benjamin Jackson was outgoing, serious, short, dark brown, and the seventh-grade school principal. His wife, Stella Marie, was more reserved like Mom; attractive with soft curly hair, tall, skinny, fair-skinned, and a teacher. They made an odd couple. The four adults would get together every few weeks, alternating houses and forming a bond of relationship that lasted for life. Benjamin brought out a side of Dad I never saw with anyone else—they were equals in terms of intelligence, social ideals, and values of education. We'd find the badminton net ready for action and the barbecue pit stoked at the Jacksons' on Saturday evening. Dad would volley the shuttlecock with Robert and me for fun, while the wives cuddled my sister and prepared dinner—steaks for the adults and hot dogs for the kids. I thought it was unfair putting the smell of steaks right in front of me, but Dad said, "Money doesn't grow on trees. When you're grown, you can have steaks."

As mosquitoes gathered for their nightly meal, the two women took turns fussing over my sister, swaddling her in a security of pillows pulled from every bed as she fell asleep. Entertainment for Robert and me took on its own chiseled identity—listening to a recorded fairy tale of "Peter and the Wolf." My focus split on the narrator talking and pressing my nose against the window screen watching the competitive match. Dad played Benjamin Jackson with every ounce of conviction in his body—running, stooping, screaming, stumbling, yelling at Mom, "Hurry, get it, get it, get it," grabbing his racket with frustration when she didn't. The game took precision, speed, stamina, and alertness, causing Dad to sweat with excitement and yelp in the air when he won. He seldom suffered defeat.

My parents' relationship with the Jacksons provided me with the first glimpse of what friendship offered—placing my trust in another to tell me the truth and do no harm. I'd see smiling faces, respect, and genuine camaraderie whenever watching the home movies with my parents' best friends. I knew behind the veneer stood *real* people.

From "Peter and the Wolf," I learned to depend on myself and never ask others for help except in extreme cases. From badminton I learned to play fair, hustle, and use every ounce of energy in my body against competitors. Winning was all that mattered. I never got over eating hot dogs instead of steak, though; I made a promise that I'd never do that to my kids. It was just plain unfair.

WE RICH

Taking a bath and seeing bubble creatures, sitting on my bed looking up at the sky, kicking dirt while walking home from school, lying on the grass under the big fig tree in our backyard, pumping up higher on the swing, I'd think without interruption and worry that Dad was going to see me and ask, "What are you thinking about?"

I'd think about singing or playing the piano on Ed Sullivan, visiting the castle splashed against the television screen at Disneyland, how Curly was treated mean on *The Three Stooges*, and all the pictures in the encyclopedia in Dad's study. I'd think about werewolves, Frankenstein, the feeling of kissing I'd see on romantic movies, people dying on airplanes, people dying in bank holdups, and people dying for our civil rights.

I'd think about my brother and wonder what his secret was because Dad never whipped him. I'd think about God, who His mother was, and Dad getting tired of me asking, "Where did God come from?" I had a hunch a bigger world existed out there somewhere and I wanted to know how to find it so I could be happy all the time.

I was thinking that afternoon when I turned the corner from school and saw a big truck in our driveway. "What's that truck doing here, Dad?" as he scribbled his signature on the clipboard. We both watched the truck back out as I gave him my daily hug, waiting for an answer. As soon as I walked through the front door, I saw it. My jaw dropped open, but there was no sound temporarily until I could inhale again.

"Ohhhhhhh my, ohhhhhhh my," grabbing my head, shrieking in disbelief, panting, jumping up and down. Briefly, I scrolled through my memory, *What good thing did I do?* as Dad read my mind. "It's either your late birthday present or your early Christmas present from your Mom and me." All feelings of mistreatment or abandonment vanished as waves of joy pushed me toward the bench of my Wurlitzer piano. My brother joined the celebration by reaching up and banging on the keys. Possession only took a few seconds, vibrating like a neon sign. "No, Robert, it's not a toy." From that moment on an imaginary label hung over the instrument. "Anyone wanting to play this piano needs my permission."

I thought nothing of asking Dad, "Are we rich?" after my piano arrived. Dad's answer, "No," did not do away with my hunch he wasn't telling the truth because having one carried a symbol of status in my mind.

The thought of being rich had first occurred to me when we moved to our brick house and again, a few months after Kelesha was born. I heard Mom and Dad talking about Mom's teaching job. That's when I knew we were rich. First day Mom went back to school, a little lady, Mrs. Miles, showed up early on Monday morning to watch over my sister. She reminded me of the big-breasted colored lady dressed in the white uniform and white shoes with the stockings tied at the knees that I met at a white lady's house once with Dad. We had only gone to that great big house once, when I was seven, but I had never forgotten her kind smile and the ice-cold glass of lemonade that she offered us.

She jumped whenever that white lady looked at her and Dad explained to me on our ride home, "She helps the lady around the house like a maid." I figured there was no harm in asking Mrs. Miles, "Are you the help?" that first day. But when I did, she turned and gave me a mean look like I had called her a bad name.

I liked the change. Mrs. Miles cooked breakfast, cleaned the kitchen, straightened the house, and left little treats for Robert and me on the stove every afternoon. My sister would be fed, bathed, and dressed in the cutest outfit every day by the time Mom walked in from school. She sure seemed like "the help" to me.

Dad preached money was the root of all evil. It made no sense to me as I'd watch the ushers walk proudly up to the front and prepare for offering, wearing gold-fringed shields neatly pinned on their left arm as if to say to the congregation, "Give me your money. You can trust me." They'd ceremoniously pass the plate from left to right and back again so people could place their hard-earned cash in silver-looking trays to pay Dad's salary. I was expected to reach into my pocketbook and pull out ten percent of my allowance. I was supposed to be cheerful too, but shucks, I'd have rather spent that money on buying paper dolls. After giving was over, we'd sing a song, hear a trustee say, "The more you give, the more you will receive," and sit down. Now you tell me, how could money be evil?

᎒TOUCHING MYSELF᎒

Flocks of birds made haste as if late for an appointment as yellow grass turned hard and dirty brown that winter of 1957. I grabbed my coat, wool cap, and mittens as the gray skies accentuated my mood—making logic of the life I had been dealt. All that mattered was keeping warm, while feeling the sensation of freedom coming down the steep hill on roller skates.

I tackled school subjects with vigor, my hands waving in the air. "Me teacher, please me," and by report-card time the A's and B's reflected my best efforts. Obedience became a shield pinned on my chest like a scarlet letter. Robert and I galloped around trees and hid behind corners of the house looking for opportunities to shoot each other point blank with his red cap guns. Jacks, Pick Up Stixs, and long hours of running my fingers across the piano helped the loneliness I felt beating against my face like a light mist.

There were plenty of girls on our street, but Dad wouldn't allow any fraternizing unless the whole family was saved. I had no idea why the hollow feeling visited me whenever I wasn't looking, but it did. Quite by accident one night, I started playing with the hairs on my hot spot, moving my thumb up and down until a most unusual and pleasurable feeling took over my body. I was sure it would never happen again, but with practice I found I could duplicate the feeling any time I felt lonely. It was my secret and I planned when I did it—late at night or early in the morning, when I was sure my parents were asleep and Jesus was busy looking somewhere else in another country. Afterwards, I felt relaxed and ready to face any obstacle that felt like dropping in on me.

One morning Mom surprised me, tiptoed in real quiet-like and caught me just as the good feeling was coming.

"What are you doing?" she demanded. I didn't know what to say.

She called Dad.

"Touching yourself is a sinful thing," she told me. "That's what bad people do. You must be a bad person. You must ask Jesus to cleanse your evil ways."

Dad just looked at me, shaking his head like I had killed someone. I felt like an awful sinner.

Masturbation had become a regular activity in my life, and I was sure I had discovered it. But I wondered, *Why are good-feeling things always so bad?* A month ticked away without television, roller-skates, ice cream, or playing with my dolls, but I didn't protest once, just thankful of escaping another whooping. After my punishment my hearing became acute. *I'll have to be more careful for every movement next time!*

A FAMILY AFFAIR

Dad's mind moved like a monkey on steroids swinging from branch to branch, dreaming up ideas and schemes to raise money for the church. One of the most successful and legendary events was the annual church musical. It was a family affair with my relatives traveling to come join the cast. I listened as the musical unfolded over long-distance calls—how many songs to fill a two-hour program, how to entertain people with both spiritual and contemporary music, whose soprano or alto voice fit the solo, would there be poems, would I play the piano, would Mom sing? It went on and on. Dad pretended to leave the decisions up to the group but I could hear him persuading my grandparents, aunts, and Mom toward exactly what he envisioned. I loved it when Dad was distracted.

My relatives arrived on Thursday to freshly waxed hardwood

floors, a perfectly manicured lawn, bathrooms that had been scrubbed with a toothbrush, and the smell of gumbo. Mom and Dad gave their room to my grandparents and moved into my room with Kelesha. My aunt moved into my brother's room and Robert and I stayed in Dad's study. It was like one big slumber party and reminded me of the days we lived in California.

Dad began our Saturday practice with a speech. "We must remember that we are an extraordinary and talented family. We're going to give a presentation that this city will never forget. I expect you to give your all. Make our parents proud. We will be victorious with the strength and guidance of Jesus Christ our living savior." I clung to every word.

The recital replaced the Sunday evening service. I fidgeted in my chair from excitement and worry that I would forget my piano solo. From time to time, Dad would stick his head out the door to see how the people were gathering in the sanctuary. As I peeked out around 6:30 to wave at Robert and Kelesha who were sitting with Mrs. Miles, I noticed most seats were empty, but Aunt Bea reminded Dad, "A singing concert is a very different way to celebrate and rejoice in the Lord. Don't be disappointed, R, if the audience isn't full."

At 7:00 sharp, Mrs. O'Neal played an organ overture, alerting the latecomers the program was beginning. A moment of silence filled the dimly lit sanctuary. My heart beat, bo-boom, bo-boom. Playing Follow the Leader, we walked out the door into a packed audience and Dad bowing.

We sang the first song together, "Lord, Make Me an Instrument." The applause was deafening and never stopped as one song flowed to the next.

Mrs. O'Neal had given me something more advanced to play: "Piano Concerto Theme from the First Movement" by Tchaikovsky. I was dressed in my favorite yellow satin dress, gold-colored Twinkle

Toe shoes, and fresh ringlets of curls. I sat erect, spreading my dress across the piano stool. My fingers sank into the ivory keys and the first note rang out with perfection. I leaned into every chord, my fingers dancing as my body swayed to the melody. There was clapping and more clapping, as I curtsied and took a bow. *Wow, I like this! I really like this. Maybe I will become a concert pianist.* Dad squeezed me and I became butter. "I am so proud of you. You've stolen the show." I didn't know if it was true, but I loved the attention of being in the spotlight.

Dad had often said, "Mother Dear is the reason I am such a great speaker." That night I understood why, as she walked out on stage looking like the famous Negro opera singer Marian Anderson—long black velvet skirt, white silk formal top, gloves that covered her elbows and a fancy scarf draped around her neck.

She cleared her throat. "The Creation, by James Weldon Johnson. And God stepped out on space"—she took a few steps—"and he looked around." She turned her head, and continued, "I'm lonely, I'll make me a world...And the light broke." She startled the audience by clapping her hands together. "Darkness covered everything...He hurled the world." She threw out her arms, "Fishes, fowls. And God said, that's good. And then he blew the breath of life and man became a living soul. Amen, Amen."

Mother Dear had acted out each adjective in the long poem, and when she finished there was nothing but silence. People were stunned. I had never seen anything like it in my life—the command of words, gestures, movement, and sounds with such feeling, emotion, and perfect diction. Mother Dear was a performer—an actress, and as she bowed under the thunderous applause, I knew my search for a profession was over. I would become a musical actress!

ᵍᵉDISNEYLANDᵉᵍ

I marked time by three seasons—the beginning of school, the ending of school, and three months off in the summer. I was always happy when the school year began; equally happy when it ended, knowing that, as I got bigger, I could make my own decisions, and even throw away my secrets and grief. The great thing about three months off in summer, though, was vacation. Dad believed in taking a vacation, and when he said, "We're going to Disneyland," I screamed.

Arriving back in California for the first time since leaving in 1953, my relatives tried to outdo each other by cooking country meals. "Putting on the dogs," they called it. Every day was filled with visiting popular San Francisco sights and I bragged to Robert and Kelesha, "I've been here before." I made up my mind to listen to Dad like I had on a hearing aid, making sure I didn't upset him in any way. After a week, we said our goodbyes and by nightfall we pulled into the Disneyland hotel. Sleep tap-danced through my body that night.

I ran a marathon ahead of Robert, yelling out, "Come on, slowpoke!" as soon as I saw Sleeping Beauty's castle. It was already 10:00 and Mom and Dad were walking too casually with my sister in her stroller. Dad bought four "E" tickets, enough for eleven rides. "That's $5.95 for adults, and $2.50 for children," the ticket agent said. *Eleven rides, not nearly enough*, I thought. Dad called a family meeting, while I blew big puffs of air out my mouth.

"We will all stay together and walk through each adventure and decide which rides we want to go on."

"How will we decide?" I asked Dad, disappointed I couldn't choose rides on my own. His look said it all; you know how, I'll decide.

It was the hottest day of the year in Orange County with way too much stimuli for one child who was tucked away in the slow-moving

South to take. I rode the Alice in Wonderland teacups, Jumbo the Elephant, the river ride, and It's a Small, Small World, following the rules without one grunt, but thinking, *Dad is torturing me. When can I ride the Matterhorn?* We had passed the screaming riders twice, and I was very conscious, *Five tickets left.* But the lines looped around the barricades and went on forever. I didn't care about waiting, but Dad insisted, "We'll come back."

Memorabilia hung from every side of my vision—Tinkerbell dolls, mouse ears, Mickey Mouse stuffed animals, snow castles, coloring books, puppets, Snow White shirts, Cinderella bracelets. I was allowed to purchase one souvenir, but the choices were endless. Each time, we went to a "land," Dad said, "Remember, you can only buy one thing, and you might see *something* that you like later," as I picked up a doll, a Jetson poster, a jeweled ring, a pirate's hat. I felt time was running out, and I wanted to have *something* to show the kids back home. By the time we entered Frontierland, I had a squirrelly feeling in my stomach I came to know over the years as acute anxiety and settled on a Davey Crockett hat. Not sure why, it wasn't feminine or girly, but Davey was strong, fearless, tackled bears, killed Indians, brought the bad people to justice, and lived in the wild, full of adventure. I liked those qualities. I plopped that beaver tail right on my head even though it was hot as hell, and wore it to school and every chance I could after we got home.

Robert and I joined the Indian circle as Dad recorded us mimicking the hatchet dance. I could see the sun moving to the west as the sound of the drum beat to a steady cadence, "boom, boom, boom, boom, boom, boom, boom, boom." It wasn't until Robert and Kelesha needed a nap that Dad spoke up. "Ready to take a ride on your Matterhorn?" Ice cream dripped down our fingers as we waited ninety minutes, inching a little bit closer until we were next. I jumped in the front seat as Dad handed over the tenth ticket. We crept up to the top s-l-o-w-l-y, inch by inch, and then whoosh, the wheels sped up and down over the tracks as the force of gravity took over. My body jerked from left to right, snapping my neck back and forth making me s-c-r-e-a-m. On the last descent we came down superfast, splashing through the cool water and getting all wet. I couldn't stay still. "That was the best fun I ever had in my whole life. Dad, can we go again? Please, please, pretty please?"

It had been a long day, so I wasn't surprised when he said, "Maybe we'll come back tomorrow." I beamed, hoping we could.

As we left, I walked backwards and watched a whole new park come alive at night with dancing spotlights, music blasting, parades, and colors like the rainbow. I wished for a magic wand to turn me into Tweety Bird so I could land on the ledge and watch until the very last light blinked off.

Instead, we headed home the next day through San Diego, stopping to cross the Mexican border to eat tacos and hit piñatas. Robert killed me with his rubber hatchet while I pretended to die over and over again. Kelesha stuffed her face with animal crackers all the way home. I couldn't get Disneyland out of my brain and kept replaying meeting the characters, eating junk food, and riding the Matterhorn. It was the only day that had ever gone by too fast. I wanted to stay for a week and promised myself, *One day you will come back and ride that Matterhorn fifty times.* I kept Davey's hat on my dresser to remind me, *Keep dreaming; fantasies do come true!*

☙DEVIL MUSIC☙

O ver the years, I would see bright-colored flyers wrapped around telephone poles and white posters stuck in barbershops and beauty parlors with James Brown, Bobby "Blue" Bland, Johnnie Taylor, B.B. King, and the Impressions plastered across the front. Our family loved music and I wondered why we never went to these concerts.

I asked Dad, "Who are these people?" and he reminded me, "That's devil's music. We are Christians. Christians don't listen to any music that makes your body jump around like that." I wanted to know so badly what made the music so devilish because I knew kids at church listened to music all the time, and they didn't act like devils to me. The only music I was allowed to listen to was classical. I loved Mozart, Debussy, Beethoven, Chopin, and Haydn; the melody calmed me down and gave me inner peace. But I sure was curious, because my toe just started tapping when I heard the beat blasting from some of the cars that stopped beside our car at the stoplight.

Dad avoided Milam Street, where the poles with the most advertisements were, even though it was the quickest way home. The curiosity kept nagging me when I heard the kids at church talking about the rock and roll man called James Brown. He was coming to town for a concert and some of the kids from church were going. I knew it was out of the question for me. So I asked Jesus, "If I want to listen to that music, does it make me a devil. Will I go to hell?" Everything inside me said, "No, don't believe everything you hear." Then I remembered the scriptures, "Obey your parents and your days will be long."

It was times like this having another adult like Aunt Bea to trust would have saved me from heartache. I'd beg her to tell me the truth about growing up, making friends, keeping Dad happy, being a better Christian, and knowing how to make the best decisions in my life. If Jesus was going to show me the way, I sure thought He should get started!

Just when I thought Jesus had gone deaf, a miracle happened. Mom won a radio from a raffle she entered. She was so excited about being lucky and I was too, because she planted it right on the counter in the kitchen where I washed and dried the daily dishes after finishing my homework. Everyone had gone to bed the first night as I turned it down real low. Station KBBL was what all my classmates listened to and sure enough first song was "Lonely Teardrops" by Jackie Wilson. My toe started first. Before I knew it my whole body was moving as I washed and dried every dish in the sink. Next morning I didn't feel anything. Nope, listening to devil music hadn't changed me one bit; it just gave me a way to be happy while I scrubbed pots and pans until they shined.

❦ BUDDING ❧

In the Fall of 1959, seventh grade hit me in the head like a horseshoe. New route to school, new classmates, more choices of subjects, and singing in the choir. I also found out while Dad was reading the newspaper out loud, We no longer colored. We Negro. Apparently, our labels had been redefined to make us less inferior. Even with all the newness around me, it seemed the biggest transition happened in me—in my body. One day at school, I raised my arms to do-si-do and caught a whiff of myself—phew, I didn't smell too good. I had bathed like always, but this odor was pungent. "You've got to raise up your arms, Ronita, when you square dance," my teacher insisted.

I asked Charlene after class, "Do you have any perfume or toilet water?" I figured it would camouflage the odor, at least for today. She
gave me Tabu and I sprinkled it all under my burgundy sweater. The
musk mixed with the sweetness made it worse, so I walked around
all day like a robot, with my arms pressed tightly to my torso.

My body odor concerned me, but I didn't dare say anything to
Mom in case she thought I wasn't cleaning myself properly. Mom
had bought me a brassiere in sixth grade that felt like a harness. I
hated my breasts sticking out, drawing stares from boys and men.
Mom wasn't very sensitive. When I slumped my shoulders to hide,
she said, "You must learn to wear foundations. You're blossoming,"

One day after school started I found two pamphlets on my bed:
"You and Your Body" and "All About Men-str-ua-tion." I flipped
through the pages wondering, *What's this? Does this have to do with
my body odor*? The pictures were bright pink, red, and purple and
the text read, "Females have eggs that can be fertilized by sperm to
make babies."

Oh, gross. Eggs, sperm, a real baby! I wasn't the least bit interested. I figured Mom left this for me. But it was Dad who hollered
out, "Did you read those pamphlets?"

Confused, I responded, "Yes, Sir," and wanted Mom to sit down
and explain what I just read. But Mom's explanation never came.
What I would come to know is I had just been given my parents' version of the "Birds and Bees 101."

Learning about my body became even more gross a couple of
months later. All the girls had to crowd into the auditorium. Our
principal, Mr. Jackson, wasn't present, and we were all looking
around asking each other, "Where are the boys?" Mrs. Brodin, the
gym teacher, climbed on the stage. "Girls, we're going to look at
a movie." I sat up as the female teachers started pulling down the
shades. I loved movies.

The music sounded like vampires would burst through the screen any moment, as the male announcer said, "Human reproduction." *Oh, it's those diagrams that were in my pamphlet*, but now they were wide across the screen.

"Ewww," echoed around the room, as they showed the male organ.

As I thought of Horace a heaviness settled in my chest. I hadn't seen Horace's penis or remembered blood, but I sure remembered the feeling. I was petrified.

Do I have a hymen? What does it look like? Should I be able to feel it? What if I don't have one? What will Dad do? The thought of a boy ever putting his penis in me again was revolting. I swore I'd lock myself between the sheets and the mattress on my honeymoon night and never have children. And I got scared that Dad would somehow twist what had happened to me as all my fault. The lights went on and hands started flying in the air as I sat shuddering, only one question stuck in my throat. *How am I going to get my hymen back?*

The next morning in homeroom, my three tablemates were already dissecting the movie when I arrived.

"It was so stupid and dumb," Georgia said.

Judy said, "It's not dumb at all. That's what people do when they're in love."

"What do you know about love?" Casey blurted out.

Judy giggled like she knew something we didn't. I was still worried about my hymen and what I would do if Dad found out. I tried to dismiss all of it as absurd and was sure my parents didn't have intercourse. They loved each other fine without it. But as the second bell rang signaling time for roll call, I found myself wrestling with secrets once again. *What am I going to do?*

Too bad I couldn't keep my worries to myself. When I got my first report card, I scanned down the subjects—no surprises, A's and B's. I looked at "conduct" last. With my body changing, and so many questions about growing up, some kind of chatter hormone had been released, causing me to yap nonstop with my tablemates. I had no idea there would be this kind of repercussion. I couldn't go home with a D in conduct. *Maybe I'll be kidnapped and my parents will be so happy to see me when I'm recovered, they won't think about my grades. Maybe a car will hit me. I know, I'll run away from home. Where will I go? Aunt Bea, maybe? How much money is in my red bank? I have no defense. Lord, please don't let Dad kill me. Lord, if you save me, I'll do anything.*

My lips trembled at the sight of Dad's Oldsmobile in the driveway and I began to hiccup as the front door opened. Dad was in the kitchen putting mustard greens in the pressure cooker.

"So how did you do your first quarter of seventh grade?" There was no time to pad myself for the whooping that came next. Dad's words kept ringing in my ears. "Getting good grades is important, but even a moron can keep her mouth shut. If you don't know how to behave, all the book learning means nothing." I didn't believe Dad, because if I came home with C's and D's in any of my major subjects, I knew I'd get the same whooping.

The next day, I resembled the three-statue monkeys; see nothing, say nothing, hear nothing when I sat down with my homeroom buddies.

Keeping my mouth closed was one of the hardest things I'd ever done. After a week, I asked my teacher, "Can you please change my seat?"

&WHITE IS THE MAGIC COLOR&

One Negro dentist lived in our neighborhood, but Mom drove across town to the white dentist for reasons I never knew until years later. I'd hear her talking about professional people of our own race. She had strong beliefs. White people were better than Negroes. She didn't trust Negroes to work as hard, perform as well, or complete a task up to her standards.

Old feelings of being a nigger filled my body as we walked through the steel doors and sat in the room marked "Colored." I could see copies of *Reader's Digest* and *Life* sitting on the tabletop in the white waiting room and wondered, *Where are our magazines?*

Adrenaline rushed through my body when my name was called. Looking back at Mom, you'd have thought I was being led away to the electric chair. In a way I was. A big needle pierced my gums while I clutched the chair asking Jesus, *Why do I deserve this pain?* Life wasn't getting any easier. I waited for the numbing to take effect as a fat tear ran down my cheek. I shrank even more in the chair as the loud drill went deeper.

Dr. Gray's stern voice reminded me of Dad. "Stay still."

How was I supposed to stay still, it hurt something awful. Every five minutes, Dr. Gray would command me to "Spit." I'd see red splotches of blood swirling around the water bowl and thought he was hurting me on purpose because I was Negro. I imagined him laughing his head off as he told his racist friends, "I pushed that drill in her teeth and she yelped like a wounded dog."

I asked Mom, "Why can't we just go to the Negro dentist! Whoever he is, at least I won't be scared to death." But Mom wouldn't budge, especially after Dr. Gray explained. "She needs something durable to take her through the teenage years. You've got two op-

tions, plastic caps or gold teeth. I recommend gold." Now I was dou-
bly sure that Mom and Dad would not allow me to wear gold on my
front teeth, because I'd heard Dad say, "That's a characteristic of boys
in gangs, devil worshippers, entertainers, and fast women." I didn't
know any girls with gold teeth and thought they looked awful. But
Mom agreed with Dr. Gray and I had to go see him every other week
for two months.

SEVEN UP

It was a steaming hot Saturday. One bottle of Mom's favorite, 7-Up,
sat in the refrigerator. I kept looking at the green bottle staring at
me, whenever I opened the door to get cool. With my dental work
in progress, soda pop was forbidden. The fourth time I opened the
door, I popped off the cap and took a big gulp, enjoying the bubbles
tickling my nose, forgetting all consequences. I figured Mom would
never know; there was plenty of time to run to the corner grocery
store. Right after I had swallowed several big gulps, I heard the car
door slam. Wheels turned frantically in my head searching for ideas.
I filled the bottle with water, popped the top on and placed it back
where I found it. As soon as Mom entered the front door, I volun-
teered my services.

"Do you need anything at the store? What about if we had peaches for dessert? I need a new pencil. Kelesha wants a Fudgesicle." Mom
paid me no mind.

Mom took a swig of 7-Up right after dinner, scrunching her face.
"There's something wrong with this soda." She took another swig. "It
tastes flat." Dad grabbed the bottle, took a sip and agreed something
was wrong. Now, if I had just kept my mouth closed, everything

might have been fine, but I started asking questions, motivated by guilt.

"What's wrong with it? Let me see."

It was enough for Dad's ears to perk up. "Who drank this 7-Up?"

"Not me, not me," Robert and I chimed in.

"Somebody drank this 7-Up and I'm going to find out who. Now just tell the truth and it will be all over," Dad said, trying to be calm.

It was a lie! I'd tell the truth and get a whooping anyway. The truth was, I had learned; not telling the truth worked just as well and even saved my butt sometimes. I honestly felt Jesus should have been whipping Dad for lying about not beating me if I told the truth. It was hypocrisy, the word Dad talked about constantly in his sermons.

Dad started his analysis. "Robert Jerome would have to get a chair and reach way up. Kelesha is a toddler. Hmm, who's left?" He looked at me.

I'd become used to whoopings by now and even deserved some of them. But I didn't start out each morning with getting the belt as my goal. The more belts landed on me, the more I became concerned about turning into *The Bad Seed*—the movie about a little girl getting into mischief, hurting people, and causing a man to die. She was electrocuted at the end, but nobody grieved. I felt cursed—born with a curious mind yearning to be liberated from restrictions, at the same time hoping I wasn't a bad seed like her. So I wondered, *How do you keep yourself from being yourself?*

There was an old piece of furniture with a record player in the hallway. It had never been used for punishment, but when Dad shouted, "Climb on and lie down on your stomach," I knew, *This was going to be bad*. He got his special belt—designed just for me, with slits and no buckle. I took a deep breath and held it as the first lick made contact with my skin.

"I hate a liar, I hate a liar. If you lie, then you'll steal. If you steal, then you'll cheat. If you cheat, then you'll kill." I had no intention of killing anyone at twelve years old; I just wanted a 7-Up and was trying to get out of a whooping.

I was never one to pretend a whooping didn't hurt, so I wailed with each downward motion until Dad got good and tired. He punished me again after he finished by sending me to buy Mom another 7-Up, so that anybody visiting the store would know Dad's belt and my legs were getting it on.

I felt resentment, not remorse, as I slid off the furniture. *Where is the love and compassion Dad talks about in his sermons?* I wanted to call him out so badly, and tell him he was wrong to be whooping me all the time. But I was scared that he would whoop me again.

By now, I had a constant dialogue going with Jesus, just like the ones I used to have with Doris. I would talk with Him all the time and tell Him about my troubles, even though I knew He knew before me. Looking up at the stars, I had a little talk with Jesus that night. *Jesus, is it right for Dad to whip me for lying when he lies himself? What about the love? You're always talking about love, forgiveness, and gentleness. Where is it?* Jesus sent no clue to me that night and there was no friend to console me, because we kept "family business" at home. And there was certainly no mommy to pat my head. There was just me, once again feeling abandoned and alone.

I reconciled that I needed to accept the most important task of my life that night—surviving Dad's wrath. I promised myself, *Get good grades, excel in music, keep your mouth shut tight, stay out of trouble, tell the truth, and serve the Lord.*

It was a promise I could not keep.

❧FRESH ORANGES ❧

As tiny buds filled tree branches, bumblebees stuck their bodies into tulips, and wool sweaters got put away in dark hiding places, I watched my classmates talking with boys and walking home with them. It all seemed innocent and a part of girls and boys socializing together. I also knew it wasn't part of my survival kit. Maybe it was my imagination, but Principal Jackson seemed to follow me around the campus and was always standing out front at the end of the school day. I think Dad asked him to, "Keep an eye on my girl!" So it caught me off-guard when a boy from band walked right up to me at the end of class one day. "Hi, I'm Lonnie. You really like music, huh?" That's all the attention it took. Over the next few weeks, I listened as he talked about playing the alto horn, being an only child, and growing up without a dad. He asked me, "What's it like being a preacher's daughter?" I only told him the good parts about being invited to dinner, standing while people applauded, and getting recognized for no special reason.

For my first music field trip, I agreed to sit next to Lonnie on the bus. I boarded the bus under the watchful eye of our female band and choir directors. They were constant companions, always laughing and eating lunch together. I dreamed one day of a girlfriend like that coming into my life; someone I could trust with my secrets. My classmates called them *peculiar* but I had no idea why, and didn't care because they always looked happy.

The bus was half full, kids scattered from front to back. More than once, I said "No thanks," as kids asked me to sit. It was warm and I found a seat halfway in the middle with a window already pulled down. I waited, wondering where the swell was coming from in my heart. I saw Lonnie running down the school's stairs with his horn case, tripping on the cracked sidewalks just as the bus was about to pull off. He looked particularly handsome in his band uniform, a white shirt, black tie, and dark pants. As he walked down the aisle, a couple of the girls seated alone said, "Want to sit by me?" He smiled politely and said, "I'm sitting in the back." When he got to me, he slipped awkwardly into the seat, and we both smiled. We rode for forty minutes in silence, taking in our existence—middle-income Negro and white neighborhoods, shotgun houses with barefoot children waving, vegetable fields, red dirt ditches next to unpaved rural roads. A warm new feeling arose in me as we reached our destination and he spoke softly. "We'll sit together on the way back." My smile was my answer.

On the way back he wasted no time grabbing my hand, but no words passed between us. I wondered why I hadn't noticed before, *he smells like fresh oranges.* As we turned the corner a block from school, Lonnie did something unexpected. He leaned over and pecked me on the lips. It happened so fast I didn't know whether to slap his face or blush. I did know a weird feeling jolted me in my stomach, a feeling I'd never had before, and I wondered, *Is that natural?* As the bus door opened, I pulled my hand away, worried now about what my classmates would say, and not sure if Dad was waiting for me out front. Silently, we unloaded the bus. "I'll see you tomorrow," he said. My feet didn't touch the ground.

Judy brushed up against me as I hung up my robe. "I saw you two." Her comments shook my nerves. By the time I walked out of the schoolyard, Dad was waiting and talking with Judy. Fear jumped right in my throat. *Is she turning into a tattletale? What if she tries to blackmail me?* I knew I'd give her whatever she wanted, because for Dad, a peck on the lips qualified me for the title of wild girl. Next day at school, I pleaded with Judy, "Please don't say anything to your mom." She laughed. "I wouldn't do that; I'm your friend, and anyway

I've got a boyfriend too." Relief flooded my body, but I corrected her. "Lonnie is not my boyfriend!"

Lonnie and I talked a few more times, but never held hands again. I could never get him to tell me what Mr. Jackson said when he was called to the office right after our excursion. He moved to Dallas during the summer and our paths never crossed again.

⚞EXPLORING⚞

W e were an unlikely foursome. Collie was the fashion plate. She took after her mother who walked into church every Sunday wearing a spectacular outfit with a feathered hat or a boa around her neck like she was a top model for *Vogue*. Collie was from a broken home and was spoiled by her grandfather, who owned the only Negro newspaper stand in town and bought her anything she wanted. She was an original—first with the trapeze, chemise, and sack dress; Revlon makeup, pantyhose stockings, suede heels, or flip hairstyle; and the first to show off her figure and talk about boys. Collie lived in a shotgun house in what was referred to as "the bottom."

Judy was the extra-smart one. I knew because our moms compared our intelligence scores. That kind of information should have been "family business," but Mom shared it anyway. We were rivals in the youth activities at our church, competing with speeches and piano recitals. She came from a big, extended family of aunts, uncles, grandparents, and cousins who all attended our church. Judy had recently started to look unhappy because her mother was expecting a fifth child. She dressed plain, never made waves, and was always pleasant. All us kids knew about her boyfriend, Lennox, who wore starched beige khaki pants and wore his hair like Elvis, because her dad caught her with him once and whooped her worse than Dad whooped me. It didn't keep them away from each other, however, so I guessed her parents accepted him as long as she kept making straight A's.

Ann was my Twinkle Toe friend, the only girl I could visit. Once in a while, Dad even allowed me to spend the night. Ann lived in the section of town with the lawyers and doctors, where lots of kids went to Catholic school. We went to the same hairdresser, shopped at the same expensive clothing stores, and occasionally showed up with the same outfit. Deep down, I thought Ann was better than me, poised and polished, mostly, because she didn't seem to have a care in the world except growing up.

And then there was me.

We were granted our wish to room together at the annual church youth conference, held at Grambling College a week after school closed. It was the first time I had ever been with girls my age for an extended period of time overnight. I was fumbly and fidgety, shy about show-ing any of my body parts, so I dressed in the bathroom with the door locked, remembering all the hints I'd been told about keeping my chastity, as if these girls were going to molest me. But Collie stepped right out of her underpants in front of us and pulled up her pajamas without the least hint of shame. I turned away.

After active days of attending Bible study, we'd crawl into bed and talk about the day's teachings, until we nodded off to sleep. One night the talk led to boys. Judy said, "I wonder what it's like to be married and have intercourse?"

I didn't want to hear anything about sex and told her so. "We're too young to be talking about intercourse."

We all got quiet except Collie, who couldn't help snickering. "I bet a boy's organ feels squishy like a baked sweet potato."

We laughed hard, which eased my nervousness a little on the

subject. I chimed in, sharing my position. "I'm going to tie myself to the mattress on my honeymoon night. My husband will have to work so hard to get to me, he'll give up." Unable to forget about Horace, I couldn't image anything pleasurable coming from such an intrusion of my body. I wanted to disclose my secret to the girls so bad, but I couldn't chance it; they might not like me anymore.

Judy got serious. "Want to know what happens?" Even though I didn't want it to happen to me, I was all ears and propped myself right up on the bed. "First you tongue kiss for a long time...then your ears and neck get kissed...then your breasts and nipples get kissed. You take off your clothes and lie on your back, while your husband gets on top of you still kissing your breasts." It sounded mighty awkward to me, all that kissing and getting out of your clothes at the same time. "His organ will grow and that's when it happens."

"What?" I asked.

"He sticks his organ in you and you both move around."

"And then what?" Ann asked.

"Don't y'all know anything?" Collie interrupted. "Then you're filled with feelings of undying passion and love," Judy continued. I thought about all the passion I'd seen in movies, and had to admit, "Love does look wonderful." But I knew from the movie *Johnny Belinda* there were at least two sides to Judy's romantic picture.

I can't tell you where the suggestion originated or how we paired together, but the conversation had stirred us up and we all wanted to know what it felt like to touch someone else. Collie and Judy landed in one bunk and Ann and I in the other.

We were slow to unbutton our pajama tops and take off the bottoms, awkward at knowing where to begin, what to touch or not touch. We laid together in our panties, not saying a word—hugging each other real close, never kissing or caressing developing breasts but moving our bodies. The sensation of rubbing together against a warm body felt comforting. With my eyes shut tight, I was sure one of life's mysteries was being revealed as little sounds and sighs escaped from our mouths. I waited, expecting the feeling of relief that came when I placed my hands between my legs, but it never did. The only conclusion that made sense to me was the feeling would come on my wedding night.

Later, lying alone in my bunk, worry entered my bed uninvited as I thought about Jesus. I hadn't been touching myself; I had been touching another girl. My sin mushroomed.

Next morning we acted like our tongues had been slashed off, looking straight ahead and avoiding each other's eyes.

Returning home, I was preoccupied, wondering, *Will our friendships be strengthened or compromised? Will our secret be shared with parents? Will we ever look each other in the eye again?* I worried for nothing. Weeks turned into months and nobody said anything. Once or twice, I had to think hard, *Did it really happen?*

GRANDMA CARGO

Mom attended graduate school that summer of 1959 in Washington, D.C., where her sister lived. She took Kelesha with her. Robert and I had Dad all to ourselves. Mid-July, he shipped us to my grandmother's for a month.

A whole month with my brother and Mother Dear wasn't my idea of the best summer. "May we stay with Aunt Dorothy too?" I asked Dad. "You'll have to ask my mother," which I took as hopeful.

The drive to Abbeville was 208 miles. I made one tuna fish sandwich each, hoping we'd stop at the Dairy Queen for the best-tasting hamburger an hour away from Shreveport. We still had to go to the back window, never knowing for sure the meaning of the snicker on the face of the sullen-looking male attendant with a cigarette hanging from his mouth. Red, yellow, and brown stains covered his white apron and his fingers had lots of cuts. He took Dad's money and threw the bag in front of us with a frown. I wanted to say, "We didn't do anything to you, Mister. Why are you looking so mean?" But I knew better than to speak. I'd check for cigarette ashes or foreign items that didn't look like they belonged on a burger because we could never trust what white people put on our food. I'd bitten into more than my fair share of mildewed buns and pungent-tasting meat in my young years. But on this day, I tore into the warm sesame-seed bun, spilling mustard, onions, and pickles all over myself, as if I had been on a barren island for months without food. It remains the best burger I ever ate in my life.

The upholstery in the turquoise-and-white Oldsmobile made me sticky as I stuck my head out the window, passing town after town, tasting the flavor of hot dust. We'd come to stop signs beside carloads of white children. They would stick out their tongues, mouthing "N-i-g-g-e-r." I accepted my distinction but wondered why Jesus let segregation keep happening.

We sped through spaces of open fields, sun beating down without mercy on dark-skinned bodies covered from head to toe with strawhats or bandannas and thick shirts or dresses of burlap or gingham. Bodies bent over, moving methodically picking cotton. I had picked cotton once for fun and made eighty-six cents after two hours in the hot sun. Oh yes, it was still a way of life for some people.

Dad had a lead foot, but managed to never get stopped by the highway patrol. I suppose being a good soldier for Christ got a little monotonous, and speeding was Dad's way of having a little fun. I often wondered why Dad never got stopped, though. The only reason I could figure was the highway patrol thought Dad was a speeding white man.

Four hours after we left Logan Street in Shreveport, we pulled up to Mother Dear's driveway at 706 Hawthorne Street.

My grandmother reminded me of the wealthy women I saw in movies. She had a big four-bedroom house, a gigantic backyard with pecan trees, a white picket fence, and a wrap-around porch with a white swing. She still kept the latest model car and this time a black Cadillac stood sparkling in the car stall. Dad's "toot, toot" announced our arrival.

"Hey, Shaa, did you have a safe trip?"

Dad couldn't contain himself. "Mother Dear, is that a new car?"

"Oh, that's old, Shaa," she told him and shooed us right into the kitchen.

Dad and his mother talked all through the day and next morning he gently grabbed my shoulders and looked me right in my eyes. "You mind your grandmother and watch over your little brother."

"Yes, Sir," I replied and waved until the car was out of sight, calculating when I'd ask to visit my liberal-thinking Aunt Dorothy.

Over the years I had come to know my grandmother's house so well that each bedroom bore a name. Mother Dear slept in the Abraham Lincoln room because the heavy black furniture reminded me of pioneer days. The princess room had a turquoise chiffon bedspread with ruffles, an ivory dresser with gold trim, and a fancy rocking chair. It was the room I had slept in years before when my grandfather Bud died. His body was set out in the maroon-upholstered living room and one night when everybody was asleep I tiptoed up to the casket. His hand felt cold and hard. I asked him, "What's it like to be with Jesus?" and was sure I saw his mouth curl, even though my grandfather never went to church.

The fun room looked like an army barracks with ten beds, where I'd jump from bed to bed like Goldilocks. During Christmas when my aunts and uncles came, we'd sleep, have morning coffee, play checkers, open presents, and listen to stories until late at night. Sometimes

Mother Dear had roomers, but I didn't see one man lurking about. My favorite was the shoe room where she kept seventy-six pairs of shoes. I'd pass the day slipping my foot into each pair, fantasizing... Hollywood, New York, and Paris wrapped in a mink coat, a long shimmery dress covered with sequins underneath, and carrying a diamond cigarette holder. I'd step out of the limousine, wave to fans, give big tips to the doormen, drink champagne, and chat with the celebrities until I heard, "Ronita, put my shoes back!"

On Sundays, we had to be dressed by 6:00 a.m. Mother Dear broadcast on the radio at 7:00. Forty minutes later as the sun continued its rise, we turned onto a dirt road where I could see up close the letters "WFCC" printed prominently on the outside of a shack-looking house. Expecting elegance, I said, "That's the radio station?" as Mother Dear swung into the space, leaving a trail of dust. Surprisingly, a white man stood in the doorway with earphones in his hand waving us inside. "You better hurry up, Orea, you're on." *I didn't know white people liked Negro music.* In a soothing baritone voice the man talked about sponsorship before holding up his fingers, 3-2-1. "And now we bring to you 'Fellowship with Christ,' featuring Mrs. Orea Thomas." Her fat, stubby fingers started playing the piano, as her head swayed from side to side. I watched as she played and sang, unable to fully comprehend my Negro grandmother on the white radio. I waited for the feeling to come over me making me weep like at church with the organ, but not even a little tiny tear felt like dropping that morning.

"We'll be right back," the announcer told the microphone, while Mother Dear sat relaxed, waiting for his finger to point again. All the rushing to get ready was over in twenty minutes! I was proud anyway and couldn't wait to tell my friends, "My grandmother's a celebrity."

❦ GOD'S TALKING ❧

Mother Dear was an entrepreneur too. She called her establishment The Shop and it was located at the recreation center close to the school, where all the kids hung out at the swimming pool during the summer. After thirty-five years of teaching, she knew everybody.

"Hello Miss Orea. How you doing today? Those your grandchillin?" the kids would say as they dug into their pockets, looking for pennies and nickels. The scorching heat was ruthless. Kids flocked to her store, the only one where Negro children could purchase ice cream, chips, pickles, soda pop, hot dogs, popcorn, and candy. Her number-one seller was the snow cone—twelve flavors from strawberry to lemon-lime. Every time the door opened, a little bell rang and I would put away my summer novel, *Little Women*, and say to Robert, "Prepare for a sale." He'd perk up, knowing whatever shaved ice was left would be his. I couldn't work fast enough most days, grinding ice and pouring juice all over the top, especially on days the thermostat hit ninety degrees. There was this one girl, Dolly, who asked for the same thing every day.

"Can I have a mix?"

I wanted to tell her so bad, "It's 'may I,' 'cause you always can."

I'd see her trotting down the road in her wet bathing suit, dripping water and working her yo-yo, as I prepared to do a lot of pouring. By the time I'd get to the sixth color, there'd be syrup all over the floor and I'd be making a mighty mess. I sure liked working at The Shop, though, 'cause I got to be important being Miss Orea's granddaughter.

Best thing about The Shop was that it was close to the swimming pool. I was mostly a shallow-water dog paddler and Mother Dear didn't swim either, but she allowed Robert and me to swim unsupervised anytime we wanted, as long as I promised to stay out of the deep water and watch him.

We had been swimming happily one afternoon when raindrops broke through the blistering sunshine and started to pelt our skin. I repeated what I had heard so many times but didn't understand, "Devil beating his wife," I told Robert. Dark clouds covered the sky and the rain got heavier. We made a game of counting raindrops by opening our mouths. "I got that one. You got that one. You missed that one," and dunking our heads in the water. I half-thought I heard my name being called after several dunks but I didn't pay it no mind. Next big dunk, I jumped out of the water and saw Mother Dear peering down at me.

"Ronita, GET OUT OF THAT WATER, NOW."

She didn't startle just me; all the kids started jumping out of the water too. Robert and I scurried to the dressing rooms, as she followed me, repeating, "Don't you know better than to be swimming in water when the Lord is speaking?"

"I didn't hear the Lord say anything," I said, and she gave me the look I'd seen before in Dad's eyes. Still wet, I pulled up my shorts, not in the mood for a sermon as Mother Dear charged out of the girls' dressing room and walked into the boys' room. She brought Robert out with one shoe off and one leg in his pants. He was just as confused as I was. She barked at us all the way home about the Lord speaking.

The sky got dark gray and black as the thunder roared. Pecan tree branches and duck feathers blew all over the yard.

"Cover all the mirrors and make sure the lights are off."

I ran from room to room, throwing whatever loose material I could find over the mirrors, while Robert stood shivering with a wet towel around his body. With every mirror covered she ordered us to

"Get on your knees and pray." The thunder's roar was deafening and the whistle from the wind blew so hard that the windows started to rattle. I wasn't afraid. I had seen rain like this before and wondered, *What's all the fuss about*?

After listening to the ticking clock and Mother Dear mumble for half an hour, my knees started aching. It wasn't my intent to be irreverent, when I asked her softly, "Mother Dear, how long…" "Silence," she commanded sharply. I didn't say another word. The howling rain had turned to showers and periodic thunder could be heard in the distance by the time she finally said, "You can get up, but stay quiet and don't move. The Lord is still talking!" As the three of us crouched in the corner with the Bible, I thought, *Mother Dear is a real scaredy-cat.* But I snapped when I looked at the fear on my brother's face. "You are scaring us. You're not supposed to do that. You're the grown-up. You're supposed to be brave. How do you know what Jesus is saying? We want to go home!" I couldn't believe the spewing and cupped my mouth with my hand. The look on Mother Dear's face told me, *Uh-oh, now you've done it!*

I could hear the number being dialed on the rotary phone. She was beside herself. "Son, you need to teach your daughter some manners. She is an ungrateful, insolent child and deserves to have her mouth washed out with soap. Come get them. Yes, yes, no, no, fine, okay." I waited for the click. *Maybe I should apologize, 'cause I know a real storm is coming my way.*

❦THE RALLY❦

While we were away, racial tensions had kicked up like dandruff back home. Dr. Martin Luther King, Jr. was coming to speak at a big rally. Shocking news came in every day on the television, the Negro newspaper, and from the locals: Mrs. Washington suffering a heart attack when white boys scared her on the bus, a little boy getting beat up looking for his lost dog, Reverend Obee losing his livestock and crops when the barn was set on fire, beatings and burned crosses. I'd eavesdrop, wondering if I'd ever stop hearing bad things about white folks. From the pulpit, Dad talked about segregation and bigotry and how we had to stand up for ourselves as a people. He called white people "the devil's hands and legs" who would answer to Jesus on judgment day and would burn in hell forever.

The thirty and forty-year-olds like my parents would shout and stomp, as Dad ignited the crowd. "Do not accept apathy by accepting inferiority! Some of us will be brutalized. Are you ready to put yourself on the line for freedom; freedom for your family and generations to come? Are you ready to meet your heavenly Father for our cause?" The teenage kids would stand, clap and shout, "We will fight, march, die for our freedom!" I couldn't die yet because I wasn't sure Jesus had forgiven me for what Horace did to me, and I didn't want to go to hell and burn for the rest of my life. But the old grannies seemed reluctant and would mumble, "Y'all gonna get yourself kilt."

Dad was one of the leaders of the movement, along with pastors from various churches around town. They met secretly, never knowing whom to trust with their plans for speeches or marches, even though news of protests headlined the newspaper and television daily. I understood civil rights as a dangerous business. People died so I could sit on a clean toilet seat and drink clean water.

Dad's commitment to equality wasn't a secret to Mom, but during the weeks she was away, his involvement deepened. I had been preparing myself for the worst after sassing Mother Dear, but when Dad picked us up two weeks before the rally, he wasn't focused on me at all. On the drive home, he couldn't stop talking. "Segregation is coming to an end. We will no longer be treated like second-class citizens." We passed the Greyhound bus station, saw the dark faces in the last four rows and the big sign, "Colored." Dad got agitated. "Look at that. Segregation's got to come to an end."

I wasn't concentrating on the bus or the big sign. Talking back to Mother Dear was like committing a federal crime, except there would be no judge or jury to hear my plea. I thanked segregation that day for saving my ass.

Dad turned on the TV right after we returned home and we watched dogs tearing human flesh, water hoses forcing men, women, and children into sewage drains and blood flowing from heads. I'd sit with my hands over my mouth gasping and wondering, *How can white people be so mean*? It impressed upon me how important it was to hear Dr. King who was coming to town. Dad shook his head. "It's too dangerous—I can't take that chance." Members from the rally warned him too. "Best not take your children." I kept asking, "But Dad, I just have to go." He stuck to his ground. "I promised your mother. She would never forgive me if anything happened to you."

At Sunday school I learned some of the kids were going to the rally, and told Dad "Charlene, Betsy, Donald, Vincent, Herbert, Willis, and Margo are going to the rally with their parents. Remember what you told me a long time ago about how I'm the example? How the other children and the congregation look up to me? It will look funny if I'm not by your side. I think it's what Jesus wants me to do." And then I threw in the last appeal, repeating what Charlene had told me about why her mom said yes. "Dad, we get special credit in our civics class if we attend the rally." I didn't know if it was true or false, but I was desperate and willing to try anything. Dad stared at me and then gave in. "Okay, but don't tell your mother."

The night before the rally, I thought about my decision—maybe our march would be on television or in the newspaper and we'd see ourselves standing right next to Dr. King.

"Hold my hand tight and stay by my side," Dad instructed me as we drove to the big Baptist church at 6:00. All the pastors were up front making speeches, looking serious. Candles with paper napkins were handed out to anyone who wanted one, and after a while it got dark. The flames began to light up the street, as the person next to me moved her lit candle next to mine until the candle flames formed a pattern of unity around the stage.

Dad was speaking as the crowd shouted, "Freedom, freedom, freedom." He stood tall. "YES, it's time for freedom and justice. God created all people equal. We MUST stand up," and he clenched his fist, "peacefully for ourselves because God loves everyone and He gave us the strength to fight for what is rightfully ours." It felt like church when the Holy Ghost took him over and notes became unnecessary. People continued to shout, "Freedom, freedom, freedom," pushing, causing pressure on the back of my body. There was no air. I felt queasy. A stout woman passed out and we stood back, fanning, as they lifted her over the crowd. I remembered Mom's words about cleanliness. "Never go out with dirty underwear, you never know if you'll be hit by a truck and carried off." A woman fainting didn't stop the speeches from continuing. I covered my ears as the crowd interrupted almost every other sentence, "One Man—One Vote." *Where was Dr. King?*

One of the pastors gave instructions. "Now we're gonna line up in rows of ten. No pushing. We gonna march peaceful-like. No pushing. We don't want to give no cause for anybody to get hurt. No pushing please." I grabbed Dad's hand and walked slowly down Milam Street, singing freedom songs. "We shall overcome, black and white together," "Oh'o freedom, Oh'o, freedom, and before I'll be a slave, I'll be buried in my grave. And go home to my Lord to be free," "This Little Light of Mine," "I woke up this morning with my mind, stayed on freedom. Hallelu, Hallelu, Hallelujah." The singing never stopped until the sporadic shouting began, "We want freedom, we want freedom."

I saw policemen with helmets scowling on the sidelines, beating the palms of their hands with billy clubs. I moved closer to Dad, grabbing his hand even tighter. He shouted out, "Don't show them your fear. We walk under the protection of God." I eased the grip of his hand picking up my feet with intention as if marching to Zion, while the warm wax trickled down my fingers. I raised my voice as high as I could, "We want freedom, we want freedom."

Despite the agitation we'd seen on television from similar marches, none of us was harmed. I was relieved when we got to the Jones Memorial church where the crowd continued to sing and chant before it dispersed. Safely home, Dad turned on the television and started switching channels. I hoped to see myself, but all I heard from the announcer was "Dr. King...in Selma." It turned out Dr. King's itinerary had changed at the last minute, and he wasn't even at the rally. I was disappointed but proud of my bravery...I marched for freedom! Dr. King arrived with his full entourage a few weeks later and it was one of Shreveport's biggest rallies. Dad marched too, right up front, but not me. Mom was back home.

⟨TAKING A RISKY STAND⟩

After Dr. King left, Dad was agitated more than ever. "It's time for less talk and more action," he kept saying. Doors to the bedroom and study were closed; Dad ate his dinner in a hurry and left; we stopped visiting the Jacksons and the camera equipment collected dust. Sunday morning, Dad broke the news in the pulpit. "I have decided to run for school board." After the sermon people lingered, shaking his hand. "We're with you, Reverend." I didn't know the purpose of a school board, but with all the well-wishers, I figured it was an important job.

While Mom spooned ice cream and peaches, we found out more from Dad. "I picked up an application for candidate. I'm getting in the race late, but I've got lots of support around town. I think I can win." I thought he could too. Dad was a terrific motivational speaker, respected and well-liked in the community. He didn't flirt with the women, steal money from the church, smoke or drink whiskey—all the bad things I'd heard about some of the other preachers in our town. Mom's reputation as a high-school counselor had brought her recognition, and I had never been sent to the principal's office. To the outside world, we made the portrait of a perfect family—aside from our private "family business" of abuse, that is. Just one problem threw a monkey wrench into the equation: a Negro had never run for school board. Dad wouldn't have even gotten an application if the clerk had known his race. She was young and figured no Negro in his right mind would ask for an application. "Y'all almost missed the deadline," was all she said. "Get that paperwork back by Friday."

With green or blue eyes and wavy hair, Negroes passed for white. One of our church members, Mr. Selber, looked just like a white man and it was rumored he was the offspring of the Selber Brothers store owner. And I knew two brothers, Sherman and Jeffrey, who sat downstairs in the Strand Theater, rubbing elbows with white people all the time. That's how the rest of us found out about the plush seats, juicy hot dogs, fresh buttered popcorn, and clean, shiny bathroom. I chuckled to myself, imagining the faces of white teenagers if they would have ever learned rubbing elbows or urinating next to a Negro is what they had been doing all afternoon.

All the commotion about civil rights and running for school

board had overshadowed where I was going to begin eighth grade. I wanted to go to the new Catholic school and had already told my friends I could. As the kids from church started sharing news about uniforms, I got brave.

Dad said, "We're Methodist. You can't go to a Catholic school. That would be betrayal."

I tried to make a case. "Lots of the kids from church are going. They teach discipline and religion and will have a great band."

"I don't care what they teach," Dad continued. "I've spoken to all the parents and hope they will change their minds. And YOU can't do what everybody else does. I'm running for office. It wouldn't look right for the preacher's daughter to go to a parochial school."

I didn't know what I was going to say now, since I had told everybody I was going too. It was ironic; even the vice-principal at my public school sent his daughter to the Catholic school. I didn't understand. I thought Dad wanted me to get the best education, mingle with the good kids, and hear more about Mary and Jesus!

Overnight, our house turned into an election office. Boxes of 4x6 cards and large posters with Dad's picture crowded the dining-room floor. The buzzword was "strategy." Dad's picture in his clergy collar made him look serious enough, although I wasn't sure wearing a collar was the best idea. What about the people who didn't go to church? He needed their vote too.

I learned when you stood up for integration, you stuck out—white people looked at us with disgust whenever Dad was with us. But the Negro people patted Dad on the back, told him "You've got our support," and honked their horns when we passed. I was so proud. One day halfway through the campaign, the phone started ringing. Mom answered it, but all she heard was heavy breathing. It kept ringing over and over again, and she told me, "Somebody keeps dialing a wrong number." By the next day Mom started slamming the phone down. I got a talking-to after that. "Don't pick up the phone."

The ringing wouldn't stop the day Mom and Dad left me in charge. I put toilet paper in my ears. It didn't help. So I figured I'd tell whoever it was to stop calling.

"Hey, Nigger," the male voice said, "We're going to come and get you and your mammy and we're going to take you out in the woods, gang-rape you, cut you open and skin you...." I dropped the phone, my ears on fire with the venom. My imagination took over. *They're coming to get me. How do I defend myself? Protect Robert and Kelesha? Where are my parents? Who can I call? Are they watching the house?*

My parents found us hunkered down in my room. I apologized to Dad. Boy, was he angry when I told him what happened. He wasn't upset with me, though. I wasn't entirely clear about how rape happened, but I knew it had something to do with Horace's privates, the pamphlet, and having babies. And I just knew it was a bad thing because the lady in the next block got raped. I'd wave at her working in the garden when we passed; she was so beautiful. After the rape, it was like she disappeared off the face of the earth. The thought of being raped gave me nightmares of wolves with deep red eye sockets hunting me down in a desert. I kept running and running, until they caught up with me, tearing me open. I must have screamed that night, because when I woke up Dad was leaning over me. "It will be all right."

A month before the election I was walking home alone from school on the road that ran parallel to the high school. It served as a dead-end connector for twelve different streets. On one side tall shrubs camouflaged the cyclone fence. On the other all you could see were the sides of houses. I had just switched sides to give my hands a rest from carrying my French horn. Band practice had been later than usual and I felt tired. The late fall day had left a smoky haze punctuated by an early chill in the air. A car came out of nowhere.

"Nigger, we're going to get you, Nigger, we're going to get you! When we finish with you, they ain't gonna know who you are."

I almost peed my pants; I slowly turned and saw four jeering white boys in a white convertible with a red interior.

The engine revved. "Come on, baby, give me some sugar, we're going to treat you real good, come on, let's go for a ride."

Nobody prepares you for a moment like this. No reading the Ten Commandments, saying "Amen" to sermons, or getting good grades. There is no pamphlet to casually leave on the bed or movie show in the auditorium about what to do. All I had was my basic instinct, and no time to waste. *Run home—won't make it with this French horn. Bang on someone's door—don't see lights anywhere. Start screaming, scare them away, Don't see anybody. Reason with them—no, they hate you!*

The car bumper inched closer, making a jerky racing sound. I could feel the heat of the steel snapping at the back of my legs. My brain acted out the worst-case scenario. *One of me, four of them— easy picking. Plenty of time to jump out, grab me, throw me down in the back seat, and hit the accelerator. By the time they find me, if they find me, I'll be too far gone to ever recover from the physical and emotional trauma.* I knew this was possible because I'd heard about it happening to girls in Georgia and Alabama in the newspaper. I had one choice, "Our Father, which is in heaven..." as the taunting continued. I took one purposeful step at a time, keeping my head bowed, hoping I wouldn't stumble or fall and wondering, *Where is everybody?* Cars usually sped by me at dusk. I kept praying, one more block to go, as perspiration became my new friend and the engine revved.

I almost kissed the Logan Street sign. The motor raced as the car made a U-turn, burning rubber and sped away. I couldn't stop shaking. My knees moved into a faster gear as I climbed the hill, looking up to heaven. I had just enough energy to run the last half block, frantically huffing and puffing, pouring out the episode to Dad when I got into the house. His face turned crimson as he slammed his fist down hard.

There was no place to report this kind of harassment. Well, you could report it, but nothing would happen. We had never heard of white boys cruising around in all-Negro neighborhoods. Dad figured I was targeted because of the campaign, which caused Mom and Dad to talk behind a closed door that night. I don't know what they talked about, but next morning Dad poked his head in my room. "Are you all right? I've got to press on and you've got to be a good soldier. I'll pick you up from school until this is over." I felt like Dr. King's child after that, a strange mixture of pride and fear. The phone kept ringing.

We were counting the weeks until the election when Mom noticed the plant knocked over on my piano several days later. Blood was all over the window and had formed a path out to the driveway, where it stopped. This time, Dad called the police. Two days later, an officer took Dad's statement. I was beginning to wonder if running for school board was worth it. No sooner had Dad made the report than we heard banging at our front door early one morning before dawn. Dad walked out with no protection except his faith and peeked through the door. "Stay in your room," he called back to all of us. He found a poster with a burning cross and a dark-skinned man hanging from a noose with fire under his feet. It was signed "KKK." For the first time, I thought seriously, *We might all be killed.*

Racism had never made sense to me. I didn't know why God allowed white folks to hide under sheets to scare, beat, and murder. I couldn't comprehend how the God who saved me from the heckling boys was the same God those boys prayed to. I couldn't understand why the white police officer showed up with his gun, billy club, and handcuffs dangling without showing any empathy; with so many questions, you'd have thought we put the poster in our own yard.

Dad lost. He wasn't ever going to get any of the white votes, but the registration drive and bull-horned trucks driving up and down the streets turned the election into a real race. Dad was encouraged and entered the pulpit cheering. "We sure stirred up that wasp nest. We'll get them next time," he joked. But next time never came; Dad's political aspirations were over.

ANGEL WITHOUT WINGS

The election ended just as I entered the second month of my eighth year of school. Chewing my nails calmed me. One day in class, my teacher called out my name. "Miss Kennedy wants to see you." The mere sound of my name being called to go to the administrator's office was enough to send a chill up my spine. As I made my way to her office, I backtracked over all my activities and found nothing that alarmed me. Most of the kids knew who I was by now and that Dad had a reputation for high standards. They teased me, "You can't do n-o-t-h-i-n-g." Knowing it was true, I still wanted to show them, "Y-e-s I c-a-n." When boys tried to say something nice to me, a classmate from church would warn them, "Do you know who that is?" and that boy would retreat so fast, just like Lonnie when Mr. Jackson got through speaking to him. On one hand, I liked the respect it gave me, but on the other, I didn't like being seen as a square. It wasn't so much the label of being a preacher's kid, either. It was being Dad's kid.

Miss Kennedy was a plump woman who dressed very stylishly

and wore a lot of black. She wore thick, oversize, black horn-rimmed glasses that reminded me of Egghead Jr. from "Looney Tunes." I liked her, but she was no pushover. I had no idea what I could have done, but moved quickly, nervous about what was coming as I entered her office.

"Sit down, Ronita. I notice you bite your nails," she said, pulling out a little manicure set. "Why do you do that?" Her words felt soft and gracious. "You are a beautiful girl. But biting your nails makes you less attractive."

I had never thought about it before, but as I looked down at my hands, I realized she was right. I hardly had nails and what I had were jagged. My cuticles clung to whatever nail was left and my hands felt rough. Miss Kennedy's hands were soft and she moved tenderly, soaking one of my hands and then the other in a bowl of warm water. Then she took each of my fingers and pushed back the cuticles, filed the rough edges, and finished with clear polish. Over the next several months, she performed the ritual once a week. I wondered, *Why did she choose me to favor*? But I could only say "Thank you" timidly through my gold teeth as I left her office. A peace fell over me after my nails grew. I had been noticed. Somebody other than my family cared about me. It was the first time I felt a desire to live in the joy of my existence. I knew then we are all given at least a couple of angels we can see in a lifetime, and I had met mine.

⚭STUMBLING INTO LIFE⚭

A week before my thirteenth birthday my stomach started to ache with a strange, dull discomfort. I curled up in bed and closed my eyes, telling myself it would go away. A few days later, I looked down and saw a red stain in my panties. The pamphlets were true! I could have a baby now. Ugh! Lacing the tabs of cotton gauze through the loops of the contraption Mom bought me proved to be more complicated than the diagram on the box. I was afraid my secret would be broadcast all over school campus because walking felt like two boxes of tissues were tucked between my legs. Mom said, "Congratulations, you're a young lady now." Honestly, I didn't know what was so great about it!

Arriving at puberty caused me to take a long look at my body. I stared at myself, cupped my hands over my breasts and hoped, *Please Lord, don't make me like Mother Dear*. I saw little patches of soft hair lying freely between my legs. Well-built calves, small thighs, but no behind or hips and a short waist. *There's plenty of time*, I thought, praying I'd fill out.

Examining my body's potential was more involved when Dad and Mom left me home alone. I would carefully pull out Mom's bra, stuff it with a little tissue paper and put on my green evening gown Aunt Bea had bought me at the secondhand store on one of our California visits. I'd strut up and down the hall using a sultry voice like Marilyn Monroe or Susan Hayward, take out an imaginary cigarette, get interviewed by *Life* magazine, and talk about my latest movie. I'd propel myself into the future—fearless, able to speak my mind and make my own decisions. When Dad told me, "You've got to do what I say," it was my turn to say "NO!"

Lost in pretending, I'd scramble to fold Mom's underwear as the car door slammed and would scoot to my red cherrywood desk like I'd been studying the whole time. Mom never guessed my hands had felt everything soft and lacy in her drawer. I couldn't wait to run fine silk over my body!

My becoming fertile correlated with Dad organizing more youth activities to keep us out of trouble—hayrides, picnics, Friday night games, and Saturday evening religious movies. I loved hayrides the best and would wait until the last minute to jump in the truck with the hip kids—the truck Dad wasn't riding in. It only worked twice. It started to dawn on me that Dad didn't trust me.

We had the first church band in the city with fourteen members and hosted basketball tournaments with concession stands of popcorn balls, hot dogs, and sodas in our educational facility. Kids from all over town came, whether they were members or not. Dad's office was open to the kids whose parents didn't have time to listen to their problems. I'd see boys and girls spilling their guts to Dad and watched him pull out tissue and pat them on the head. It was strange, I never felt he was sorry for me.

Plenty of gossip was going around about "the game." It only happened on the nights we had band practice. The boys would go upstairs and the girls would come from downstairs, meeting at a small, dark entrance corridor connecting both floors. From what I heard, you never knew whose tongue would enter your mouth until the couple burst out the door, laughing and giggling. Mr. Hallowell, the janitor, would chase the boys downstairs, but they managed to slip right back up to the second floor every time. I nearly got pushed in the door one evening when I was standing too close. Being Dad's daughter was the only thing that saved me; nobody, I mean nobody wanted to face Dad with that news. A few months later, Dad began practice with a lecture and the game stopped immediately. Still, it sure looked like fun.

Dad organized speaking contests and piano recitals with first, second, and third prizes. "It's good to build character and help you compete in the real world," he said. I spent time reciting in the mirror, enunciating words, making facial expressions like Mother Dear, and sitting on the piano stool for hours, practicing. It was expected—I must be first.

I'd heard Dad's speech, "It doesn't matter if you're a dishwasher. Be the best you can be."

As the competitions began, I'd impatiently wait my turn, hoping the other kids would forget sentences, stumble over bad notes, and overall make a flop of their performance. Dad said, "Winning isn't as important as playing the game fairly." But cheating never entered my mind. I'd cross my fingers when any first prize was announced and when I won, the trophy sat right on top of my desk for the whole world to see. And when I came in second, I'd scold myself, *You didn't prepare hard enough. Winning is everything.*

❧ BROTHER AND SISTER ❧

I grew impatient waiting for my brother and sister to grow up. Stories of Hansel and Gretel; Wendy, Michael, and John in *Peter Pan*; and Meg, Jo, Beth, and Amy in *Little Women* filled me with gleeful anticipation. As the oldest, I knew Dad would shine the spotlight on me to get it right and be an example, but I was sure the three of us would fuse into a ball of fire, oxygen, heat, and fuel together. Instead, Robert and Kelesha could have been on Mars or living in their own galaxies. My expectations became clearer over the years. Weren't brothers and sisters supposed to be interested in each other's welfare? I was their big sister, their scapegoat as well as their buffer against Dad, and would have defended them with my last breath. But I never felt my attempts to protect them were reciprocated. I'd brood, *Why can't they speak up for me?* It was a silly notion for children six and ten years younger than me, but I felt the injustice nonetheless.

But I liked being left in charge. I could bark at my brother and make my sister cry just like Dad did to me, even though neither of them did anything to provoke me. I wasn't very good at keeping up the charade because the spot of anger I provoked in Dad just didn't live inside of me. You need that spot to forget how you really feel about a person you love, like Dad did for me. I couldn't help but try, anyway. I figured there must be something good gained from hurting or scaring another person to death. Maybe practicing with my brother and sister would help me to understand the spark lighting the fire under Dad, since neither of them ever got in trouble.

But when it came to play, my brother and I clicked together like tinker toys—we chased chickens, roller-skated and biked, swung hula hoops around our waists, soaked up cartoons, climbed the Jungle Jim, and made his bed our trampoline, as if child's play would shake us free from the invisible chains we never spoke about.

Respect for each other felt natural and organic. I dreamed of the day Robert would grow strong, tough, and brave, so he would stand up to Dad whenever adversity struck me. But he was like a Persian cat—gentle, calm and affectionate without much motion around him. Armed with Gideon's Bible tucked safely in his shirt pocket, he simply was too timid to take a stand and, strangely, I grew more protective of him, rather than the other way around. I tried not to hold it against him, but for a while I was disappointed in his lack of masculinity.

Kelesha was the box of chocolates Dad had waited for all his life. I brushed her long, wavy hair, helped her dress, watched her grow into herself and listened to her antics. As she got older I hid my face behind a scowl, as if doing so would help me to understand why she had it so easy. I never figured out what motivated her and found her unwilling or unable to care about much, except what she wanted. From the beginning, she and I sat in front of a canvas in search of a finished picture of imagined sisterhood. But the paint never dried and too often our brushes became bristly. She was oil and I was water, except for where we merged around music. And I wouldn't know how much she had watched me from afar until decades later, when she gifted me with these words:

Piano Ro,

You gave me a special love gift, so many years ago.

You played upon the piano resembling birds we both know.

Sometimes quickly like a hummingbird, playing sixteenths on a run.

Other times slowly like an owl, until your Sonata was done.

And though our ages seemed far apart, music bridged our differences,

My big Sis, Piano Ro.

You played with such expression, that it made my feelings swell.

To a place high above the mountains beyond the cares and strife.

You played each piece so beautifully, each composer you knew well.

From the moment that you took me there, I knew it would change my life.

And now I play the piano with memories of Piano Ro.

As real today as ever, as my fingers feel that flow.

Over chords I never imagined playing to a place I always go.

You gave me a special love gift, a long, long time ago.

For the gift you gave your sister, now lives inside my heart.

And I will carry it with me always never to depart.

I guess the most common thing the three of us shared was being the preacher's children. We were expected to absorb Dad as he welcomed the Holy Spirit. For the rest of my life, no matter our age differences or proclivities, it would remain the one thing we did together, without fail, as siblings.

⌖THE PRICE OF BELONGING⌖

I walked to school alone every day, even though plenty of kids on our street attended my junior high school. The problem was Mom and Dad weren't sociable with anyone on our block and were suspicious of how our neighbors raised their children. I planned on changing that situation with Victoria who lived in the next block and waved at me from her mom's car every morning. She was an A student, played the clarinet, and invited kids to her house on the weekend; plus her mom taught at our school. The only catch was I wasn't sure where she went to church, and she didn't have a father.

Winter had left the ground hard and barren that day in 1960, and I wasn't looking forward to walking home with frozen knees, when Victoria spotted me in the hallway.

"The bell just rang for class break. Come on, get your coat and join us. The girls are huddled up in the teachers' parking lot."

"Victoria, it's freezing out there, I'm trying to stay warm. Don't want to catch a cold."

"Oh come on, Ronita. We're not staying out there long. You know everybody. I've got something to show you." Greedy for crumbs of acceptance, I waltzed over to the huddle, blowing hot air in my hands to ward off the chilly air.

I wiggled in right next to Veronica from math class. "Hey Ronita, coming to join the party?" I didn't know how to respond.

Victoria stuck her hand in her pocket, moving back and forth like a "bobblehead" doll. "Look what I've got, fresh out of my mom's pack this morning." I stared at the cigarette and felt a little angel and a little devil land simultaneously on opposite shoulders.

The little angel whispered, "You know how your father feels about smoking. You've seen his face watching Camel advertisements. It's a filthy, dirty habit he detests. Tell the bell to ring, ring now, so you don't have to take a puff."

The little devil whispered, "Aunt Bea, Uncle Claude, Aunt Dorothy, and church members smoke. Can't be that evil. Ain't they all going to heaven? Don't miss your opportunity to be a regular teenager."

The little angel whispered, "Walk away," but my feet seemed locked in cement. The wind blew hard; the matches blew out as Victoria kept trying to light the cigarette, while the little angel whispered, "Walk away now."

"This damn wind," Victoria cursed, as match after match blew out until one was left. The little angel whispered, "Aren't you cold?"

The last match caught fire and Victoria took a long hard drag as I realized, *She's a professional.* My nose turned up from the smell as the wind swirled the smoke right in my face.

The little angel whispered, "Last chance to run, it's your turn next."

"Cough, cough, cough!!" It tasted bitter. I spit, trying to rid myself of the aftertaste as the first warning bell for next class rang.

The little devil laughed, as I took off running like a jackrabbit. *No more experimenting with smoking for me.*

Over the Christmas holidays Dad had been tutoring me in math and in January walked into class without even telling me, to observe my progress. The kids all stared; nobody's parents came to class. After Mrs. Duncan called on me a couple of times, I figured he'd heard enough of my right answers, so I relaxed. My relaxation was momentary when he leaned down and spoke up close to my ear with a stinging voice, "I'll speak with you when you get home." My face turned crimson. *Didn't I answer the questions correctly? J-e-s-u-z, what have I done now?*

Dad was like a certain breed of snake that could strike at any given moment. Sometimes he acted like a python curled up on a branch, waiting to drop around his victim without notice or provocation. Other times he acted like a rattler, shaking and threatening before he struck. He was waiting for me when I got home.

"No daughter of mine is going to smoke cigarettes."

I couldn't believe it. *Who blabbed?* I was instantly angry, especially with Victoria, as I prepared for the thrashing that came next.

Afterwards, Dad smiled. "You might as well face it. I've got a direct highway to Jesus. Everything you do in secret, I'll find out. Be thankful, it's God's way of protecting you." I didn't want to admit it, but he was right. Dad had special powers—radar—when it came to me. Next day, I stomped to school.

"Victoria, did you say anything about my smoking?" She burst out with a laugh, "Who would I tell? Who cares, anyway?"

"My Dad," I burst out louder than intended.

I asked every one of the girls the same question, but couldn't find one clue.

"How did you know?" I finally asked Dad.

He told me straight out in a gloating manner. "When I visited your school, the girl sitting next to you in class was doodling. She wrote her name under the list of Class Smokers and right under her name was your name."

I didn't speak to Veronica for two weeks.

Dad became more obsessed after that incident. "We need to protect her from bad influences," I heard him say to Mom. He didn't know I was a nun compared to all the other kids who passed dirty books around school, talked incessantly about sex in gym, and engaged in unmentionable acts when their parents weren't around. Dad was just plain suspicious and wanted to keep me in the glass house he had created where I was better than everybody else and the world was always good. I didn't know it then, but a tsunami was coming. And it was headed straight toward me.

&LITTLE PRINCESS&

I was budding like flowers in Spring, but had no bouquet of flowers until Ann's mom invited me to join a girls' club right after St. Patrick's Day. My hunch was Mom had noticed how hard I was working trying to balance growing up with Dad's strictness. I had no idea what kind of group it was, but it didn't matter; I'd have made friends with schools of fish, given the chance.

I tossed and turned the night before, thinking about the orange pedal-pusher set I had laid out for the first meeting. It was set for 12:00, but the hands on my clock moved like tires stuck in mud. I flipped my hair to the left, right, and down the middle, nervous I wouldn't look right or be good enough. Dad dropped me off promptly, but not before getting out of the car to look over the chaperone mothers who greeted us. Ann's mother walked him to the screen door. "Don't worry, Pastor, I'll bring her home." I was so relieved. *Now, he can't quiz the girls or lecture me.*

The first thing I noticed was each girl's complexions—not a chocolate chip in the group. Two-thirds of the girls were mulatto, with what we referred to as "good hair," and three girls looked white with green eyes. I elevated each girl on a pedestal as Ann gave the introductions and polite hands stretched forward.

"This is Patsy. We go to the same school and her mom's a nurse.

This is Glenda, she plays first clarinet in the band and her dad's an attorney. Rosalind plays second clarinet and her dad owns the funeral home. This is Loretta, her dad is the principal at Hamilton High School. Joyce's father is a doctor. Mileen and Seville's uncle is the band director at our school and our hostesses today."

After Ann finished, Patsy and Rosalind said, "Aren't you a student of Mrs. O'Neal? The daughter of Rev. Thomas at The Temple?" I let out a sigh of relief when I was recognized, as the pressure of prestige was weighing on my shoulders.

The two hostesses stood. "Attention girls, Little Princess is now in order."

I had never witnessed such graciousness and poise as old business and new business were entertained. It was a social club, but they were organized just like the conference meetings at church. The conversation swung from one trapeze to another.

"Okay, who got the follow-up on the volunteer Red Cross project?"

"Who's hosting the next meeting?"

"What about the social event during the holiday?'

"Did you see the Nixon and Kennedy debate?"

"What's at the Strand Theater?"

Rock and roll music was placed on the phonograph and some girls danced the Twist, while others talked about what boy liked what girl at school. I urgently wanted to contribute as the noise level rose to a delightful hum. I soaked up every word and expression like a dry sponge—feeling validated, for I had known for some time that sophisticated, uncensored girls like this existed and that I was uncensored too.

The afternoon brought laughter, burgers, and vanilla ice cream and with each spoonful, I sweetened up to the long unanswered prayer of inclusion. We formed an assembly line to pass the food as we cleared the table, then washed and dried the dishes—all equal in the process. A light shower cooled the afternoon sun right at 5:00, as the club meeting was about to adjourn.

Loretta, the principal's daughter, stood. "Wait, what about Ronita? Do we accept her into our club? Raise your hand." I looked around nervously and counted: nine hands high in the air. Home, I was home free with girls Dad was surely to accept as *good enough*.

The get-togethers floated from house to house and the girls met every month, sometimes twice. I guess it was too frequent for Dad, who would say the very morning of our meeting, "Got to finish all your chores before you can go." I'd have two extra pillowcases sprinkled by Mom waiting for me in the already full basket of ironing. I nearly burned the clothes taking out my frustrations.

When I was able to attend, my world expanded like an accordion. I practiced the skills Mom taught me about etiquette and setting up a formal table. I listened to devil music and was introduced to blues and jazz while learning to swing dance. But mostly, I got to practice social skills, playing the role of boy or girl. It was a challenge for my "real" self to show up uncensored for four hours, but over time, I embraced a more natural way of allowing each moment to be an adventure, at least for a little while.

The more I watched the girls, the more perplexed I became about the role religion played in my development. *These are serious girls practicing Catholicism, and they know a lot about the world.* I was so envious. I could see how each girl had been given the opportunity to mull things over, speak her mind, and debate because there was no shyness about any subject. I kept asking myself, *How can I get THIS kind of freedom to discover the meaning of life?* Observing the girls helped me believe that an existence far beyond being Dad's daughter was waiting to eclipse, and I would be in the perfect position to embrace it with wonder when the time came. It was a holy thought!

ᏣᎲᎡ. PHYSICAL FITNESS ᏣᎲ

When the 35th president was sworn in, you'd have thought Jesus Christ was taking the oath. Any words that dropped from Kennedy's mouth were gospel. Exercise had never been much of a family value, but when Kennedy spoke at the podium of an "Urgent call to strengthen all programs which contribute to the physical fitness of youth" on July 19, 1961, Dad wanted to follow in his footsteps and made an enthusiastic plea from the pulpit.

"In support of our president, I'm inviting the youth of our church to show how fit they are. We plan to take a twenty-two-mile hike out of town to the Greenwood Elementary School. I want you to encourage your children to come along and you can come too. Let's see, how many of you parents feel this is a good activity for our youth?" I noticed hands of half the congregation pop up.

Ten kids—all girls—showed up at our house on the Saturday morning of August 5. Dad called us the Twelve Healthy Disciples. Prayer and toilet relief began our 6:30 a.m. journey, hoping to beat the heat. Conversations of what our day would bring sprang up as we bought into Dad's vision. People we recognized and people we didn't passed us on the street and honked, as we waved and said to ourselves, *Walking is fun*. Dad walked in front, telling stories of being in the army and pointing fingers at us, saying, "You're going to fall out first with your tongue hanging out. You will need a wheelbarrow to carry you home. You'll need an oxygen tank." We all laughed. I loved it when Dad was free like this!

He slowed the pace as we passed the last gas station outside of town. We had been walking over an hour. The temperature gauge read 89. "Let's stop to get some water. Don't want to poop out," he said. Sweat dripped down our faces. We moistened our bandannas and took off again. By lunchtime, I felt like I had walked to Dallas, Texas.

"What you got, what you got, what you got" was all I could hear as we held up sandwiches of tuna, bologna, fried chicken, and egg salad. I wished for a strawberry Nehi soda pop that had been sitting in an ice bucket all day and a shade tree.

I wasn't in a big hurry to continue, when Dad said, "Pack up your belongings, time to hit the road." He slipped into his army sergeant role with ease. "Let's get hopping...Gimme your left, your right, your left, your right," bringing laughter and helping us to forget our fatigue. It didn't take long before we all tired of repeating Dad's drill, "Sound off, sound off, one, two, three, four, one, two, three, four."

There were periods of silence when we were each left to our own thoughts, periods when our shoes hitting the pavement was the only sound you could hear, frequently interrupted by periods of loud grunting and moaning as we walked. We sang church songs and ballads as bullets of sunrays pelted our heads like hail. The heat was relentless, and I was parched. When I looked at Dad, tiny pricks of red had popped up all over his arms and I was sure the pace had slowed.

"Okay, we've got eleven miles to go," Dad announced, wringing the water out of his bandanna.

"What?" we all screamed, thinking we would see the roof of the school as we turned the corner of the next mile. A chorus of exasperation overrode our determination, "My feet hurt. It's too hot. Too many flies. My clothes are sticking to me. Where are we? Where's the water? My hair's all sweated out. I want to go home!" Dad tried to encourage us. "What do you think the disciples did when they found themselves in a situation like this? They kept going in spite of being weary. Let's all get a walking stick."

My legs and arms felt like I was dragging around fifty-pound dumbbells, as the last chuckle of laughter escaped my lips. I found a sturdy four-foot walking stick and leaned on it with all my weight. Visualizing a cold bath with ice kept up my cadence—stick, left foot, right foot—stick, left foot, right foot. These were country miles, so I can't tell you how long we walked that day. It didn't matter to Dad, because once he set out to do something, nothing or nobody was going to keep him from his goal. That afternoon, however, all of a sudden he stopped.

"Girls, we've done really well. I know our president would be proud of what we achieved today. He'd say like the good book, 'Well done my faithful servant.' Who wants to start heading back?" I wanted to say, "What about the twelve disciples? Would they stop now?" Instead, I rolled my eyes at Ann. *Finally, thank you Jesus.*

A rusty black truck passed us with an old Negro man smoking a cigarette. Dad started yelling and waving his hands in the air. "Hey Mister, stop, stop, please stop." We joined him. The man came to a shrieking halt and started backing up slowly as gray smoke coughed from his exhaust pipe. "What y'all doing out here walking in the sticks?" the man asked. "Don't y'all know you could get tarred and feathered and nobody'd know it?" Dad started explaining right away about voting for Kennedy and our fitness walk while the man blew smoke rings in his face. "Y'all crazy. Get on in the back," the old man said as he spit out something brown and mumbled to himself. We tossed those sticks on the ground, and jumped in the back quicker than jackrabbits on fire before he changed his mind.

I was waiting to see how Mr. Physical Fitness was going to explain his way out of this one. I didn't want Dad to be embarrassed, but to tell you the truth, I was glad. Failing at something made him more human and vulnerable and I softened toward him that day. But as soon as my feelings toward him softened, he turned clever and came out smelling like a rose as parents began flying up the church steps.

"I am responsible for each girl's welfare. I'd hate myself if anything happened. They were all weary, the best thing was to stop." I can't say he lied exactly; we were hot and exhausted, but Dad had pulled the plug. We never quit!

Next day, you'd have thought Dad was ninety-nine years old when he crept into the pulpit with his sunburned skin. "Lord, I don't see how those people walked all over Jerusalem without tennis shoes, rubbing alcohol, or suntan lotion." The congregation roared. As always, Dad used the experience for his sermon. I sat envious and captivated. For months, his sermon stuck in my mind.

You know, it's better to have a dream, go for it and give it your all. Failure is only in the eye of the beholder. I decided right then to be stronger, have more courage to stand up for myself, and believe my little light was going to shine, shine, shine.

PEARLS

Stephen Todds sat two seats over from me in geometry. He dressed like a teenage model. Closely cropped hair, fine quality shirts, jackets and slacks of greens, grays, and blues with saddle oxford shoes. Nobody dressed like he did except his older cousin, Trevor. Stephen didn't care about my label or Dad's reputation. "You're different," he kept telling me. I had blossomed—long pressed hair, attractive nails, shapely legs, and just enough curves in the right spots. Socializing with the girls had increased my world view to more than school and church, and I had mastered holding my lips just enough to camouflage my gold teeth from shining too much.

You could hardly call it romance, because we never kissed, but I did have a tingle in my chest whenever he was near me. We both liked learning and I shared my dreams of becoming a classical pianist, actress, or a pediatrician, my latest interest spiked by babysitting my sister. He looked straight in my eyes as I talked about Paris, Hollywood, and being famous. He talked about civil rights, becoming an attorney, defending people, men's clothing, being an only child, and his mother. His voice softened when he spoke about her. The first time the possibility of being his girlfriend entered my mind was at my fourteenth birthday party. Kids were having house parties all the time, but I never attended. "Too young," Dad said. "There is a season for everything."

Mom fixed little dainty sandwiches of chicken, tuna and liverwurst, a big bowl of Hawaiian punch with lime sherbet and chocolate cake. I stood waiting in the chill, displeased with Dad's decision to hold my party in the garage. Inside the church parsonage was no place for a party, not even an innocent one. Ann showed up first, then Collie and all the Little Princess girls, and some boys came too. Now I had my own idea of my first teenage party and hoped some of the girls would bring rock and roll music. I wanted to swing dance and see ruffled petticoats moving. But Dad had his own ideas, and planned the party from beginning to end. I was embarrassed—he acted like it was his birthday!

We started with Pin the Tail on the Donkey, taking turns spinning with handkerchiefs tied tightly around our eyes and laughing as thumbtacks landed all over the wall. Name That Tune was next, and would have been fun except the music was Connie Francis, Nat King Cole, and Perry Como. By 5:00, soiled plates and balled-up napkins filled the wastepaper basket as the kids started lingering outside the door. By 5:45, singing "Happy Birthday" was a memory. I started begging, struggling to keep the tears from falling, "Please stay, we're going to play treasure hunt." Henrietta was the only one who told me the truth as the crowd quickly dispersed. "Versie invited us to her house to listen to rock and roll." I was crushed. I tried to make a case with Dad to follow the crowd, but he wasn't having it. "You can't leave your own party," he reminded me, but nobody was left except Stephen and Ann.

My party was a flop. The only saving grace was Stephen. "I bought you a present. Open it." He handed me a slender box wrapped in beautiful, light-pink glossy paper with a tiny white bow. I had never received anything from a boy. Mom had taught me to open presents with respect, so I carefully peeled back the wrapping to reveal a velvet black box. Inside were tiny pearls with a gold clasp. Stephen fumbled to place it around my neck as feelings of love warmed my heart. My head began to swim. *What do I do now if Dad walks in?* Dad had turned my party into a fiasco, but the pearls cheered me up, even though I couldn't bring myself to tell the truth about who gave them to me, too afraid Dad would make me give them back.

Ann cornered me the next Saturday at Little Princess, whispering in my ear.

"You're not going to believe what I have to tell you. Guess who is getting all dressed up to come to church?" I couldn't imagine.

"Stephen, silly. He likes you."

I squealed like a pig.

Stephen knew dating was out, but I had to give him a star for cleverness: meeting Dad on his own turf. Sunday morning, I prayed, "Stephen, please don't walk into church late." Dad hated folks making noise, interrupting the spirit after church began. I kept hoping, maybe, just maybe if Dad likes Stephen, sees he goes to church, sees how intelligent he is, maybe I can talk on the phone with him like the other girls.

Sunday school let out at 10:30 and I could hardly concentrate on the lesson. Stephen was already present, looking suave as I entered the sanctuary. We sat in the balcony, which had become the young people's section. I beamed like headlights on a new Thunderbird, happy to be near him, my pearls hanging perfectly around the collar of my V-neck dress. Dad looked up intermittently throughout the service, shaking both legs back and forth like he had a twitch. His eyes stayed open, unlike the meditation he always practiced before his sermon. But I was oblivious. During spaces in the service Stephen and I leaned toward each other, momentarily whispering, as our shoulders slightly touched.

After Dad's first point in his sermon, I felt the floor shake as a heavyset usher—the woman who had gotten the spirit and nearly sent Dad to the hospital after she hit him in the ribs—walked down the balcony stairs. She stopped right at the pew where I was sitting and wiggled her stubby index finger. "Come here." I had to step over Stephen's feet and the three kids sitting next to him. "Follow me," she said. Except for the words coming out of Dad's mouth, silence came over the church as every eye followed me down the aisle, as if I were being rolled down to the front in a casket. Dad pointed, "Sit." My head dropped. I wished for Houdini to wrap me in his invisible cape. How could Dad be so cruel in front of Stephen and all the church folks?

When service was over, I shamefully scrambled through the thick crowd, avoiding the stares and snickers, but the balcony was empty. Dad said nothing on the drive home.

At school the next day, Stephen said, "So what they say about your father is true. He's really strict." By January, Stephen had moved to South Carolina to a private school, and the warm embers that had been stirred slowly died away.

ᢒᏨTHE PLANᏨᢒ

One Monday night in February of my tenth-grade year, Dad dropped Mom off at the train station—another teachers' meeting in New Orleans. That's when I hatched my plan. I'd been doing a lot of comparison with the other girls about how I dressed. Girls at church and my classmates shopped alone, but Mom had continued to buy dresses, sweaters, and skirts that fit loose with silly ruffles and bows, so that any boy sizing me up in the "physically attractive" category was going to have to use way more imagination than I was worth. Plus, no girl in my class was wearing socks, except with black-and-white saddle shoes or penny loafers. No girl, that is, except me. Did my parents think keeping me looking like a child would stunt my development? It wasn't working.

My mind was developing too. I was constantly thinking and asking questions to myself. Mostly, who made God? Why was Dad so strict? Why did being the preacher's kid feel unnatural? What was going to become of me when I grew up? I didn't want to believe that God wanted Dad to hover over me with such possessiveness. And anyway, wasn't life about trying new things, stumbling and dusting yourself off?

I had been studying myself in the bathroom. A girl had to know her fine points. That's what my physical education teacher had said, and I wanted to believe she knew best. I even gave myself a grade compared to the girls and the movie stars I admired—face B+, teeth F, breast B, legs A, waist D, feet A, and hair B. I wished my grade averaged out to an A, but B wasn't too bad. My light skin color helped too. I kept waiting and waiting for Mom to say, "Okay, you can wear what you want." But nothing changed. I just wanted to look like the rest of the girls. And today I would!

I went through my checklist like a pilot about to take off—slips, panties, bras, and socks were tossed this way and that. *Where's my underarm shields*? Just as my frustration level peaked, and I had pulled out every article in my drawer, I found them. Mom constantly talked about dry skin, so I had rubbed Vaseline petroleum jelly over my legs and feet until I looked like a greased pig. I put on my underwear, slip, and navy-blue pleated skirt. All that was left was Mom's sweater and stockings. I grabbed my robe, covered myself for breakfast, and sat on the bed, trying to figure out what I needed to check off next. Most important was how to get out of the house without being discovered. I paused for a moment. *If Dad knew what I was cooking up, he'd say*, "You think you're two bits slick."

I'd say, "It's not that at all." I'd say, "Take everything I have, even my piano, because this burning desire to be normal like everyone else won't go away."

As I slurped the last two spoonfuls of cereal, I figured I had two choices. Wear a coat or sneak out quickly while Mrs. Miles was preoccupied with Kelesha. I figured wearing a coat would defeat my purpose and by midday, I'd be too hot. Creating a distraction was my only other choice. But what? Timing was everything.

Every morning Dad dropped off my brother at school, leaving right before me, and would occasionally give me a ride on days when it rained. I liked morning walks. I preferred the peaceful time for my own thoughts, even though it meant lugging my heavy French horn. It wasn't raining that morning, so I was a little surprised when Dad asked, "Want a ride?" Of all mornings, I certainly did not, and tried to hide any hint of deception with my answer. "Thanks, Dad, it's a beautiful day the Lord has made, so I'll walk." He looked at me. Oops, I had never said that before.

My mind started spinning like a top. I had a lot to do—finish dressing, create the distraction, and get to school before the bell rang. I glanced at the clock; twenty minutes left to get ready. *No time to create a distraction.*

Mom's departure had given me plenty of time to find her V-neck sweater. She kept it in the bottom of her dresser drawer neatly folded among the sachets. She looked so radiant every time she had it on. It was fine-quality wool and the deep red reminded me of the lipstick movie stars wore. I ran my hands over the soft fabric before sticking my head through the opening and gently pulling it down over my underarm shields. I hurriedly put my robe back on. And then it was time to roll up the dark-blue stockings between my hands. I had watched Mom hundreds of times, but had never actually worn stockings. The nylon felt so silky and I didn't know what I was doing. Mom had bought me a garter belt just like hers and promised, "I'll get you a pair of stockings." That day had never come. I decided I'd waited long enough.

I looked up to heaven. "Please don't let me get a run in these stockings." I rolled the first stocking slowly up over my knees and carefully up to my thigh, hooking it on the plastic snap. Shucks, the seam was crooked. Twisting it around my leg didn't help, so I began again. The clock was ticking. Seams straight, I stood up and felt like clicking my feet together like Dorothy in *The Wizard of Oz. I'm leaving Kansas*, I thought. I picked up my books and darted in the bathroom, as Mrs. Miles made her way down the hall to see to my sister. You'd have thought I was a jaguar as I ran out the front door.

The only thing on my mind was Murphy, the quarterback. "I'm going to show him," I kept saying over and over to myself. After he had tossed me aside like a shoehorn, I thought my feelings for him would just go away, but each day my throat felt like I had swallowed a big fish bone. I needed some bread to wash that bone down. Actually, I just missed the attention and things like holding hands while talking about sports, band, and what we wanted to be after growing up. I remembered the first time. We were yakking away when he reached over and placed my hand in his. I expected his hand to be rough from cuts and bruises, but it was smooth as a baby's bottom. When he touched me, goosebumps prickled my arms. I imagined, *This is what it means to fall in love.*

We held hands for two months and then one day he totally misread my invitation to spend time with him alone. If a neighbor hadn't knocked at just the right time, I don't know what might have happened. Still, I was shocked when he told me a couple of days later, "I can't talk to you anymore."

I shuddered, reflecting back on the ordeal, as I puffed down the stairs to the band room to put up my French horn and got to my locker before the first bell rang. I ran into Betty and Verna who sat next to me in band. They squealed when they saw me.

"Look at you. Stockings, you're wearing stockings? And when did you get that sweater?" I blushed.

Judy and Irene from band joined them. "Turn around," they said. "Hey, what happened to you?" I was attracting more attention than I wanted.

Henry and Evan from the football team whistled and turned completely around, running into the lockers. The second bell rang and we all scattered in the same direction, knowing we'd have to be in our seats by the third bell. The attention continued as I took my seat in the second row, right next to the window. And then I had another thought, *I hope I don't look like Marilyn.*

Murphy spotted me during lunch, chatting away with Betty and Verna. He had broad shoulders, a magnificent smile, beautiful white teeth, and a soft, smooth voice. I sighed, thinking of how that was once mine. He walked over, leaned against my right shoulder, and whispered, "Can you meet me after practice?" I wasn't sure what I was expecting, but I had gotten his attention. And now it was my turn to teach him a lesson and tell him "No" when he begged me to hold his hand again. Instead, my throat got dry and I blushed, batting my eyes. "Okay, I'll meet you out front."

It was unusual for me to dart across the street to the hamburger joint after school, even though kids from band would get French fries, burgers, or hot dogs to last them until dinner. Truth was, Dad had declared the burger stand was off-limits because of the older kids who blasted radios, talked loud, smoked, and used vulgar language. But I was starving. Too much excitement. As the light turned green, I walked into the middle of the intersection, preoccupied with what I was going to say to Murphy. *Toot, toot, toot.* I heard a car horn, and looked up. *Oh my God! Dad!* I was suspended in the moment, glancing away, gasping for air, before staring back into his face. His index finger wagged from left to right. My appetite was gone.

Band practice was a cloud. I left as soon as rehearsal finished, oblivious to meeting Murphy. Each leg felt like I was dragging a steel tank, and the toes of my shoes were scarred by pavement as I drew closer to the front door. Dad wasn't home.

ᏜTHE LETTERᏝ

My intention was to undress quickly, return Mom's items to her drawer, and rehearse my answers again before Dad got home. There would be an inquisition and I had better get my story straight. I practiced what I'd say. *We had a pretend dress-up day at school. Dad, you know my favorite celebrity is Marilyn Monroe.*

The envelope was lying on the coffee table, staring at me with its jagged edges. Never before had I thought about reading my parents' mail, but that envelope commanded me like I was under a spell: "Come here." It was a cheap, plain white envelope; nothing like the sweet-smelling stationery with the embossed rosebuds that Mom kept in her nightstand. It was addressed to Dad with no return address. My heart pounded through the red sweater, my hands started to shake, my mind swirled. What are you doing picking up this paper? Why are you invading your parents' privacy?

The blue-lined notebook paper was folded with three creases. The handwriting was terrible. My eyes gobbled up the words.

Dear Reverend Thomas:

I am writing to you because I don't want the same thing to happen to your daughter that happened to mine.

I know your daughter has been seeing this boy Murphy and that she invited him to your house alone when you and your wife were gone a couple of months ago.

I know your daughter is too young to date and that you don't know anything about this. I feel it is my responsibility to tell you because I respect your family and I don't want you to experience what I am experiencing. You see, my daughter is pregnant and we don't know what we are going to do.

Mrs.

The name looked like chicken scratch.

I got dizzy, the chair catching me. I read the letter again, slower this time. I slipped the letter back in the envelope and closed my eyes, trying to remember, *Who is pregnant at school?* Mom's sweater flew off my head and I placed it back in the drawer. I washed the nylons quickly—no runs—and hung them to dry in my closet. Then I sat on the bed, waiting, my mind like a basketball. *What am I going to do?*

When the front door opened, I braced myself. "We'll deal with this when your Mother comes home Friday." I couldn't believe it. Four days of torture.

I can't tell you what I did from that moment on, except my imagination swung me around like I was on a merry-go-round. *This is what Marie Antoinette must have felt like when she was waiting to be executed.* Verna and Betty asked me, "Are you sick?" The band director pointed at me twice for hitting the wrong note. My homeroom teacher threatened to send me to the nurse, concerned by the tautness of my face. I stepped into the crosswalk on a red light and failed my English exam. By Friday night, I was exhausted.

Mom's train pulled into the station at 6:05. Nausea rose in my stomach as the car door slammed. The one saving grace was that it would be over—I would take my medicine, whatever it was, and be done with it.

I detected no hint of agitation in Mom's voice as she greeted Kelesha and Robert, and I thought, *Maybe it won't be so bad.* Dad's voice burst my bubble. "Your mother is tired, we will deal with this in the morning."

Clutching myself between the sheets, the wolves tore me limb from limb, leaving a smooth white carcass. Next morning Dad called out at 7:15. "Meet us in the living room in fifteen minutes." It had been the longest night of my life.

I decided to put on layers—a long-sleeved yellow nylon pajama set, two pairs of panties, and a thick quilted robe. The buttons were secured, the collar turned up. Just in case. I felt like a steel ball and chain had been attached to my feet. They were seated already, Mom on the couch and Dad in his big chair. A cold, hard look burned from his sockets. Mom sat with no expression. I hung my head low, placed my limp hand in my lap, and waited, wanting to offer an explanation but afraid to speak first. I hadn't meant any harm. I just wanted to be normal like all the other girls. Couldn't Dad see I was a good girl and could be trusted? I realized it wasn't a very good explanation. I wanted to be trusted, but had done everything not to be trusted. On the other hand, maybe I'd get points for realizing my own disappointing behavior if I spoke up. I didn't enjoy being sneaky, who would? But at the time it seemed like the only way to normalize my reputation. Was that such a bad thing?

Dad began with a lecture about responsibility and then catching me in Mom's clothes. He called me "common and promiscuous," speaking calmly, as if purchasing a screwdriver from the local hardware store. The very next second, his voice changed and moved up an octave like climbing an escalator. "The more serious offense is the contents of the letter." He wanted to know the truth and in a split second I had to decide what words would be spoken, remembering how he felt about lying.

⚬MURPHY⚬

I had spent every waking moment since reading the letter trying to figure out how Mrs. Whoever knew. I had licked and sealed the silence of what happened. Yes, I had been foolish allowing Murphy to come in the house. But how was I to know? I just thought having a few minutes with him alone would be nice. Girls my age at church had company. I wanted it too, but Dad had turned serious when I asked permission. "You're too young to have company or to court." I tried to explain. "It's not courting, Dad, just clean fun." But it was like talking to a brick wall.

Preoccupied with fitting in, I had taken advantage of the situation earlier in the fall when Dad and Mom had gone to a convocation conference. My sister stayed with Mrs. Miles, and my brother and I stayed with a church member who lived six blocks away. On Thursday, I told Murphy, "You can walk me home." When we got to the front door, I invited him in, "You can stay for fifteen minutes." *Somebody in the neighborhood saw us.*

Murphy and I sat nervously on the couch when it happened. He reached over with his full, broad, juicy lips. His tongue slipped inside my mouth, flickering like a snake. I could hardly breathe. He tasted like Juicy Fruit gum. I couldn't believe the most famous athlete at school was kissing me. My body was tense from wondering, *Was I doing it right*? Fairies pitter-pattered through my heart as our lips pressed together. His arms held me in a gentle embrace until he mumbled through our lips, "Let's get more comfortable." I was sure it was time for him to go; yet the warmth of his body made me dizzy. Resistance fled like bank robbers. "Okay, but only five more minutes." I spoke before I could think. "Promise me you'll leave after that." He smiled with his deep dimples. "Okay."

As we lay side by side, the feelings in my body swirled around me. I became his breath mint. Without warning, he became an acrobat, climbing on top of me, licking my neck, panting, holding me down. The memory of Horace's body entered into my present consciousness as I said, "What are you doing? Get off me," but his body stiffened and grew stronger as he kept licking, groping at my breast. *I'm good as dead if Dad sees a hickey on my neck.* I could feel Murphy's penis growing, rubbing against my thigh.

"Stop, stop," I said, but his hands grabbed mine as I tried to push him off me. "Stop, stop this minute!" I continued, wondering why he couldn't hear me. His muscular body turned into dead weight. Tears exploded. "Stop, please stop," I whimpered. "Get off me, please stop, why are you doing this?" But he was deaf.

Suddenly, the doorbell rang. It gave me just enough time to jump up run to the front door, and fix my blouse. With trembling fingers I peered into the worried face of my guardian, Mrs. Washington. *What should I do*? I opened the front door, happy to be saved, as the back door slammed. "I came by the house to get some clothes and I fell asleep," I told her. She poked her head in the living room, and then as I produced some clothing from my bedroom, she seemed satisfied. Most importantly, she didn't see Murphy.

I didn't share any of these details with Dad. I just confessed, "Yes, I let Murphy come by the house, but only for a few minutes." I hoped telling the truth would reduce whatever punishment was being planned. Dad's hand met the side of my face, snapping my head to the right. "I can't believe you want to give yourself to that boy!" he yelled. "I don't, Dad, I just wanted..." and then I stopped, as I saw Dad's golden leather belt. "Get up, you made your bed hard, now lie in it. If you go to hell it won't be because I didn't try my best," he said. I braced myself, hoping for the first time in my life, Mom would intervene. He caught my glance. "Your mother won't save you."

⧽BROKEN⧼

I sucked in my breath, bracing myself as the first lick landed perfectly in the center of my hand like a bee sting. By the sixth lick, I bit my lip, determined not to cry out. By the twelfth, my howling was deafening. I tried to count, foolishly believing a magic number floated in Dad's head associated with *the sin*. After twenty-five, I became lost in a fog with no memory, as what felt like hot coals accosted my flesh. He was all over me—arms, legs, back, elbows, buttocks, swinging blindly and wildly as I turned, twisted, trying to keep my robe pulled tight in anticipation of where he'd hit next. Spit foamed from his mouth; his breath was labored as he kept repeating the same thing over and over again. "Do you want to go to hell? I'd rather see you dead." I wished I were dead as I screamed "Noooooo, Daddy!," believing he meant what he said.

My robe fell to the floor from all the twisting, while my body became exposed, virgin hands protecting my face, as his strikes continued to land—leather to flesh. On my leg, red stained my pajamas as Dad continued to swing wildly. Every nerve in my body felt bruised as the leather landed one more time. Half naked on the floor I coughed, choking on my own mucus, delirious, asking for mercy. "Please, I won't do it again." Mom watched in silence as the attack kept building. Finally, she spoke out with a little more force than I was used to. "Robert, stop, you're going to kill her."

It was as if a pack of wolves had brought me down. Fine welts and red ooze covered my hands, legs, and arms. I tried to stand and fell back on my knees, unable to stop whimpering, wishing I had a gun to stop the misery. Dad stood over me, wheezing. Mom was a shadow. The room was spinning as they walked out. I was alone, falling and forsaken in darkness, a wave lost at sea. It took a while for strength to come as I gathered my rags and stumbled to my room still whimpering, closing my door tight.

Hours passed as my pillow caressed my tears. When I looked in the mirror, an unrecognizable monster with slits for eyes stared back at me. Weeping started over, softer this time as the thought kept ringing in my head. "You want to give yourself to that boy." It wasn't true, and I realized how little Dad knew me. The stake moved the ache deeper down into my heart.

The house was quiet, except for doors slamming in the distance as I sniffled all afternoon. It wasn't until right before dinner that Robert climbed onto my bed and hugged me. "Kelesha and I stopped counting at eighty-seven." I looked like yellow hornets had eaten me for lunch and could hardly swallow the dinner that sat before me. Silence covered every morsel of our food. By Sunday, the swelling was more visible, but it didn't keep me from church. I didn't have to explain anything because my brother had blabbed about my beating at the Music Mart where we both took lessons. It was the only time I ever remember Dad whipping Robert.

That night after the house was still, my cold feet tiptoed quietly to my cherrywood desk. Homework was due on Monday. I looked up at the sky, searching for God. Where had He been? Why had He let this happen to me? I was a good girl. A thousand stars bumped against each other forming a jeweled crown on the night. That's when I knew.

One day I will tell my story.

I wore shame like a new coat, turning black and blue, then yellow and purple over the next few days. Three days later Verna drove in the final blow. "Your dad found Murphy working at the barbershop and told him to stay away from you."

My body healed. My internal wounds left track marks. I became addicted to quietly shooting fury, outrage, and resentment through the needle into my arms. Dad's secret was out! He was the villain, the monster, the devil lurking in the dark. I no longer believed in him as a man without sin, for I knew God would never allow a holy man to beat another human being the way he had beat me.

The beating threw me out of alignment, left me unprotected to reconcile the good with the bad, the angel of heaven from the demon that sometimes escaped from him and from me. I collapsed into self-pity and prayed my nature would become extinct. And then I remembered Dad's sermon about cutting off the part of the body that doesn't serve God. I walked to school talking to myself. *Cut off your nature of curiosity. Stomp it out. Stop wanting to know how everything works, stop wanting to be like everybody else. Stop wanting attention. Stop, stop, stop.* It felt unnatural, shrinking from myself, but it was the only noise my mind could distinguish. Somehow, I had to survive. I kept to myself, fell asleep most nights against the rough edges of my books, sat transfixed at my piano and read my Bible. Murphy and I never spoke again.

&RESIDUE&

The circumstances of my beating changed Robert forever. After his whipping, he grew quieter. In his eight-year-old mind, Dad became a giant breathing fire and devouring the land; a giant capable of pain, destruction, and annihilation. He figured the best way to cope with the angry giant was to read, pray, become a nonentity, and be the example of peace. Encyclopedias and his pocket Gideon Bible became his best friends, and he dreamed about how to live vicariously through all the historical people he read about without drawing attention to himself. Eventually his fear internalized into a speech impediment. It was most noticeable with Little League.

"Robert, where did you get your baseball glove?"

"I, I, I, I, I, I, I, I, g, g, g, g, go, go, go, go, got, got..."

"Wh, wh, wh, where?" they'd all laugh, as parents and kids watched.

He grew afraid of conversation. Developmentally, his social skills became limited to speaking with his eyes and through his clarinet. Dad encouraged him to join Cub Scouts, but your chances were better at picking the winner at the Kentucky Derby than getting a sentence out of him.

I watched Kelesha fold herself in Dad's arms, no longer wishing his hands to touch me. She continued to rule the house, whining whenever she didn't get her way. I'd hear Mom complaining.

"Robert, you are spoiling her rotten. She doesn't listen when I talk to her and you don't make her mind. You think it's cute, but one day you'll pay for your leniency."

"Ah, Juanita, she's so sweet. She's my knee baby—keeps me young at heart. She'll grow out of it, but let her be a child. Before she knows it, she'll have to take on all the world's troubles."

I couldn't understand how Kelesha got away with behavior that brought so much trouble to my world—refusing to eat vegetables, talking back, telling Dad and Mom "no," screaming for no apparent reason. I resented how Dad perceived her selfish mean streak as "sweet." But like he said, she was his "knee baby," a flower too delicate to be whipped. My resentment grew as he coddled her, forcing me to accept her permanent position as adorable daughter in his life.

Dad never allowed his demon dragon to rise up again—his secret stayed chained within him forever. Instead, he resorted to less physical forms of punishment.

"No piano for a week."

"No movies for a month."

"No recreation or socializing until I get good and ready." And when I came home one Saturday after getting my hair done, a new punishment awaited me. He'd found a paperback romance book hidden under my mattress. Everything in my room was turned upside-down—shoes, panties, school books, ink pens, hair rollers, glass figurines, pictures, jewelry—intermingled with shredded newspaper one-and-a-half feet deep.

"Clean your room before you go to bed," was all he said. I only slept three hours that night.

⟨⟨LOST FOOTING⟩⟩

In the Fall of 1961, Dad's name came up again at convocation. The educational annex constructed under Dad's leadership had produced a state-of-the-art building and the church coffers had grown with the increased membership. Dad's reputation as an intelligent, articulate, entertaining, fire-and-brimstone preacher had spread and the word was out. Dad was headed toward becoming a bishop. I wasn't surprised; people treated my dad as if he was God.

I had become less animated or spontaneous, thinking carefully before I spoke. I spent more time in my room alone and hours on my piano, as I started experiencing life like it was a pomegranate—tasting one seed at a time. It kept me hungry, but safe from myself. Most of the time I walked around feeling sorry I was born. I'd stare in the mirror for hours, wondering if I'd ever see the wide smile and bright eyes again. All that was important was that I stay out of trouble and show deference to my parents as I accepted my fate and Dad's flaws.

In September 1963, disappointment fell on me like heavy bricks as the church assignments were read off. We were moving to Oakland, California. Dad's tenacity had paid off and he was on his way to claim his gold star. A tightness filled me—happiness for Dad's reward of hard work and the unfairness to me. Eleventh grade had started. I'd folded into the rules of accepting who, where, and what was there for me. I was looking forward to running for student body officer, joining the drama club, attending the national band competition, becoming a debutante. Soon I would enter Howard University. It was all I thought about!

I moped around silently, mourning the place I had found for myself to survive. There was nowhere to speak my feelings or unburden my sadness. Dad kept saying, "This is God's will. You will love California." The week before we left, the church asked to take a family portrait to run in the local paper. The photographer tried jokes and charm, but I wouldn't smile. There wasn't anything to smile about. My eyes watered constantly as I thought about the last seven years—how much I had endured and how I had grown.

During the last few weeks, there were a variety of church guild goodbye parties, and Little Princess surprised me with a farewell gathering. "We'll come see you, you come see us," they all said as my multicolored autograph book overflowed with addresses and phone numbers. I knew they wouldn't.

On the morning we departed, I looked over my room one more time—so many memories, some I didn't want to remember. My eyes started to tear up again as Mom and Dad waved to Mrs. Miles and the Jacksons. All I could hear was, "Bye, bye, y'all write us, drive careful, come back and see us." It was too much. I broke down, not caring anymore who heard me sobbing. We were almost in Dallas by time my tears dried up and I experienced my first migraine headache.

Three days later, we climbed the creaking steps of our new home, and once inside inhaled the smell of fresh paint. The brownish-colored shades against the pale orange and rose pink walls reminded me of sherbet, but didn't cheer me up. Mom wasn't smiling. New paint couldn't hide the truth; this parsonage was old.

Our new home gave me a new roommate and gave privacy to my brother. My five-year-old sister made Kleenex animals, collected live insect critters, and left dirt on both our sides of the room. I didn't take kindly to sharing a tiny closet, turning off bedtime lights or her rights to half of the room. Kelesha and I seemed to have nothing in common except our heritage. It gave me one more reason to speak obscenities in the shower—my newest form of coping with life.

Our new church was one block down the street. We could have walked, but instead we drove into the parking space marked "Pastor" as people stood waiting to shake our hands. Remembering Dad's old talks, I mustered up a smiling face. It was expected. Inside, I felt like a wasteland. "Good morning," we all said, as the men hurried up to shake Dad's hand and the ladies started gathering around Mom. I thought, "Here we go again."

We had moved two thousand miles away and the Holy Ghost had followed Dad straight into the pulpit of Beebe Memorial C.M.E Temple. After the sermon the ushers opened the back doors of the church for the invitation to discipleship. It was time. Mom, Robert,

Kelesha, and I stepped forward, I hoped for the last time.

 MACK

Oakland was divided like most cities into north, south, east, and west. We lived in the west, once home to elite Victorian houses. Now it was a mixture of forty-something homeowners, the elderly, welfare mothers, revolutionaries, hoodlums, drug addicts, and abandoned ghosts. Since West Oakland was considered a disadvantaged school district, Mom drove me to the most prosperous part of town to enroll in school. Early enrollment was over. I didn't care much where I finished high school; I just wanted to graduate and get on to college.

We arrived at McClymonds, referred to as Mack, by second period and waited in the reception area for Miss Lee, my new counselor, while she finished talking with a student. Through the glass of the closed door I could see she was white. Her skin color got my attention. I mumbled to myself. *I don't trust white people. I hope she doesn't try to sabotage my chances of graduating.* Having been a school counselor herself, Mom knew all the right jargon and the two of them started chatting away about the joys and challenges of steering young minds. I stared at diplomas and searched for pictures of a husband and children. There were none. Miss Lee assured Mom of my status.

"With her B+ average, she's guaranteed a place with the college prep kids. Let's get her paperwork completed, so we can scoot off to third period class."

Music had been the cauldron to hold my expressions of joy and grief. There were times I'd sit for hours and just play. Eagle wings spread through me that morning as we rounded the corner and opened the door. "You'll Never Walk Alone" filled the room. The three of us stood in the doorway, while the white teacher swung his arms through the air, closing his eyes to the harmony. The sound was perfectly pitched.

"Doc, you've been asking for a musician; you've got one now," Miss Lee announced. I didn't know what to say. Nobody had asked me if I wanted to play, but I sat down on the piano stool, waving goodbye to Mom.

Doc extended his arm, shook my hand and said, "Welcome, we really need you." I thought, *Could it be possible a white man will accept my ability to play piano*? All my experiences of the South told me I wasn't good enough. But I shook off the fear as 120 eyes stared at me, waiting.

Doc broke the spell. "You play the introduction, and I'll bring the choir in." By the time the bell rang, you'd have thought I had been playing for the choir all my life.

Guys from the bass section surrounded the piano, but were cut off by two girls I'd seen at Sunday service. "That's the reverend's daughter at my church," they said. "Watch what you say." It was not the way I would have liked to be introduced, but it was out. All I had to do now was prepare myself for the scrutiny I knew would follow. A boy named Reuben said, "Your dad's a preacher?"

The word spread like measles. The next day when I sat on the piano stool, I heard my new name, "Sister Thomas." I didn't know if they were laughing at me or welcoming me, but within a week all I heard was, "Sister Thomas this, Sister Thomas that." Playing the piano had given me instant recognition. I was grateful.

᚛FILLING NEW SPACES᚛

Our move had given me something quite unexpected—girls my age living right across the street.

Suzette and Yvonne were the daughters of a couple who attended our church. Suzette and I were exactly one month apart and we immediately became friendly rivals—studying together, competing for grades and recognition. She was the sophisticated type, reminding me of Little Princess girls with flawless brown skin and the cutest short-styled haircut. I was in awe of her poise and would have changed my name to sound French like hers, if I could. Her sister Yvonne was a year younger. At least once a week, Yvonne and I would dart out the door at the exact same time and walk the seven blocks to school. I found her easygoing and comfortable, like Ann.

Yvonne and Suzette had their own rooms, decorated in their unique style. I envied their closeness and wished my sister weren't in first grade. On weekends after chores, the girls colored in the blank spaces of being teenagers. I paid close attention—how they spoke, what they wore, how they moved, what books they read, what movies they saw, lessons about certain teachers, protocols of makeup, who to talk with at church, what boys went with what girls, choosing a profession, and being a Christian. From what I could see, punishment didn't exist. All week I'd hold my breath, encouraged that with them on the weekends, I could be myself. I don't know if Suzette and Yvonne ever knew the strength they infused in me—the life jacket they threw me whenever I began to drown.

Mom used the last three months of 1963 to reorganize our family. She enrolled Robert and Kelesha in an elementary school four blocks from our house. She joined the PTA and began sewing again. She placed woven shelf paper in drawers, replaced chair and couch coverings, hung pictures and planted shrubs. Weekdays were filled with cooking dinner and helping my siblings with homework, and weekends were as familiar as ever—housework and church. Dad scheduled just enough time on Saturdays to model maleness for Robert.

"Boy, stop being cooped up in your room. Let's cut the lawn, trim the shrubs, wash the car. Afterwards, we'll watch football." But Robert preferred to stay in his room reading, mixing up ooze and blowing it up with his science kit or feeding his pet lizard. Kelesha's Kleenex animal collection grew and I kept finding dead bugs. I worked hard so Dad wouldn't see me rolling my eyes at her.

By Thanksgiving, the house was organized and Mom had started the Winter session to complete her Master's degree.

ᢒ‌NOT AN ORDINARY DAYᢒ

Weekdays, I'd iron my school clothes while listening to Mom's radio. The Supremes blasted, "Baby, baby, baby, where did our love go?" and the news announced that President Kennedy was landing in Dallas, Texas. Dad loved Kennedy and often quoted him in his sermons. I guess we all loved him. He was always described as doing something positive for Negroes' rights and being willing to stick his neck out so we could be equal. I had fallen in love with Jackie—the way her clothes hung on her body like skin, her glamour and style, her maiden name "Bouvier," her soft voice and how she decorated the White House.

It had been eight weeks of settling into my college prep classes. There was no teasing about being a preacher's kid. The only teasing was over my thick Southern accent, more pronounced when we read the classics. It was my turn as Lady Macbeth, wringing my hands.

"Out, damned spot! Out, I say. Hell is murky!..." when my teacher Mrs. Hill was called out of the room. I was glad to stop as my class-mates were laughing at me. When she returned, the color in her face had changed. "President Kennedy was shot and is reported in se-rious condition." Everyone gasped and started asking questions. A moment passed while she tried to calm us before the door opened again. Our band teacher yelled out, "President Kennedy is dead."

Some of the kids started to cry. I couldn't believe it. Like peo-ple all over the world, I wanted his death to be a joke, some awful mistake. A prayer was offered by one of my classmates as the door opened once again. I hoped this time, the news would be that it was a hoax, but we were asked to come to the auditorium. I could see the grief on the faces of all my classmates as we stood for a moment of silence with our heads lowered. We were let out of class to mingle around the auditorium and cafeteria to share stories of Kennedy and watch the story unfold on television.

When I arrived home, Dad was upstairs in the bedroom, watch-ing the news. Walter Cronkite's face was somber. Every detail of what they knew was being repeated. "This is the motorcade...shots were fired...President Kennedy's body...Mrs. Kennedy's pink mo-hair suit, stained with her husband's blood." At 1:30 in the morning, Mom sent me to bed. My obsession with untimely death started all over that Saturday. I sat motionless, staring—at my eggs getting cold, gray spaces outside the bedroom window, a pimple on my face as the tragedy continued to unfold. *Wonder what it's like when you die?* Our church service was morbid; even the nursing babies didn't whimper. Dad cut the sermon short. I sprinted up the stairs and ate dinner in front of the television.

I watched Lee Harvey Oswald, a skinny, hollow-eyed man in a jacket being escorted by police, wondering what could have possessed him to commit such a senseless act. He looked like somebody had roughed him up. Suddenly his body contorted; his expression changed. Pandemonium broke out. A man in the shadows had shot Oswald and now he was dead too. Monday was declared a national day of mourning, and everybody stayed home. I watched Mrs. Kennedy in her black suit and draped veil, going through the motions of brokenness with such courage, beauty, and grace. I felt a strange sort of kinship with her, like we could have shared tea over feeling pain. The fragility of existence hit me by storm when John Boy saluted his father. One moment you were alive, President of the United States, a father with a beautiful family—next moment you were dead. I asked Dad, "How can this be?" but the only explanation he could muster was, "We don't know the day, month, or year when our life will end. That's why we must do good in every moment, because it could be our last." I didn't find his words very comforting.

THIN VEIL OF LIFE AND DEATH

Each year, one weekend event was organized for all the grades to co-mingle at my high school. I had been accepted into a group of eight to ten kids from seniors to sophomores, including my friends from across the street. We ate, critiqued subjects, teachers, politics, each other, our parents, and sometimes even participated in the milk fights. Now that was fun! Everyone was college prep, active in band, drama, the class newspaper, or student government. We were the first ones to hear of school activities and the yearly event—a ski trip to Northern California.

I couldn't wait to tell Mom and Dad.

"Oh boy, my first time in snow! I can't wait. I know you're going to let me go! My grades are A's and B's. My chores are complete. I've learned my piano solo. There aren't any church activities." Plus I thought to myself, *No boys calling the house and I've kept my mouth shut.* Mom passed the decision to Dad and he said, "We'll see." I thought, *No worries, it's a mere formality.* I knew Aunt Zemma's secondhand store filled with clothes from rich people would offer the perfect place to find a chic ensemble. I was patient until the forms were due and asked Dad again. This time, he surprised me with an absolute "No." I wasn't giving up so easily—"Dad, don't you want me to be well-rounded in preparation for college?" It didn't work. I was smart enough by now to cover my face with a mask, so Dad couldn't see my disappointment.

Each day after choir and during lunch, I was asked the same question, "Sister Thomas, are you going on the ski trip?" My disappointment deepened. The only silver lining was Suzette and Yvonne weren't going either. But they didn't want to experience snow!

The Saturday morning of the trip, my imagination was caffeinated by adventurous thoughts of building snowmen and sliding down mountains of ice. The day dragged on like the sixteenth inning of a tied baseball game, and my mood matched the gray sky. I couldn't wait to move out and make my own decisions.

The evening news came on at 6:00. The phone rang a few minutes later. Yvonne was talking fast. "Did you hear, did you hear?" she said. I had no idea what she was talking about.

"No, what?"

"The ski trip. Gloria, Clinetta, and Melvin are dead. They drowned."

"What?"

"The ice broke, they fell in and drowned," she continued. "It's on the news."

I wanted it to be a mistake, but television confirmed my shaken disbelief. Dad gloated just a little as we watched the reporter confirm the deaths again. "Now, aren't you glad I said no?" It was a wild speculation that I resented; sixty-three kids had gone on that trip. There was no reason to believe I would have been a fourth victim.

Once again, I was reminded of Dad's love for me. It was like a jigsaw puzzle, and sometimes the pieces went missing. I believed there was nothing he wouldn't do externally to protect me and keep our family safe. But he was a zealot. When his mind crossed the lines of Christian devotion the generous, compassionate, logical person I knew crashed. In its place a powerful irreverent energy rose up, threatening and consuming anything in its path.

As Suzette, Yvonne and I listened to the eulogies, each sermon burned a memory in my heart about living in truth and dying with peace. I sat transfixed, remembering my encounters with Melvin and Gloria in the library the Friday before the trip, and my last words, "Have a good time for me." Now they were dead, like Kennedy. I wondered what their last thoughts were as the breath left their bodies, or if they felt pain. I kept asking God, "WHY?" Gloria had the highest GPA in the school and was going to some Ivy League college; she wouldn't harm a flea. Clinetta was the head cheerleader, adored by the whole student body and accepted to the University of California, Berkeley. Melvin was smart, a star football player with a scholarship. As I glanced at the cold body freed of its spirit, I kept asking God, Why do good people get hurt, suffer, and die? The only consolation came from the belief deep within. *Now they are in heaven.*

WHEN DREAMS COME TRUE

I was twelve the first time I saw the movie, *The Reluctant Debutante*. I didn't understand the word *society*; I just saw the elegance and splendor of people looking important and special. Leaving Shreveport before I was presented had been a hard dream to banish, as I would have been selected as one of the city's "good girls." The old green ballgown that Aunt Bea had bought me years before had given me plenty of opportunity to waltz around our backyard, and I had worn it until the netting fell apart.

I had never been able to count on Mom to nourish my heart. Mom seemed cool, disconnected from her real feelings. She excelled at taking care of our family's day-to-day needs and supported Dad's ministry tirelessly. But she seemed emotionally aloof. Little did I know at the time but she was quietly watching me, and how the toll of lost friendships and Dad's extreme expectations had shaken my self-confidence. And so one May afternoon as I cooked dinner, she gave me the shock of my life.

"You've been invited to be a debutante."

I stopped chopping. "What did you say?"

"You heard me, you're going to be a deb."

I could feel adrenaline pumping through my veins as I caught a string of balloons floating up. "Does Dad know about it?" I didn't want to get excited for nothing.

"Yes, it's okay with him."

"For real? Don't kid with me, Mom. You know how much I want to be a deb."

"I'm not kidding. You've got a sponsor. "

"How did that happen? What do I have to do? When is it?"

I acted like the chicken Dad killed, jumping all around like my head was chopped off, exploding with joy. Mom had struck gold. During the Spring she had entered an internship at one of the high schools and had been partnered with another counselor. Mrs. Wilson belonged to the national Negro organization called The Links, who sponsored the cotillion each year. As soon as Mom shared my dream, Mrs. Wilson decided to sponsor me. My feet began to levitate. I wouldn't come down until the first meeting in June.

My stomach filled with more butterflies than I'd ever had in my life on the ride to the first meeting. I figured whoever lived in the big Victorian house close to the UC Berkeley campus must be very rich. I turned and waved to Dad as he peered out the car window, waiting for an acknowledgment from whoever was inside.

Mrs. Wilson wrapped her arms around me as if she knew me. "It's so nice to meet you. Your mom has told us about how you always wanted to be a debutante. We love her, she is such a wonderful addition to our counseling staff." I politely thanked her, overwhelmed about how nice she was, not at all sure of what to expect.

I had never seen such perfection—fingers held perfectly around teacups, bodies straight and shoulders back, smooth skin, coiffed hair, silk suits, empire dresses, gloves, hats, manicured nails, and hip talk. I opened my ears, stood real straight and tried to look like I belonged. I'd never been good at small talk and made a beeline when I saw the only two girls I knew, one from church and one from school. My signature gold caps sparkled in my mouth and I hoped the girls wouldn't think I was ugly. Chatter created a steady hum about private school, second languages, plans for college, living in the hills, and summer vacations in faraway places like France, Spain, and New York. I couldn't help but think, *What am I doing here? Look where I live and go to school.* Then I remembered words spoken many times in our family. "Remember, no matter where you are, always carry your head high." My fingers eased a little around the teacup.

Each girl stood, spoke about her background, how proud she was to be the daughter of doctor so and so, attorney so and so, businessman so and so. When my turn came, I spoke with every language skill I had ever learned.

"My father pastors Beebe Memorial C.M.E. Temple and is building one of the largest churches in the Bay Area. My mother is one of the first Negro high-school counselors. I'm attending Howard University, majoring in drama, music, or medicine. I am the pianist for my high school choir, have competed in piano recitals and won trophies for oratory speaking. I'm on the honor roll and I sing in the church choir. I love reading, writing, and fashion. My ambition is to become an actress, doctor, or concert pianist."

When I finished, I looked around. Smiles, head nods, clapping, and pleasant faces told me, *Whew, you passed the first test!*

My parents had no idea what it meant to be a debutante. For me, it represented values extracted from years of listening to my parents—virginity, pedigree, and excellence—the cream rising to the top. Mom and Dad's constant reminders about being a decent, moral girl lived deep within me and I had every intention of graduating from college, becoming a professional, meeting Mr. Wonderful, falling in love, having an elaborate wedding, fancy house, two children, and living happily ever after, in that order. That's the way it happened in the movies, and that was going to happen to me! But being a debutante meant even more. I would be recognized, presented to the world as the special girl I desperately wanted to be—the "good" girl Dad had always desired of me.

As the sponsors began to discuss what was ahead, I was surprised by *the other responsibilities* of being a debutante: writing an essay, community service, and parties to attend. There was even a business side to solicit at least $750 worth of advertisement for the souvenir book. Seven-hundred-fifty dollars was a lot of money. We were encouraged not to worry, but I couldn't help myself. Who could I solicit? The last bombshell was selling tickets; we were expected to fill at least one table of ten. I didn't know what I had gotten myself into. Then details about the actual ball began—Sunday afternoon rehearsals beginning in September; warnings about exposing bare skin on arms, necklines, and backs; which fabrics were too sheer for our gowns; what gloves, shoes, necklaces, earrings, nail polish were acceptable; and being on time. I would be presented to society at the Hilton Hotel in San Francisco during the Thanksgiving holiday, hanging on the arm of my polite young escort. I gasped. My sponsor saw me. "We have young boys available who meet the standards in case you have difficulty." I was toast. There wasn't a boy in the universe that Dad trusted, plus using a reserve boy felt so pitiful.

By the time the requirements were completed, my eyes had begun to blur. *Oh my goodness!*

White-and-cream-colored invitations with gold linings started arriving in the mailbox immediately. I tore open the first envelope as if it contained the key to life. "You are invited to a pajama party and gourmet breakfast on Saturday at the Claremont Hotel." I showed it to Mom first, jumping up and down, hoping she would talk to Dad about staying overnight.

Dad wasn't having it. "We go to church on Sunday. What would the members think if they knew you were at an all-night party and couldn't come to church? You can be a debutante but it mustn't interfere with school or church." That was the last comment he made about me attending parties.

In my sixteen years, I had never missed going to church, except for measles and chicken pox. I had never humiliated Dad in a public way, had participated in every youth activity, won awards, excelled at music, been an excellent student, taught the little children at Sunday school, raised my hand and spoken up even when I didn't want to. Hadn't I fulfilled Dad's speech to me so long ago about showing Jesus how much I loved Him? Where was the fairness? It hurt me to believe he still needed proof of my cooperation. I deserved leniency and acknowledgment for all I had endured. I couldn't chance speaking out—what Dad had given, Dad could easily take away. So I pouted just a little and prayed a whole lot, but the party came and went. I lived vicariously through the invitations, hopeful one would penetrate his steel heart. But those girls only saw me at one event. And Dad wanted me home early, so you might as well say I never went.

&TENDER TRUST&

After moving to California, one of the few bright lights that kept me going was my aunt and uncle. They were childless and although Aunt Bea never spoke of it, I sensed a tender sadness whenever she looked at her nieces. Aunt Bea and Uncle Claude were the lively kind with many friends cultivated from their being educators— Claude was an elementary school principal and Bea a first-grade teacher. I'd find any excuse to spend the day, night, or weekends with them, free to say or be whatever I wanted. They were so hip—cigarette in one hand and a glass of liquor in the other. Playing cards with friends, telling off-color jokes about sex or politicians, dancing and occasionally saying a bad word. We'd frequent art galleries, street fairs, fine restaurants, and the golf course. Aunt Bea would cook my favorite red beans whenever I asked and surprise me with articles of clothing and shoes she picked up from her sister's secondhand shop or trinkets from weekend excursions she took with my uncle in Monterey and Napa. I learned the Twist, the Mashed Potato, the Jerk, and the Slop just in time for small, chaperoned parties with the teenagers of their friends. I felt indebted for the exposure and came to appreciate the feeling of being trusted, careful not to spill the beans about the boys upon returning home.

Uncle Claude would smoke and drink gin and tonic without a care in the world on the Sundays we met for family dinners. Claude respected Dad as a holy man, but he was his own person without need of anyone else's approval. I longed for that kind of self-esteem to land within me and decided I wanted to be just like my uncle when I became an adult. During one of these dinner outings, Aunt Bea extended the best invitation ever.

"We know how much you love jazz, so we're taking you with us to the Monterey Jazz Festival in September for your birthday." And before I could open my mouth, Aunt Bea said, "Yes, your father has already agreed to let you go with us."

"Are you sure Dad said I could go?" It didn't sound like him, especially because I would miss church.

Dad looked me in the eye when I asked him again. "Yes, you can go." I wondered, *What's got into him*?

Uncle Claude was a jazz collector extraordinaire from what I could tell. Herbie Mann, Modern Jazz Quartet, Miles Davis, John Coltrane, Dizzy Gillespie, Thelonious Monk, Sarah Vaughan, Dinah Washington, Carmen McRae. I loved them all, especially Miles. Uncle Claude didn't mind me listening whenever I came over, after showing me how to handle each LP.

"Hold the record with your thumb and your middle finger, so you don't get grease or smudges on it like this. Wipe the record with this soft cloth and put them back in the jacket when you're done."

Sometimes I had the house to myself and when they returned I'd be snapping my fingers, twisting my rear end, and bopping to the sound with my eyes closed. Aunt Bea and Uncle Claude would laugh and I laughed too. Being around them stirred my imagination of being "hip" and filled me with a thumping inside. *Things are going to be all right!*

But I was bewildered by Dad's willingness to allow jazz in my life. I had learned not to trust him. When we got home, I asked again. "Dad, you're going to let me go?"

He spoke with lightness and patted my head, "Yes, you've been a good girl and I don't see any reason why you can't go with your aunt and uncle. I know how much you enjoy music." I couldn't believe my ears. *Dad must be real happy or hypnotized. Or maybe he's too preoccupied to bother with watching over me anymore and understands I'm all grown up!* I hoped that was it. I had come to understand that moving to Oakland had been calculated. His charge had been to build a new cathedral and educational building. Completing the facility would set Dad up strategically for his appointment as bishop. I knew he would be successful. God just came through for Dad. And although I had paid an enormous price, I was proud of his success and proud to call him my father.

Dad's good mood was unexplainable and unexpected, but I decided to roll with it, be grateful and hold on to my belief that better days were ahead of me.

ᚙPLUCKEDᚖ

The ninth Monterey Jazz festival was scheduled for the third week of September. With four weeks to go, I'd lie across the bed visualizing myself in dark glasses, black Capri pants, a cowl neck sweater, and a red scarf around my neck. I was spotted by photographers looking cool, paper and pen thrown in my face by admirers desperate for my autograph. The jazz musicians would notice, invite me to the front row, play a song just for me. I'd laugh and smile, enchanted by the attention. Hours would pass, while I imagined...

Wearing the latest, hippest outfit filled every cell of my brain, especially after Aunt Bea hinted, "A few teenagers from the party will join us on Saturday."

Sitting on Suzette's bedroom floor, I engaged her and Yvonne to help think through my outfit choices. Yvonne kept staring at my eyebrows. "You need to have those things shaped."

It was true; they sprouted over my eyes like owl feathers. It took an hour as she plucked and wiped, plucked and wiped, causing my eyes to water. When I saw myself in the mirror, I kept staring. My brown eyes stood out like lightbulbs. Funny how one small gesture could make me feel so beautiful.

At breakfast Dad kept squinting his brow. "What's wrong with your face, what did you do to your face?" I didn't know what he meant, but his tone alerted me as he turned my face toward Mom. "Look at her face. Who told you that you were grown-up enough to get your eyebrows done?"

I humbly looked him right in his eyes and spoke softly, "Dad, I'm almost seventeen, what's wrong with getting them shaped?"

The volume turned up as Dad's agitation spilled over the pancakes and bacon. I had learned a simple technique when dealing with Dad's tirades; I bowed my head in silence until he blew off steam. This time it backfired. "Tell you what, think you're grown and can make your own decisions? You're not going to Monterey!" he barked. The room became silent. Robert and Kelesha looked on, confused, gulping down their food and relieved that Dad wasn't barking at them.

I ran upstairs to bury my tears and beat my pillow in frustration. At first, I was mad at Yvonne, vowing to stop speaking to her forever. But as the hours passed, I knew it wasn't her fault. I racked my brain, thinking back. *Am I crazy to believe that getting my eyebrows plucked was inside the boundaries of my own liberation? Am I even crazier to believe that Dad would allow me to listen to music he felt could corrupt me?* I pleaded with Aunt Bea to help, but her attempts to change Dad's mind fell on deaf ears.

These were the times I felt most perplexed. Telling the truth had been Dad's soapbox, but when it came to keeping his word, he was the liar. I couldn't help but believe somewhere in Dad's world, a detour had occurred, interrupting his flow. A major snag, a haunting dark shadow he didn't even understand. But usually, there were signs—a raised voice with Mom, impatience with Kelesha, sudden absences from the house, excessive jingling of change in his pockets, no time for any of us, no jokes before his sermon, or simply overreacting, like the time he ran the Jehovah Witnesses down the street with a broom. This time, there had been nothing. Truth was, I should have seen it coming, but I had gotten comfortable over the last few months. I admonished myself, *You can never ever go to sleep. You've got to be quick on your toes. You've got to remember the cycle. You lose every time you relax into being yourself.* I felt a mighty storm brewing in me as fantasies of being hip, listening to jazz, and being with the teenagers slipped away. And I had blabbed my mouth—telling my classmates I was going!

I'm going to run away, skipped through my mind like pebbles on a lake. My only prayer was, *God please bring down your mighty wrath on my father*. In the meantime, all I could do was watch, stay alert under his radar screen, and accept his final decision when he spoke the words, "You have to learn to show us respect."

ᘒDEBUTANTE BLUESᘒ

W hen it came to my escort, you'd have thought I was getting married. My parents understood the boy would be required to be in close proximity to me for several months, and Dad wanted to ensure that he could trust whoever it was. All I heard around the house was, "That boy must come from a good background." Code for "He must be a Christian."

I was sweet on a boy from school, but Dad didn't know. Joel was from a good family, his brother went to Stanford, and his family was involved in city politics. He'd hold my hand and walk me halfway home to the point we felt Dad might see us. But Dad didn't want to hear one word about him as my escort. Instead he said, "I've already decided." I braced myself, knowing it would be some egghead with bad breath and acne. Surprisingly, I was quite pleased.

David was a man—three years older than me, tall, dark, and debonair, and he had his own car. Dad trusted him because he was the son of a church trustee my parents had known since I was a baby. Dad waited for my reaction, but I didn't say a word, afraid my body language might set off alarms in his head. I had a crush on David. He knew it too, and would tease me all the time about growing up. Dancing with him was going to be so romantic! And I could relax, confident that I didn't have to worry about Dad sticking his nose in every move we made. All that was left was talking with David's parents to make sure he knew the rules. And within a week, my escort blues were settled.

We began practicing our debutante routine the first week in September. One o'clock sharp every Sunday afternoon. Dad was not pleased, but what could he do? Our choreographer worked us step-by-step in groups of fours and eights, starting and ending, over and over again until 5:00. I was serious; each step had to be perfect. I had to show the choreographer, my sponsor and, most importantly, my parents how well I followed instructions.

Months before, I had searched for the perfect dress through pages and pages of bridal magazines. It had to meet the requirements, but more importantly, the bodice of the skirt, neckline, and sleeves had to define my uniqueness. The day I turned the page and saw the model standing with her back turned showing silk roses, I knew. Mom loved it too. There was only one problem in the tiny print.

"Ronita, do you see how much that dress costs? It's outrageously too expensive. You need shoes, and another dress for the after-party; there's your senior ball; you've got college and...." My ears turned off. *Wasn't I worth this one sacrifice?*

I was never good at faking my hand, and Mom saw my joy turn to gloom. "Tell you what, your heart is so set on that dress, I'm going to make it for you."

Mom was a great seamstress and had made clothing for us over the years, but I hadn't seen her make anything for a very long time. Plus she seemed too busy with her high-school students to create what I saw before me. "Don't worry, I'll get Mrs. Madsen and Mrs. Taylor to help. You'll see." I wanted to believe her.

I was feeling the pressure of trying to fit in and compete with the girls: bringing in advertisements for the souvenir book, having the most exotic dress, filling up the guest tables, responding to the girls' questions about why I never came to parties, and deciding on an after-party dress. I juggled preparing for the cotillion with studying for aptitude tests, piano recitals, and my church responsibilities. I knew high scores were required for Howard, and I didn't want *anything* to get in the way of being accepted at my dream college, as both my parents had said "Yes" as long as my grades and scores were good. When it came to getting a good education, I believed them!

One other thing hovered over me right from the very first time I heard it. "As you are presented, your fathers will escort you around the room." I was fine with this part of the ritual. "After your routine with your escorts, your father will greet you and perform the first dance—a waltz—like the tradition of being given away at weddings." *Uh-oh, my Dad didn't dance in public.* But I couldn't fathom Jesus or church members upset with such a respectable event as the cotillion. Still I wondered, *Will he do this for me?*

Advertisements trickled in like a plugged faucet. Mom and Dad knew a lot of people, and I was sure he could surpass what was required, if he wanted to. But I sensed a hesitation. He didn't even want to discuss getting ads for me. Dad never liked asking anybody for anything—he didn't like being indebted. The problem was the deadline for turning in money was approaching fast and fulfilling the quota was getting in the way of my studies. I assumed we'd need lots of tables—perhaps more than anybody else because of all the people we knew at the church. And I assumed Mom and Dad were excited about showing me to the community for the *fine* job they had done in raising me. Yes, it was an expensive event with formals, rented tuxedos, and seventy-five-dollar tickets. Even so, I was the only minister's daughter in the group of twenty-eight being presented and kept thinking, *I am special!*

By my birthday in early November, the dissected pieces of my dress began to come together. Mom had made modifications in the fullness of the bodice, neck, and backline as chiffon turned into silk tulle and two-inch slanted sleeves grew six inches. I was distressed until I saw the two unique features of the dress—beading on the front and twenty rolled-silk tulle roses sitting in a box. Time was ticking by quickly. Mom still had to put all the sections together, tack the roses to the bodice, make my after-party dress, make her own dress, continue to take care of our family, and work. I cooked more dinners, cleaned more toilets, played longer piano selections, got more migraine headaches, and played with my sister to keep from biting my nails again!

Dad hadn't decided what he was going to do about dancing with me, so my Uncle Claude was lined up as a back-up. I was sure it was a formality. With one day left, our annual Thanksgiving dinner at Aunt Zemma's became a giant tease about tumbling down stairs, heels falling off shoes, hair flopping, and missed dance steps. Laughter filled the air, and I was happy to release the tension.

ᏣᎳWALTZING ON AIRᏙᎦ

O ur choreographer had announced, "Report no later than 9:00 for breakfast and final practice in the ballroom." Some of the girls had spent the night, but I knew that wasn't an option for me. My stomach butterfly friends visited the whole day until we were led to a big room to get dressed. "Pictures at 5:00," the chairwoman announced. I just hoped my hair would stay in place, my deodorant would hold up, I wouldn't fall from walking in my new white satin shoes, and Jesus would see fit to allow Dad to dance with me this one time.

All the girls in my pod had described their dresses in detail from the high-end department stores like I. Magnin, Irene Sergeant, Saks, and Gump's. One girl claimed her dress came from Europe and was made of rice paper. I couldn't wait to see that! My hands took on a frostbite quality as I snapped the two hooks on the strapless lace bra, rolled up my stockings, and secured my hoop skirt around my waist while taking every precaution with my hair and makeup. It was a lot to organize at seventeen. Mom had wrapped my dress in a plastic garment bag, but I hadn't seen it for a couple of days while she put on the finishing touches. My hands trembled as I slowly pulled down the zipper, not sure what to expect. I let out a gleeful "Yea." Mom had outdone herself, and while the dress wasn't exactly how I had remembered, it was perfect. I put on my pearl earrings, necklace, and long white gloves, walked to the mirror, and saw a princess staring back at me. She had no flaws, handicaps, errors, or excuses. All she had was beauty—pure, honest beauty. With that assurance, I winked at myself just in time to notice the stares from the other girls.

We came out of the large dressing room and stood before the photographer while he looked at our faces, then our dresses, and began selecting where each of us would stand or sit. It took a long time as he selected the back row, then the second row, and finally the first row. I had the jitters the whole time, praying I wouldn't be hidden behind someone's teased hairstyle. When he pointed at me and placed me on the front row to the left of the girl right in the center, any doubt of being second-best faded from my mind. Flashbulbs started nonstop after that, blinding me as I worked hard to smile just right so as not to show my gold teeth.

It was time to line up alphabetically, time to step into the limelight of a dream. I had a long wait and could hear the applause as the announcer read out each girl's name and talked about her aspirations. As my name was called I floated up the stairs and curtsied under the chandelier light. The glare made it hard to see and I worried about the Thanksgiving Day predictions. But the good Lord was with me as I walked down the stairs and took another curtsy where Dad waited. He smiled deeply as his hand met mine and gently escorted me a quarter ways around the ballroom. I curtsied. Halfway around the ballroom floor I curtsied again and gave Mom a colorful fall flower arrangement. All I could hear was applause. All I could see were blurred faces as Dad held me steady. One more quarter-walk around the room, another curtsy, and the next girl's name was announced. It had gone by too fast and I wished I could freeze the frame. My mind flashed over the scenes of movies where I had sighed with envy and I realized in that moment; none compared with these golden moments in the spotlight.

After the last girl had been presented, we all moved to our positions. My heart was pounding as I waited for the strike of the first note. It was a classic minuet; five symmetrical steps of moving forward, backward, and to the right over and over again for what felt like forever. In the moment all I could think about were the steps, keeping my posture, smiling, and not tripping over my dress. From the rooftops tiny crystal lights began to glitter all over me and I curtsied to the last note. A deafening applause shot through the room and a standing ovation followed. We finished without a flaw. David joined me with encouragement in his eyes and held me gently around my waist as we prepared for the real test of the evening; a series of intricate configurations that began in pairs, multiplied by two or four until fifty-six bodies moved around the floor like a giant Ferris wheel. Our movements were sharp, crisp, and precise with no room for mistakes. The audience clapped wildly to our twirling and looping.

We ended to the beat of jazz, shaking our hips like we were at the high-school hop. Tension slowly released its grip on my body. We hadn't messed up once! I held my breath in preparation for the father-daughter waltz. I had never danced with my father and stretched my neck over the crowd waiting, expecting his handsome image to walk up, take my hand, and look in my eyes. Instead, I saw Uncle Claude.

Tears would have spilled if it hadn't been for his joking, "You're the belle of the ball. Ain't a girl here prettier than you, my little chili girl."

I wanted all the girls to see my father. But more than anything I wanted Dad to show the world I was more important than Jesus. I never forgot his explanation after the dance. "As a minister, it's not proper for me to be dancing. My members are here. What will they think?" I didn't understand. What kind of Jesus would frown on such an innocent act as dancing with your daughter at her coming-out gala? And why couldn't Dad for once care more about me than what the members might think? I had become accustomed to making sense out of no sense and decided I wasn't going to let Dad spoil my joy.

He kept his word; I was able to stay out until 4:00 a.m. at the after-party, but I was the first one to leave. Sunday school started at 9:30. The memory of gliding became etched in my heart and when the newspaper article came out, there I was, beaming—the minister's proud, beautiful, joyful daughter.

STUNNED

The college application process included an essay, "Why do you want to attend Howard University?" Writing a response took no time. I loved essays and had every pamphlet I could get my hands on about the scholastic reputation of the fine arts departments and the medical school. Tora Walker from church was an alumna and had filled my head with so much talk, I was dizzy with glee. During the beginning of my senior year, with the cotillion keeping me busy, I hadn't paid attention to the details of acceptance letters. But when we had to fill out the vitae for the cotillion souvenir book, there was no doubt I'd be moving to Washington, D.C. and majoring in the arts or science. I wasn't yet sure of the profession, but never the college.

As Winter waved goodbye, I realized that time was drawing near for my separation from the Thomas family. I wasn't sorry to be leaving home like some of the girls from church. I couldn't wait!

One evening after watching a brilliant Spring sunset, I could smell bad news coming as Dad and Mom sat me down after dinner, looking me straight in the face as if somebody had died.

"When we promised you could attend Howard we were living in the South. We live in California now. There are many good schools here; Mills, UC Berkeley, UCLA. We think it is best that you select a school on the West Coast."

A sharp-edged stake went through my body. "But you promised, you promised. You said if I kept up my grades, I could go to Howard!" I could feel my body getting warm all over, the tears about to fall as I listened to Dad's apologetic tone.

"Yes, yes, but we've talked it over and we think this is best. We've got Robert and Kelesha to think about, and we think this is best." I thought it, but didn't dare speak the words of broken promises that Dad had preached about in his sermons as I stomped up the stairs. It wasn't fair. Next morning my swollen eyes woke me with my own criteria for college. *Get as far away as you can from this house and Dad.*

I was accepted at all the schools my parents had identified plus more, and decided to attend the University of Oregon in Eugene.

But a gnawing feeling kept tugging at me and I wondered, *What's really behind Dad's decision?*

I'd overheard my parents talking about new schools, fabric for furniture, and making ends meet from their bedroom. And one afternoon, we took a drive to a house in the Oakland hills. By mid-April, my suspicion about why not Howard was verified. We were moving. Mom and Dad had purchased a five-level house with views of the Bay Bridge and a long bus ride across town. I was so confused; I thought pastors weren't allowed to own houses. What I didn't real-

ize was that I was simply the next victim to the legacy of Dad and
Mom. Money for their college education had been spent by their
parents. I think they both figured I'd get over it and move on. But as
graduation came and went without much fanfare, I felt crushed and
believed I would never recover from the wound. Over the summer I
moped, grieving my status as an almost-Howard alumna right up to
the time of the annual church conference.

It was almost half-past three on Sunday afternoon. The bishop's
secretary would take an hour to read appointments for the ninth region. I was hot and bored; the appointments weren't going to affect
me. A wasp fluttered freely from light to light when I felt the air thick
with quietness. I wondered, *What happened?* People were looking
puzzled and sad eyes fell on me with such consternation I ran down
the stairs searching for Mom or Robert.

I ran right into Sister Graceson, weeping. "I can't believe they
took your father away from us, I just can't believe it."

"What?" I asked. "What do you mean, took him away?"

The knot I knew well returned to my stomach as I tried to free
myself from the crowds of people bumping up around me. I found
Sister Washington, stammering. "We, we, we don't under, understand. How cou, cou, could Bishop do, do, do it?"

Drifting in my own fantasies, I had missed the secretary's announcement and thought Dad had been appointed as a bishop. Relief came over me, *Maybe now he can stop trying so hard to show
everybody what a good preacher he can be.* Sister Washington interrupted my thought, weeping. "How could they make your daddy an
evangelist?" I didn't know what that was, but it didn't sound like a
promotion. As I fought my way through the crowd of members waiting for Dad, all I could see was the top of his head as folks started to
embrace him.

"That's alright, Pastor, God will see you through, you hold your head up, we love you, Pastor." So many people surrounded Dad, he couldn't do anything but put on a good face and say "Thank you." But as his eyes came into view, I could see the arrow had gone deep.

He cuddled around Mom and the three of us as we walked slowly to the car. I kept looking at his face; the gale had knocked the wind out of his sails. A couple of the church trustees ran after us, "Follow us, Pastor, let's get something to eat." At the restaurant heads bobbed together in little whispers; we sipped Cokes and fumbled with our napkins. Afterwards, the group decided to follow us home. In our living room each person became an attorney, making the opening and closing argument in one breath, expressing disbelief and anger. I was fascinated by the passion, sure Bishop Avery would correct his mistake. As I sat back listening, I reflected on Dad's success, all the accomplishments of his ministry with one question stuck in my head. *What led to Dad's disgrace?*

At the time, I didn't understand Dad's star had been snatched away on purpose. For months tension had been brewing among some of the leadership. Rumor was the bishop thought Dad had gotten too big for his britches and needed to be taught a lesson and singled out for breaking the rules. What better way to make an example of a favorite pastor climbing the ladder than strip him of his prestige and take him away from his family? Evangelists were roaming ministers at the mercy of the bishop. They had no congregation, no regular income, no clue where they would be from week to week, and no place to live. Pastors lived in church parsonages, not in their own homes, and *this* was the crucible of Dad's troubles. According to Dad, the bishop had given him the impression that purchasing a house was okay. But over the summer, the tide had turned against the preacher with the silver tongue.

The phone woke me up early the next morning as reality sank in. *Dad doesn't have a church anymore.* I hurried upstairs, eager for the next development, and heard Dad speaking, "I'm not going to accept the appointment. Yes, we'll meet tonight."

Those words brought me to a different reality—the impact on going to college, as I was to leave for Oregon in a few weeks. I didn't know what else Dad could do to support our family. And I hoped there would still be money for me to go away. But the possibility of Dad leaving the ministry cheered me up. Religion was two-faced.

My sister and brother were oblivious to what was going on with the phone ringing and people hanging around the house. But I was front and center, curious, not wanting to miss a beat. By dusk folks sat or stood anywhere they could as Mom poured coffee and Dad sat in his favorite chair overlooking the bay. I knelt down beside him with a ringside seat. One by one, speeches strung together, echoing a unanimous message.

"Pastor, you must continue serving in the ministry. You're our pastor, you can't let them get you down."

Dad tried to comfort the group. "We'll be all right and from time to time I'll preach here and there," but his voice cracked.

"We need to do something. We need to stand up, take action. You the best pastor we ever had and we're way ahead of schedule on the building fund and construction. We need to take action, I tell you. Let's go to the bishop. Let's protest," a voice spoke out. Everyone nodded their heads with agreement and a few more members repeated the same proclamation. I thought, *This is getting interesting!*

Brother McLeary had been listening in the corner when he spoke up. "How about starting our own church?"

Everybody stopped talking, took a deep breath, and looked straight at him. It was a bold statement—sacrilegious. Every person present had been raised in the Methodist tradition and had been taught that good Christians accept the bishop's decision. It seemed so preposterous, I almost laughed. Then I looked at some of the faces and saw them light up. We closed with prayer and the group agreed to meet again the next evening. The phone kept ringing late into the night as word spread about the news and Mom found herself trying to explain the situation to her family in Louisiana.

On Tuesday night, the original dozen folks showed up with new recruits. I sat fascinated as the plan hatched right before my eyes with Dad listening, the filament firing in his eyes. It was a simple solution. Members from the old church would follow Dad into a new church, if he were willing to be the leader. The plan was to hold the first gathering on Sunday at the home of one of the former members. The original idea was scratched by Wednesday after fifty-eight people showed up at her house for the third meeting of the week.

The question on everybody's mind was, where can we hold a service?

One of the elder mothers stood and said, "Put your trust in God, it will be revealed, and we will see you all on Sunday."

Brother McLeary spoke again. "What about Mosswood Park?"

It was in a central location and easily accessible by bus. Everybody left in agreement!

On Sunday morning, we left home early. I was scared nobody was going to show up and I didn't want Dad to be humiliated again. But as we turned the corner, streams of people were walking down the street. People from the committee were having a hard time keeping up with dusting off bleachers. By the time the service began, every seat was taken, and the makeshift ushers counted over 150 people. We prayed and sang, and Dad preached like never before as people passed by in cars, curious. "Y'all having a revival?" Young black boys banged their basketballs against the rim.

By the end of the sermon as the invitation to discipleship was extended, there was no doubt about what he was to do. Seventy-five people came forward, and the next week another hundred. It had been decided. Dad would lead a new congregation, although it was foggy how.

Beebe Memorial was never the same. One-half of the congregation joined our new church, splitting husbands and wives, mothers and daughters, sisters and brothers, parents and children, trustees, guilds, choirs and boards. No department was left untouched, as both congregations began to rebuild brick by brick.

Our family was thrown into chaos—we were living in a white neighborhood where Chinese men cleaned yards, Negro women rode the bus in white uniforms, and Mercedes-Benzes cruised the winding roads. We were living in the most affluent school district where Robert and Kelesha would receive the best education and walk home with kids who looked nothing like them.

Dad had a new congregation, but as I sat in my room I'd hear conversations seeping under the closed door about Dad's ability to support our new lifestyle.

One force stabilized our family—Mom. She seemed ignited by new sparks as soon as we moved in our new house, purchasing furniture and drapes and spreading cute ornaments all over the place. One thing was clear, her job was secure and she planned to make use of the twist that had come with no warning.

SEPARATION

I watched the excitement with mixed feelings—torn about leaving for college under such vulnerable conditions and eager to turn the next page of my life with new eyes. The days passed like honey dripping from a wooden spoon and I was ready to venture into the rest of my life. I spent the last Friday rechecking the green trunk and large, cream-colored Samsonite luggage that had been a gift. I checked my list. *Sweaters, flannels, galoshes, hair dryer, rollers, toiletries, alarm clock, typewriter, school supplies, music book, my gold watch from Aunt Bea. School papers, money and, oh, don't forget your Bible.* My room looked abandoned except for my stereo, which Dad had strongly recommended stay home. I sighed. *I'm actually leaving this place.*

Saturday afternoon, my relatives gathered for my last meal of fried shrimp, French fries, and chocolate cake. Around the dinner table, Dad couldn't help joking. "I remember when she was a little girl, always asking questions. Where did God come from? Will the people born before Jesus go to heaven? Why does the sun set in the west? Questions and more questions. And now she is going off to college. Time sure flies. Well, we've taught you right and wrong, now all you have to do is practice what I preached and never forget the good Lord will watch over you."

"I won't forget, Dad," I said dutifully. Aunt Bea and Uncle Claude hugged me last, placing a cute transistor radio in my hand. "Now you're all set, on weekends. Think about us and listen to a little jazz."

I spent the evening on my brother's bed, concerned about his new status as older sibling. "I know more focus will be on you now with the new church and everything. You going to be all right?" He shrugged his shoulders. "You know I love you and I'm going to miss you. Don't worry about Kelesha's tantrums, she'll mellow out eventually. Call Aunt Bea and write me. Before you know it, you'll graduate and be off to college." We hugged, and I felt the weight that pressed against his heart.

Next morning, my parents and I left before the sun came up for the eight-hour drive, arriving in Eugene in the early afternoon. We pulled up to the dormitory and waded through a sea of luggage, confused faces, weepy eyes, and arms tangling around necks.

The resident assistants met us at the entrance, asked my name, and gave me a key. "Your roommate's already checked in." We were located on the third floor right next to the resident assistants.

Dad joked, "Oh, that's good, now she won't be able to get in any trouble."

I couldn't wait to live without his suspicious thoughts!

The three of us climbed the stairs to the third floor and there I had a glimpse of my room and roommate Katherine, Kat for short. My room was glorious—twin beds, a study desk, enough closet space for 15 hangers, and we were right across from the showers and bathrooms. I could see other dormitories, the tennis court, and trees from the bay window that spread across the entire room with green curtains to match the bed coverings.

As we introduced ourselves to Kat's family, an immediate tension permeated the room. Kat was pleasant, but her parents, especially her father, didn't want to shake my parents' hands. He looked constipated. The three of them stormed out of the room, and as they left we heard Kat's father say, "You're not going to room with a nigger."

Memories blanketed me with sadness as I heard that name again. Her father demanded a room exchange from the resident assistants, but Kat stood on her own two feet. "I don't care what you say, I want to room with her and that's the end of it."

I wanted to take lessons from this girl and decided not to let it spoil my first day.

After being smothered for almost eighteen years, I had expected some sort of ceremony or something meaningful to mark our separation. Instead, after unpacking my belongings, Mom and Dad gave me a big hug. "We need to get back on the road before it gets late. Your mother has school tomorrow and I've got a new church to organize."

"Aren't we going to have dinner together?" I asked, stunned. Dad hugged me once more. "You'll be fine," and they were gone.

I watched the car until I couldn't see it anymore, disappointed by their abrupt disappearance, like my parents were glad to be rid of me. The background noise continued to hum as eager girls leaped from car doors and dads pulled out trunkloads of luggage. That's when I remembered feeling the corners of my lips turn up, showing all my gold teeth. Want to know how fast the world turns? Sit on the shore and watch the sunrise. As the second hand ticks, watch the first rays of pink burst through a pale blue sky. Watch as the lone star disappears right before your eyes. Don't glance down for a moment, or if you do, look up again. And you will marvel. The sun hasn't moved at all. You have!

❧CONFUSION❧

I had my first punch in the stomach when I went to register for classes. "We don't have your paperwork or your final transcript," the clerk said.

Embarrassed by the previous day's label, I felt shy talking to the white lady, and wondered. *Does she think I'm a nigger too*? I didn't know what to do. "Excuse me, Ma'am, how could I be accepted into school and be given a room in the dormitory and not actually be registered?"

"I don't know, but we're real busy. I'll check on your paperwork. You come back tomorrow," she said.

I was baffled. *There must be a mistake.* The next morning, and the next, I was the first person in line and the clerk shared what she had discovered. "You've been accepted, but your transcripts went to

Oregon State, about an hour away. We contacted them and they're sending everything to us. Check back at the end of the week."

I didn't know what I was supposed to do in the meantime. *How could this happen*? My transcripts had been completed on time by Miss Lee; at least that's what she had told me. I hadn't worried, because I knew Mom would have made sure everything was in order. After all, she helped students with their college entry documents all the time and knew what was required.

I had received clear instructions. "Don't spend money calling home unless it's an emergency." This qualified. I almost ran out of breath sharing all the details, knowing Mom would immediately correct the error. But I wasn't prepared for her response.

"There's nothing I can do. That was your counselor's job."

I couldn't believe my ears as I hung up the telephone. Mom had time for her students, time to make sure Robert and Kelesha attended the best schools, time to decorate the house, but no time for me. It felt like a dirty trick was being played on me for wanting to leave so bad. It felt like Mom and Dad's invisible arms were snatching me, pulling me back to a place of darkness. From then on, I held Mom just as responsible as Dad for the deep wound that lived inside me.

Every day I stood in line waiting to see the clerk. "Nothing yet," she said, eyeing me sympathetically while I worried about getting my classes. I tried to look like I was registered, milling around the bookstore, standing in long lines, carrying schedules, and asking questions about professors who didn't yet exist. The bay window became my focus as I watched the kids go back and forth like ants. It was a new experience being thrust into an all-white dormitory, and I wasn't at all comfortable. The girls asked, "Did you get all the classes you wanted?" I didn't tell Kat the truth either, because then she would think I was a dumb nigger and that she had made a mistake standing up for being my roommate.

It took a week to get my transcripts and by the time all my paper-work was completed, I was labeled as a late registrant and could only sign up for classes that weren't filled. Professors had already gone over the syllabus for the year and didn't want to hear my hard-luck story. Schedules for academic advisors were booked for weeks. With no guidance, I signed up for all the wrong subjects, most of them not even freshman classes—anthropology, Western civilization, American literature, and statistics. What did I know, I just needed fifteen units. Even the music theory class turned out to be filled with juniors and seniors. I had gotten myself into a pickle and was completely intimidated by so many white people.

FITTING IN

Kat was friendly and uncomplicated. She lived in a small town in Oregon where as far as she knew, the population of Negroes was zero. She couldn't stop apologizing. "Sorry about my dad's bad manners. He's just backwards."

"Believe me, I know people like your dad in Louisiana. They just don't know any better. Lucky for me, you're not like him," I kept saying. Kat wasn't interested in clothes, lived a rather simple life, and worried about her mom's stamina and her baby sister with Down syndrome. The compassion for her sister and genuine expression of guilt about leaving her family drew me close to her right away.

Settled with my roommate and nothing else to do, I started watching tennis matches at the courts outside our window. I had competed in school and loved whacking the ball across the net. A black fellow played every day with the same white partner and he was really good. By the fourth day, I summoned the courage to walk out to the courts. I don't know what came over me, but I spoke out.

"Hey, I play tennis too; not as good as you, but I do play."

He smiled and said, "What's your name, where you from, where do you live?" I managed to mumble, "Ronita, California, and up there," as he zipped up his racket.

"Maybe we'll play sometime," and walked away.

History caught up with me that first few weeks as I reflected on white people's attitudes about skin color. I felt the need to prove myself in some kind of way, so I pulled out my music book and slipped onto the piano stool in our dormitory lounge, right about the time everyone had finished our evening meal. I felt like it was the one thing I knew I did well. As I played "Moon River," "The Shadow of Your Smile," and "Moonlight Sonata," the girls warmed up to me, pointing and clamoring over my music book, "Play this, sing that." I obliged, happy to be useful at something.

By the third week, I felt like a real freshman and joined Kat for the first time at the student union. The tennis player was there, surrounded by a bunch of people. I knew I had to buckle down with my studies, but I told myself learning the ropes from the other black students was also important. I wanted to play tennis too.

Little did I know Victor was a man around campus—a junior and star basketball player. I found it out when one of the black girls pulled me aside. "Stop staring at him. He's got lots of girls after him, black and white, so don't get your hopes up."

"I just want to play tennis," I said.

She looked at me and snapped her fingers. "That's what they all say!"

Before I arrived on the campus, you could put what I knew about the University of Oregon in a thimble. Some days I'd walk around trying to clear my head from the hours of reading. The campus was spread out over 250 acres and home to hundreds of species of trees.

Gothic-looking buildings covered with vines stood elegantly among sprawling modern structures. When I walked twenty minutes north, I'd run into a row of fast-food restaurants and twenty minutes south, my choice of church denominations.

From what I could tell, Eugene's economy was the campus, temporary home to 11,500 students and exactly a hundred Negroes like me: except we weren't Negroes anymore, we were Black! But my status was even smaller than a hundred. All over the country, universities and colleges were attempting to integrate. Upward Bound had been created for underprivileged students wanting a college degree. With a grade point average of C, students could receive a scholarship to supplement their incomes by working in the cafeteria, performing janitorial or menial office jobs around the college. I had entered on my own B+ average and my parents were paying my tuition. But in the eyes of some of the white students and my teachers, I was lumped in with the ninety-one Upward Bound students. It didn't sit well with me, because I certainly didn't want to be placed in the same class as economically deprived C students. I made it known too, telling anyone who would listen, "I'm not one of those kids!"

At the time I applied, I had no idea of the negative view that Oregonians had toward minorities. I figured the people would be open-minded like at home. But the upper-class black students started warning what infractions to watch out for—tampered grades, incorrect homework assignments, being lured into disciplinary arguments, lost homework, being over looked by teachers, pranks and theft in our dormitory rooms, name calling and being crowded off the sidewalk. And there were definite neighborhoods where we were not welcomed. The stories frightened me, as I thought about the South and my first week's subtle form of racism. We left our doors open, and girls kept peeking in on me while I sat under my hair dryer, like I was a new exhibit. Every fifteen minutes, someone would tap the cover and tease me, "What kind of hair do you have that it takes so long to dry? Can I touch it?" I turned up the temperature dial. At night I'd think about Howard, wondering what the freshman girls were doing—making new friends, talking about classes, not explaining the texture of their hair. But I was determined to make the best of it and not allow the color of my skin to keep me from getting my education.

There were girls from wealthy families on my floor, and one particular girl, whose father was the architect for McDonald's, invited me to her room. I loved McDonald's, especially the nineteen-cent fish sandwiches and the large, fifteen-cent French fries. I felt special being invited. I knocked on the door, and entered a smoke-filled room. The thought of my last adventure with smoking quickly came to my mind.

"Do you smoke?"

"Nope," I said.

"Well, everybody who's cool in this dorm smokes."

I had heard that word "everybody" before and knew it was code for being a part of the in-crowd. There was no doubt; I wanted to be in, especially with these white girls.

The three girls sitting on the bed kept blowing rings in the air. "Come on, we can't let our piano player be a square. Try it."

I didn't dare tell them that, in fact, I had placed a cigarette in my mouth once, but didn't inhale. "Okay, what do I do?" I figured one drag on a cigarette wasn't going to kill me.

Arisha, the leader, pushed the huge pile of clothes off her bed. "Sit," she instructed. "Now pucker up your lips and try to pull the smoke out, like this." The dimples in her face stood out as she took a drag. I put the cigarette between my fingers and made an inhaling sound, just like she had instructed. My lungs filled with smoke and I started to cough and cough. The sensation felt like a 350-pound linebacker had hit me in the chest. I coughed so much my eyes turned red and my nose started running. They all laughed. I felt betrayed, and thought they were laughing at me until Arisha said, "You're a really good sport; we like you." The next morning all the girls were inviting me to their room. I must have passed the test.

✑STRUGGLING✑

Being in didn't help much when the TA's passed back my first test papers with C's and D's. I couldn't figure it out. I loved learning and had graduated in the top one percent of my class with an A or B. Why was I having so much trouble keeping up? What was I doing wrong? I was too ashamed to ask for help. I didn't even know tutoring existed and it didn't help that nobody in the dorm was taking the same classes. I thought about calling home and talking with Mom, but did it fall under "emergency?" I determined it didn't and plus, I needed to keep up a front that I was fine making my own decisions without them, thank you very much. Once, I knocked on the door of the resident assistant. "Just a minute," she said. But then I tiptoed away, ashamed and not sure I could trust her because she was white.

After talking with Mom about my transcripts, there had been only one short phone call between my parents and me since they had dropped me off. I knew they were leaving me alone to make my own decisions. But what I hadn't anticipated was total abandonment. I sure could have used their help. I had never made one key decision about my life on my own. I was like a barefoot backwards country girl, trying to act sophisticated in the big city. And with no one to confide in, I fell further and further behind.

One cold, rainy day, I noticed a black girl walking across the campus. She had on a long, white coat with red-and-blue trim and a matching umbrella. She stood out like a Picasso. I'd see her almost every day and wondered who she was because of her fine-looking clothes and sophisticated air. One day in the student union, she came in and I introduced myself thinking, *I need a black friend. Maybe she can help me figure out how to get better grades.* Her name was Stella, but everybody called her Gin. We started meeting up at the student union to study whenever we could.

A few weeks before Thanksgiving, she asked me, "What are you doing for the holidays?" My parents had intended for me to stay on campus, as they were being quite frugal. So I said, "Nothing."

"You can't stay on the campus by yourself. You must come home and visit with me". I could hardly wait until the four-day weekend arrived.

Gin's cousin, April, was a junior and had a light-brown Mustang. She offered to drop us off at the bus station on her way home to Portland. From there we planned to take the ferry to Seattle, where Gin lived. My parents had given me an allowance for the whole term, but I had spent it all, not knowing how to budget properly and ashamed to ask for more. That Wednesday afternoon as we packed our bags in the car, I tried not to think of the money I didn't have, afraid if I told Gin she would change her mind.

When we got to the ferry, I had to confess. "I don't have enough money to go further." She just hugged me and said, "Don't worry, we'll find a way."

Gin was able to come up with half my ticket. Then we started scrounging around on the floor of the ferry building and bathroom looking for coins. I was thirty-nine cents short as the horn blew on the ferry. "Please mister, I just need a little help," I begged the white ticket agent. Amazingly, he gave me the money and we just barely got through the gate. My faith in white people went up that day.

Gin's parents were waiting at the ferry and greeted me like I was their own daughter. The temperature had dropped to the teens and the heat felt good as we climbed the stairs to her bedroom. "Watch your head," she warned as I nearly bumped it on the door entry. Her sister didn't say much, but her aunts were sweet as candy, questioning me all about school and how Gin and I became friends. By Sunday, I didn't want to leave the blanket of family that had warmed me. She must have told her parents about my financial situation because that Sunday as we packed, her Dad put enough money in my hand to send me back to school and have some left over until I went home for Christmas. Embarrassed, I tried to turn his offer down, but he wasn't having any of my foolish pride. I looked out the window most of the way home. The bus ride gave me plenty of time to wish I were Gin— trusted by my father, adored by my mother, a sister one year younger, and lots of college friends.

⊱SHOCKWAVES⊰

My academic situation continued to spiral down. When I took tests, the gray matter in my brain went on strike. I became a dunce. Intimidated by the three, four, and five hundred white students in my classes, I never raised my hand. Instead I shrank further and further in my seat, hoping to hide in case the professor decided to point right at me. I dreaded finals, and a repulsive feeling of failure swept over me as the first term came to an end.

I could see my brother and sister jumping up and down as the train pulled into the station. I stepped into full-blown Christmas and put on my happy face, temporarily putting school out of my mind.

At first, I was delighted to be home. Robert had grown two inches and couldn't stop talking about playing his saxophone in the band competition. I could hardly get my coat off before he dragged me to the piano for a duet while my sister combed her doll's hair. There were no friends to call or weekend parties like at Gin's, but I stuffed my face with cush, biscuits, fried chicken, and gumbo, returning to what was easy and known—family and church.

Services were being held at Lawson Funeral home in East Oakland. It felt eerie knowing dead bodies were stacked in the back room, while we passed the collection tray. Dad hadn't skipped a beat and his sermons were as powerful as ever. The first Sunday home, he announced my return and I felt welcomed by the old and new members.

Over the Christmas break I wanted to tell my parents so badly that my grades weren't good as Dad kept asking me, "How did you do?"

I wanted to scream and say, "Not good at all!"

But with the past so vivid, I was afraid of what he might do and choose to stay quiet. Migraines danced through my head like plies. As the weeks passed, I continued to pretend I was enjoying the break, but that old feeling of anxiety greeted me each morning as I brushed my teeth.

A week before I was to return to school, the envelope arrived in the mail. **"Academic Probation"** was stamped across the bottom of the form letter with my 1.9 grade point average.

Dad and Mom couldn't understand. "Why are your grades so low? Did you buckle down and study? Were you harassed? Roommate not working out? Did you get up there and forget everything we taught you?"

I braced myself for one of Dad's verbal attacks. But he remained quiet as I tried to explain—my lost transcripts, the advanced classes I was taking, no one to help me make the right decisions, and the racism I felt under the surface all the time. I didn't shy away from my own responsibilities either, believing I could study longer and harder. But I couldn't bring myself to go one step further and say what was in my heart. "I am scared of all those white people."

Dad got on the phone and talked with someone at the university, trying to explain, but he received one answer. If my grades didn't improve, I was out! I put on a happy face around my relatives and tried to lift myself up as I boarded the train for my second term. I thought about Howard again. *This wouldn't have happened to me if I could have gone to my dream school and studied with kids who looked like me. This wouldn't have happened to me if Mom had looked after my welfare. This wouldn't have happened to me if...* The image I had held of myself in college was fading. I didn't know how to stop the downward spiral, but I had to turn it around somehow.

℘MORE THAN TENNIS℘

The tennis match with Victor happened quite by accident. I was browsing in the student shopping area and he was working, standing tall and debonair in the doorway of a men's store. I noticed his full broad lips, and the impression of his muscular chest and solid thighs against his tweed suit.

"Haven't seen you at any of my games or parties."

I nodded. "Yes, that's true." As I looked back on what happened next, I think that was the only reason he even spoke—I wasn't falling all over him.

"Well, let's see how good you are at tennis. Say next Sunday?" he grinned.

"Can't, I'll be at church."

"All day?" he asked.

I looked serious. "Got to study."

"Okay, how about Wednesday afternoon?" and with that he held out his hand and we shook. *Not a churchgoer*, I noted.

He played me hard, volleying the ball all over the court as I scraped my racket, grunting and catching my breath. I didn't win a game, but it wasn't because I didn't give it my all.

"You're not half bad," he said as he slipped his racket in the jacket. "Let's play again sometime."

We met up over the next few weeks for tennis as he gradually revealed his life. "I'm on a basketball scholarship; I was the number-one guard at my high school. When I graduate, I'm going to play pro ball. My family lives in Salem. You ever been to Salem?"

"Can't say that I have."

"Well, you'll have to visit sometime. I lived in the dorms the first couple of years, but now I live with my sister on campus; she's a graduate student."

"How long you've been working at this men's store?"

"Scholarship doesn't pay for everything. I need to work and look good at the same time. It's a good environment, 'cause I like putting things together, being creative and working with my hands. I sell a lot of merchandise too, because the guys like to purchase from a winner."

Full of himself, I thought, and I was intrigued because he knew just what to say in any given moment and didn't mind taking time with me, even though he was a star. I could see why all the girls liked him. He was nice to me, a gentleman, inviting me for soft drinks and light conversation, but didn't have a lot of time to spare with his job, sports, and studying. In no time, I nicknamed him "Snake Charmer."

By the middle of the second term, I was rubbing my hands around those muscular shoulders. Tennis matches turned into bike rides, screaming from the bleachers at basketball games, and long, passionate kisses that made my knees buckle. Gin and I had become best friends and she dated one of Victor's buddies, a star football player named Jason. We'd play cards together in the student union, watch movies on Sunday afternoons, and never study together. I was falling in love, ignoring the rumors that Victor dated other girls until one day I caught him kissing somebody—a white girl. It must have been fate, because he had walked me to my room, but I needed a book from the library and that's when I saw them. I took off running—crying like a two-year-old. The next day, Gin told me what she had heard. "That's his *real* girlfriend." I didn't want to believe it was true, and when I confronted him, he had the nerve to be angry with me for accusing him.

All for the best, I figured. *I'm on academic probation.* But after a week, he came sniffing around like a dog. And I fell for his romantic rap. It was as if Victor's attention toward me stopped a leak in my heart and gave me a sense of security about my value and purpose. The feeling was fresh and raw. He apologized. "That girl and I are finished." When his warm lips touched mine, the ice on my mountain thawed. I believed him. He bought daisies and took me to a jazz concert at school to see Les McCann. It didn't take much. I was like taffy in his hands, all soft and gooey with no resistance.

⟪DOOMED⟫

No matter how much I studied, I just couldn't seem to make a B on anything. One of the spillovers from my first quarter was that many of the freshman classes were sequential, and because I hadn't taken the beginning class the first time, I was unable to take the next class the following term. I signed up again for classes that were way over my level of comprehension, thinking, "I'll just study more." Frustrated, I didn't know what to do except worry as the migraine headaches accelerated. By the end of the second term, the domino effect had taken over.

After arriving home for break in March, I met the mailman every day, looking for the envelope that was on its way. There were no surprises as I looked at the stamp in big red letters signed by the dean. "Failed." The pit filled every inch of my stomach. *Where will I hide now?* Dad had been pretty calm the first time, but I fretted to think how he would react to my total failure. Looking at the letter kept reminding me of my catastrophe, so I ripped it into tiny little pieces and flushed it down the toilet. Lucky for me, Dad was so occupied with the reorganization of the church, he never followed up with the school and had no clue how I had been progressing over the quarter. I wished he had, because I still didn't understand what I was doing wrong. Frightened, I decided on the only option. *Keep it a secret.*

When I got back to school, I told myself I was still on probation; that I'd go to night school and bring my grade point average up. I didn't think about tomorrow or what would happen in May when Dad found out the truth, I just created one giant illusion in my mind. All I could think about was staying in my dormitory for one more quarter—and Victor. Maybe somehow I could make it come out right.

The resident assistant called me into her room right after I returned. "You're not supposed to be here, you know."

"Yes, I know, but my dormitory fees are paid. Please let me stay; my parents don't know and I won't cause any trouble." She made me promise to go to night school, but not before dropping a bomb on me. "Kat's not coming back. You need a new roommate." I was totally caught off-balance; Kat had been passing all her subjects. It turned out she had gotten caught in a spider web of assimilation in the other direction—dating a black student. Her face broke out and her hair started falling out so noticeably by the time she got home that her parents decided not to send her back. I received a short letter a week after school began.

> Dear Ronita,
>
> My dad blames my nervous breakdown on you and has refused to pay for any more college tuition. I'm transferring next fall to a new school.
>
> I hope we continue to be friends.
>
> Good luck with Victor. Please write when you can.
>
> Kat

I saw no return address on her letter. Folding it to my chest, I felt guilty for being black. The only good outcome from Kat's departure was Gin. She moved in right away. I plowed forward, taking three classes at night school, determined to make straight A's and figure out the rest of my strategy by the end of school. Making excuses to leave three times a week for night school was draining. I wanted to be honest with Gin, but shame blanketed me like volcanic ash. I bought her trinkets to keep her questions at bay, and after a while found it easier to hang onto the pretense of being a student in hopes of surviving my shame.

ILLUSIONS OF LOVE

Victor invited me to Salem to meet his family during Easter break. I knew from movies that meeting the parents was a serious step in our relationship. I slept in the guest room, helped in the kitchen, and joined in the conversation, eager to make a memorable impression on his mother. She was sophisticated like Mom. I beamed sitting next to him at church, especially when the minister acknowledged him as a future NBA star. And on the drive home, he snuggled me right next to him as Mt. Hood, Douglas fir, and ponderosa pine witnessed our deep affection.

The welcome I received on the visit with Victor and his family intoxicated me and turned me into a love drunk. He was free to mold and shape me after that, as I wrote a short story in my head of increasing romance, leading to marriage. My childhood daydreams of being famous became real, and I saw my face on television as the wife of a professional sports player. We lived in a mansion on a hill with three kids, a shiny red Lamborghini, and a poodle. Some days in my story, it didn't matter that I didn't have a college degree. I just needed to be well-bred, gregarious, stylist, entertaining, and religious like his mother. But the more I thought about my script, the more I worried. *Will Victor marry a girl without a degree, without a career?* Inflated by my own story, I hung on to Victor's charm and struggled to keep the candles of self-pride from burning out. And when he became suspicious about school, I started buying him presents, believing I could make up for my inadequacies by purchasing love. I didn't know it then, but it was the beginning of a pattern I'd come to regret.

Free love was all over the news in 1966. It seemed the old norms of celibacy I had been raised with were slowly fading away. Girls in my dorm talked freely about taking the plunge and having sex. But these girls were white and I'd seen enough movies to believe they had plenty of possibilities for snagging a rich husband. In the back of my mind, two of Dad's favorite slogans kept rattling around in my brain: "Get your education" and "Keep your virginity, that's all you've got." I had temporarily blown the education part and began to wonder, *Is it true about my virginity? Did I still have it after that terrible day with Horace?* I decided to talk it over with Gin.

"How do you feel about having sex before you get married?" My question didn't shock her at all.

"I think it's wrong when you're not in love or it's not with someone that you're going to marry. Then the boy just gets what he wants and leaves you. Then what have you got? Nothing," she said.

"And what about getting pregnant?" I continued. "My Dad would kill me if I got pregnant. Actually, I'd kill myself. What would I do with a baby!"

"You can protect yourself so that doesn't happen," she assured me.

We continued to go back and forth about the merits of virginity and our parents' beliefs, until I said, "Do you really think it's okay to have sex with the boy you love before you get married?"

"Yes, you've just got to be really sure that he's the one."

At the time, I didn't have one reference of an intimate relationship that was positive. All I had was the extreme—Horace and Murphy. It was easy to wedge Victor in the middle as normal, while I weighed what I should do. After a couple of days, I brought it up again.

"I believe Victor is going to marry me. He hasn't tried to force himself on me, but I'm having a hard time keeping it together with so much passion."

"Me, too," Gin admitted.

I still wasn't clear if I wanted to lose my virginity before marriage, but if I decided to, I didn't want to lose it alone. We must have thought of the idea at the same time, because we blurted out, "Let's make a pact." We decided on the junior graduation party coming up in a month and shook hands. "Okay, we've got a deal."

Over the next few weeks, Victor and I engaged in long, hot caresses at the drive-in that left me panting. But I continued to protect my virginity, catching his hand firmly whenever he got too close. He'd reach his limit of "Stop" and start the car's engine before the movie was over and take me home. I didn't want him to stop whispering "I love you" in my ear, so finally I allowed him to take me to Lover's Lane, the place I had heard the girls talk about for more serious petting. Without a word about our pact, I allowed his hands to touch me any place he pleased, as I moaned. After that, all doubt about giving myself to him vaporized.

ℭℭTHE PACT℺℺

I settled on my favorite white and yellow lace outfit as the party drew closer. Gin and I whispered, locking the door to keep the other girls from accidentally hearing our plan. We were nervous, giddy, and shaky about our decision, neither of us sure of what to do, except what we'd heard from stories and rumors.

"I hear it hurts really bad at first. I don't want any pain," I told her, remembering Horace as he pierced me.

"I don't want any pain, either," Gin said.

We were stuck. "I'm not asking anybody what to do because I don't want anybody but us to know," I confessed. So we decided that the only way to dull the pain was to get drunk.

I wanted to be a poised, lady-like drunk and decided on sloe gin and orange juice, a favorite among the black girls who believed "sloe" meant "slow." It was a wild party—drinking, dancing, slamming down fists and cursing when the right card didn't appear on the table. After refilling my glass twice, I was having a blast. Gin and I hung onto each other as the alcohol started to take effect, giggling with nervousness about what was coming.

I didn't know what time it was, but it was way past 2:00 and I was plastered when Victor whispered in my ear. My head was spinning and all I heard was "Go." I pointed to Gin, incoherent but able to signal, "I'm off." The next thing I remember, I was on the bed at the apartment he shared with his sister. Miles Davis's "Sketches of Spain" played in the background. The music seeped through my pores and

I felt sexy as wet kisses covered my face. Victor checked with me once more. "Sure you want to do this?" When I slid under the sheets, he had his answer. His kisses sucked my breath away as his smooth hands touched my breasts and traveled down my slim waist. I waited as his warm body moved closer to mine. Then I passed out.

I woke up to a terrible hangover and an empty bed. The first thing I looked for was the stain. I'd hoped we would be in a motel to free me from embarrassment, but as I kept spreading the crumpled sheets left and right looking for the signs of becoming a woman, there was nothing. I tried to think back to the last moments before passing out, wondering, *Was I hallucinating? Maybe nothing had happened at all.*

Victor was quieter than usual when he came out of the bathroom. Not at all attentive like I thought he would be for taking my cherry. On the drive back to my dormitory, he said, "I thought you were a virgin." I turned, alarmed. "I am, I mean, I was." He gave me a skeptical look and I started to weep, the ghost of Horace vivid in my mind. "Okay, okay," he said, "I believe you," and gave me a hug. By the time my feet crossed the entrance of my dorm, all I could think about was the stain. Had there been one that day, so many years before? At the time, I didn't know what to look for but, yes, there must have been a stain. I was a child and I was a virgin, I was a virgin, I kept saying to myself. As I tried to convince myself of my sanity, an awful feeling came over me that I had protected a treasure that had been stolen long ago. And now Victor would think I had been a tease and a liar! I paced back and forth, *What to do, what to do?* but there was nothing except a sinking feeling that I had made a big mistake.

The words coming out of Gin's mouth drifted in and out of my ears, as I kept thinking about the stain. She hadn't passed out and yes, when he entered her, it hurt. But she had washed the sheets and pledged her love to Jason. Her romantic description influenced me to try three more times with Victor while I was sober. The last time I was convinced either Horace had ruined me by taking something precious that would never return, or it would take a while for me to warm up to sexual intercourse.

As the school year came to an end, I was numb. It was official—lost virginity and lost education. As I thought about going home, I pulled out the mask crafted from years before of happiness that I'd wear whenever in public. I tried it on that last day of school when Victor picked me up. We kissed and cuddled at the airport as I waited for my first plane ride home. I convinced myself. *Settle down. Victor loves you. He'll go pro and then you will marry.* It took the plane's jolted landing to jar me back to reality. My eyes filled with tears. I had flunked out of school! *What am I going to do now?*

❦CONFESSION❦

Secrets can be toxic; they eat away at you like poison, causing your skin to break out and corrode. They take away your appetite, cause you to chew your nails, cramp your stomach, and keep you hidden away. They make you lose sleep, play sad songs and wipe away smiles from the mirror. They cause you to lie, then lie again to keep from being rejected. But the worst thing about secrets is how lonely and isolated you feel, believing you are drifting further and further away from ever feeling sane again—a place where breathing hurts. My secret had turned me into a robot.

Every couple of days over the summer Dad asked, "How did you do? When are your grades arriving?"

I'd shrug my shoulders, "I dunno." I had become almost catatonic. I played piano at Sunday service, trying to forget my misery.

But all other attempts by Robert and Kelesha to engage me in duets, ping-pong, or bowling failed. I kept quiet, fixed dinner and wiped dishes over and over again until they squeaked. The noose of the secret tightened, stripping me of me, causing me to pretend day after day. I could feel the ghosts of my ancestors laughing at me. By early August, I was dragging around a ton of guilt. I couldn't take it anymore and decided to face up to the truth.

We ate Saturday breakfast as usual while I tried to recite the short speech I had prepared in my mind. But the words stuck in my throat like peanut butter—all I could get out was, "Mom and Dad, can I talk with you?" It was as if Dad had been waiting, but he didn't overreact.

"Give your Mom and me a little time, and we'll come down to your room." He was calm and peaceful, not at all like what I expected, but I was suspicious anyway. I could hear their footsteps descending the stairs. My heart sped up, faster and faster. Dad entered first, then Mom, and they both sat on my bed with their hands relaxed. I started to cry, a wave of shame and disappointment surging through me until Dad put his arms around me.

"Whatever it is, will be all right. We will deal with it."

The salty tears streamed down my face, hotter, longer. I couldn't speak. They both tried to comfort me. After what felt like forever, I blurted, "I flunked out!"

A moment passed and then Dad said, "Oh God, we're so relieved. We thought you were pregnant."

Dad was so understanding and compassionate, I worried that he was sick. The three of us put our heads together, mulling over possibilities. "You always wanted to go to a black school. How about Southern University, it's close to family." Mom even called her sister in Maryland, but she had four children of her own to raise. I was disappointed, because Maryland was close to Howard. But who was

I kidding? I couldn't transfer anywhere with my transcript.

Victor had sent cards with crazy drawings over the summer. Each was signed, "With love." I saved every one of them in a scrapbook and slept with it under my pillow. I missed his lightness, his humor, and his lips on mine and didn't know when I'd see him again. After my confession to my parents, I wrote him with the news, "I'm not returning." The cards kept coming; they were funnier and funnier which preserved my illusion that we would marry.

I kept calling Gin to tell her I wouldn't be coming back to college, but I could never get her at home. She finally called me one day in early September to tell me the news.

"I'm pregnant."

A knot formed in my stomach.

"We're talking about getting married, but I'm staying in school."

I could barely speak. "Let me know when the baby comes. I'll come to see you. Count on me as godmother."

As I placed the receiver on the hook I looked up to heaven. "Oh God, that could have been me." Neither of us had done anything to protect ourselves, believing the gossip that, "It takes more than one time to get pregnant."

My secret was out to my parents, but I wasn't about to tell anyone else that I had flunked out of school. Instead, I exaggerated the truth and told everyone I transferred to San Francisco State. State had an annex downtown on Sutter Street. It was like an adult school for mature people who loved exploring new subjects or wanted to continue their education one day. Transcripts weren't required; only the fees for units beginning at $35.00. The plan was I'd make up the classes I needed and transfer to State in the fall of 1967. The problem was the annex didn't offer the right curriculum necessary to catch me up. I signed up anyway—contemporary history, writing, and art. At least I was back in school, although I didn't know how drawing pictures of nude people would advance my studies.

I'd catch the bus three times a week into the terminal, transfer to the streetcar, and get off right in front of the Mark Hopkins Hotel. I passed students in the hallways, but they were older with jobs, no time for a sullen-looking kid like me. I'd come and go at our house without much fanfare, still stunned by my shame and worried that my brother and sister would no longer look up to me as their big sister.

Growing up for them had changed dramatically with our move. My brother and sister enrolled in junior high and elementary schools surrounded by wooded landscapes and scented flowers. The hills looked like white people's heaven. Blonds, redheads, and freckled children were dropped off in Porsches, Jaguars, Mercedes-Benzes, and Volvos.

The first couple of weeks Robert's stuttering kept him quiet, until he joined the band and started practicing jazzy songs on his saxophone. Mom sure looked after their adjustment. She took every opportunity to have them socialize with the upper-class black kids, signing them up for Jack and Jill, a social organization designed to build character. My brother and sister had real friends and sleepovers and seemed allowed to speak about whatever they wanted during meals. I watched and listened, wishing I had not been born first. Wishing I had not been Dad's punching bag. But I resigned myself to my fate; there was really nobody to blame for my failure but me. I had blown my one opportunity to fulfill my dreams and now the only hope I had left was Victor.

He let me down easy and gradually—first one card a week, then every two weeks, and by the new year I knew: Victor and I were over. I kept up the charade in my heart, hoping for a good excuse—maybe he had fallen from playing ball and was in a body cast or a coma. I had no phone number and no address where I could search him out.

I was miserable. In the end, I had a scrapbook full of caricatures and a broken heart.

I swallowed the bitter taste of Victor's demise and became withdrawn, scattered, and empty. I wanted a second chance, a miracle, Houdini's magic to wipe away the last year. *God, can't I do it over again.* Running my fingers over the ivory keys was the only thing that kept me from screaming at the top of my lungs, even though, sometimes, I was too weary to allow the magic to penetrate me. Most times, my thoughts closed in on me. *What good was it to keep up the charade if I couldn't marry Victor.* I kept thinking over and over again a phrase the folks in Louisiana would always say, *"Can't make a silk purse out of a sow's ear."*

Had I known the symptoms, I might have been saved from going in and out of depression over the next fifteen years of my life. I might have understood my feelings of hopelessness, worthlessness, and negative thoughts; my destructive behavior, disturbed sleep, inability to concentrate, impromptu shopping, and binges of under-and overeating as a sickness—one I could overcome with help. Instead, I accepted my sadness as a temporary reaction to the setbacks, disappointments and struggles I had endured.

One day while walking down the stairs after class, I'd had enough of pretending. I wasn't college material. I sat down, placed my head in my lap, and had a good, hard cry. I walked down Sutter Street to the first trash can I saw, dumped in my books, and walked away from college again. I was clueless as to where the footprints of my life would land next.

Mom wasn't having it. "You can't sit around the house like you're on vacation. Got to do something. I'll call people I know at Oakland Public Schools and see if I can get you a job interview." Three weeks passed and I found myself in a room with a typewriter. "Start now," the test lady said as the clock ticked and I typed as fast as my fingers would go on the black Underwood typewriter until she said, "Stop." She clocked me at ninety words a minute. With one year of college, I was offered my first job typing letters, making phone calls, and filing papers as a clerk in the supply office for the school board. I was seven months away from my twentieth birthday and made $13 a day. I gave my parents $75 for rent and food. I paid $78 a month for a new yellow Toyota Corolla with a black vinyl top. After taxes, tithing, and filling my gas tank, I still had money for clothes and didn't save a dime.

I existed by checking off the minimal requirements to get through each day—dress, drive twelve minutes to work, punch a time clock, type, file, take a fifteen-minute break at 10:00 and 3:00, a one-hour lunch at 12:00, and do enough to keep my job. I was assigned Tuesday and Thursday to prepare our family's evening meals and stuck with tuna casserole, spaghetti, and tamale pie. Every day was a battle around suppressing my dreams of what could have been. My heart hurt with the shame I tucked away in the hem of each day's garment. I sang Burt Bacharach songs—"Alfie," "A House Is Not a Home," "I'll Never Fall in Love Again"—while tears coated the ivory keys. I lived under the same roof as my parents and siblings, but felt like I had entered a place where I never wanted to be—a place where my eyes and sense of smell were useless and everything I touched or heard frightened me.

Sometimes on the weekends, I'd sneak out. I was suffocating and knew my parents wouldn't understand that parties didn't start until 11:00 and I had a 12:00 curfew. I'd ride down Van Ness in San Francisco, looking at the bright lights and people laughing. I'd drive to the ocean and watch the waves splash in and splash out, wishing I had the nerve to step in. I'd drop by a club or arrive at a party alone and become wallpaper. I would return by 2:00 or 3:00. Nobody ever missed me. And that is what I believed about my life. If I slipped and fell into the ocean, I wouldn't be missed.

As Spring shook off her showery coat and stepped into Summer, I resigned myself to waking up with a parched throat of disappointment day in and day out, with little hope in my heart. What I didn't know was everything was about to change.

⚛QUINCY FULLERTON⚛

Quincy drove the only green-and-white Fairland station wagon in Shreveport. Every time I saw that car coming down the street, I knew he was dropping off a girl who lived around the corner from my house. I'd stop in my tracks and stare for no particular reason other than the way he looked behind the steering wheel—like he knew he was extraordinary. But what did I know. At the time, I was only thirteen. Quincy attended the Catholic high school and his father was a popular doctor. His family was what we regular folks called "Upper Crust" and "Highfalutin Negroes." Mom fueled my imagination when I'd mention that I had seen him.

She'd start, "Now that's the kind of boy any girl from a good family would want to date someday." I just tucked her comments away.

Quite by coincidence Quincy had stumbled into a classmate who went to his Catholic school and now attended our new church. I guess they started talking about people from the old days because the next thing I knew, the phone rang.

"Hey, it's Quincy. Do you remember me? I'm working on a cruise ship, and getting ready to pull out in a week. Want to get caught up on old times?"

I looked at the phone like it was a piece of strawberry shortcake: Quincy and I had never had one conversation before. When I saw him I couldn't believe he was sitting in our living room looking just as special as he had years before. Over the week he visited every other day and we talked about all the kids we used to know, Vietnam and how we both hated senseless killing, the space program, Dick Gregory running for president, Timothy Leary and LSD, wild naked people running around Haight-Ashbury, the Black Panthers, race riots in Detroit, New Jersey, and D.C., and the fact that we would never see a black man become president in our lifetime. He was entering his senior year of college at Southern University and was worried about being drafted.

Quincy had lived a different kind of life with more freedom to experiment and the encouragement to go after his dreams. He believed in God, but he felt people were hypocrites, so he didn't bother going to church. We bonded around music. He had so many records: the Beatles, the Doors, the Fifth Dimension, Led Zeppelin, Hugh Masekela, Jimi Hendrix, Max Roach. Many of the artists I had never heard of before, but I liked the sound. Quincy was cool like Uncle Claude! He never went anywhere without his Nikon camera and snapped pictures of Dad's rosebushes, views of the bridge from the Mormon Temple, sunsets, and me without any obvious reason. He was tall, lean, and fair-skinned and in one week, I had warmed up to him like a frog on a rock.

He left seven days later, with a promise, "I'll call you," and a warm hug just tight enough to give wings to the one tiny butterfly that had started to flap in my stomach. I tracked his voyage on Robert's globe, wondering what port housed his ship on the China Sea.

But little by little that butterfly got weak. There was no reason for me to believe he would call back.

My hollowness returned. Over the years I had watched as men and women walked down the aisles to make their confession before joining the church again. They would tell the congregation how they had strayed—made the bottle their God, mistreated their children or parents, stole, served time in jail, and abandoned the Bible. They'd hide their faces in Dad's chest and cry about being lost and needing to come back home to Jesus. People would clap and shout, "Hallelujah, praise God," as Dad read from the little green book. The choir would sing and everybody in the church would march around to welcome back the lost soul. I hadn't done any of those things, but I wanted to believe walking down the aisle would somehow renew my soul. I wanted to feel the hearty handshakes and body warmth wrap me with support from people I thought loved me. I wanted to receive the forgiveness of God and be free of the heaviness that woke up with me each morning.

The problem was I was still Dad's daughter. And that came with responsibilities and role-modeling that didn't include open confession. My brother was a junior usher; my sister sang in the children's choir. Mom had become one of the women in white—dress, stockings, shoes and a little lace cap—and I played the piano. I couldn't just walk down the aisle and confess my sins. How would it look to the congregation? I couldn't be responsible for tarnishing Dad's reputation or image. What would people say? And I couldn't take a chance of triggering the old Dad coming back. All I could do was wake up with my heavy burden every morning, throw it over my shoulder, and carry it around wherever I went. The weight sure was taking its toll, but there was no place to dump it without being caught.

ᝢTINY EMBERS FLAMEᝢ

When the phone rang on August 2, 1967, I almost dropped the receiver. "Hey kid, what's up? I'm back." At first, paralysis set in. But then I felt the faint fluttering of the butterfly's wing. I screamed, "You're back, you're back, I missed you," with more enthusiasm than I had intended.

Quincy and I resumed our special times of listening to music, watching sunsets, and snapping pictures. We talked about the thousands of people our age marching against the war. I wanted to join them, but the prospect of being teargassed kept me away. We debated about civil rights, the South, and Dr. King. What I most noticed about Quincy was he knew exactly what he was living for—walking in his dad's shoes.

"Where are you going to medical school?" I asked.

He hesitated. "I'm not sure."

And with that, I hoped I could persuade him to study in California. But I didn't say one word.

On the surface my dropping out of school didn't seem to matter to him, but it bothered me. And since he was going to be a doctor, I wanted to be something meaningful too, something that would make me stand tall and proud. I had to admit, I felt a pang of envy that he knew the direction of his life and I didn't have a clue. Well, that's not entirely true. Music still ran through my veins and I had entertained the idea of becoming a singer or actor. But my parents had discouraged that idea. "It's a rat race. You've got to know somebody in Hollywood," Dad said. I never brought it up again. Instead, I woke up like a chameleon every couple of weeks—I could be a court reporter like my cousin's husband. He made a good salary, and loved listening to attorneys argue all day. I could be a real estate agent and broker a large house like my mom's friend. I could be a telephone operator like one of the ladies at church who always dressed to the nines. I wanted to travel all over the world, and could, if I were a stewardess. Actually, I tried out for the stewardess job with PSA; I passed the written test, but when they saw those gold teeth, I was all done. Amazingly, I even thought about becoming a Playboy bunny; I had the goods for it, but didn't have the guts.

I hid my feelings of indecision from Quincy, afraid that if he knew how insecure I was he'd stop coming over. I kept the spotlight on what I knew—dazzling conversation, shopping on Telegraph for lace vests and tie-dye shirts, thumbing through albums at Tower Records, quiet moments watching the sunsets.

We'd sit shoulder to shoulder for long periods of time on the hood of his aunt's car, watching the sun turn from golden yellow to burnt orange. One evening, right before he was leaving, the sun took its time sliding away for another day. We both turned simultaneously and leaned toward each other for our first kiss. I didn't move as the butterflies multiplied and danced the jig. He kissed me again, his lips like warm honey, and I was sure, my prince had come!

He went back to college on Mom's birthday, August 31, while our family gathered for barbecued burgers and steaks. "You kind of like that boy," Aunt Bea smiled. I couldn't help covering my gold teeth with my hand, for Quincy had left with more than his belongings.

UNDER A SPELL

Feeling as if I had taken a long swim in the river of joy, I transferred to a lateral position in the microfiche department, feeding old report cards through the mouth of a pewter-colored machine. A mechanical arm could have done the job just as easily. The dusty old stacks of cards in the stuffy room made me drowsy, but not the conversation with the other two girls. One was raising a four-year-old son, trying to collect support from her estranged husband every month. She was tired of struggling, and flooded her desk with her son's pictures. The other girl was eighteen, just out of high school and engaged to be married. They both watched soap operas—*The Guiding Light* and *All My Children*—and would share their shock about who was sleeping with whom. I lived vicariously through Pearl's daily reports of wedding checks and balances as she pulled out her white wedding planner, yapping about bridesmaids and cake. I'd trail off into my own fantasy, imagining the words "I do," while Quincy and I stood at the altar, pledging our undying love. And then I would snap myself back to reality.

When he called every six weeks or so, I'd listen to him ramble about papers due, roommates, marching band competitions, and his eagerness to graduate. Our conversations never got mushy with sweet nothings, although I wished they had. There was no exchange of Christmas presents, but the phone rang on December 31 with a pre–"Happy New Year" and an invitation.

"You are coming to my graduation, aren't you?"

I was delirious with gaiety when I hung up the phone.

I slept more deeply than I had for a long time, waking up every morning to an ever-inflating fairy tale that kept multiplying like atoms. We would get married after his graduation and take a romantic honeymoon to Tahiti, Fiji, or Hawaii. I'd continue to work and support him through medical school before returning to college. I needed him to see me as an equal. Somewhere in between we'd have a couple of children, a boy and a girl. We'd settle in a rich neighborhood with rich friends on a winding street high in the hills, with a dog and a red convertible Mercedes-Benz. We'd never harm our children or make them cry and would buy them expensive clothes and take them to Disneyland to ride the Matterhorn. Oh yes, I spun the story like yarn. But there was one snag that I didn't want to admit. Motherhood. I felt a fiery dragon lying in suspended animation inside me named Abuser, Beater, Persecutor, Tormentor. She would only awaken with childbirth. The thought alarmed me, because husbands wanted offspring. Temporarily, I put it out of my mind, desperate to erase my own premonition.

❧BELIEFS UNDER FIRE❧

April 4, 1968, started off like any other day, but by the evening commute I could hardly see the road from the tears pouring down my face as the news spread. "Dr. Martin Luther King, Jr. was assassinated today while standing on the balcony of the Lorraine Motel in Memphis." We huddled together around the television, trying to piece together what had occurred. My heart ached for the King children. We watched riots and looting break out in Washington, D.C., Baltimore, Chicago, and seventy other cities, despite pleas from ministers and Congress. Quincy and I couldn't believe the paradox. Dr. King had stood for nonviolence, yet people could only find violence as an outlet. I understood the frustration and pain, but couldn't reconcile why struggling black people would burn and destroy their own communities. It brought back memories of marching in Shreveport, dogs tearing flesh and the 16th Street Baptist bombing.

Somewhere inside, I wanted to believe that human beings were basically good. I knew racism existed. I witnessed it at work. The three black women who worked in my office were all in different departments but we had similar experiences of two standards—one for whites and one for minorities. We had the lowest pay and were passed over for training and promotional opportunities. There was no leniency or consideration for being a minute late from breaks or lunch, or we'd face discipline without warning. We'd walk into a room and it would become so quiet you'd think the Pope had stuck out his gloved hand. The word "nigger" was still spoken, but not by us. We found out about birthday celebrations as the icing hardened on the last pieces of cake and were given menial jobs that our coworkers turned down. Our supervisors provided little constructive feedback on performance evaluations that played our successes down and our failures up. And we were closely watched as if we were planning an office robbery. Most of all, we weren't privy to the *unwritten rules* about the culture, an essential element if you ever wanted to get out of a dead-end job. The prejudice was subtle, hard to prove; and we didn't like it, but we took it because we had no choice.

The popular song "Free Your Mind and Your Ass Will Follow" piqued my interest. It spoke about being brainwashed as a black person, but I started to think of it more as it applied to my life. Could I be brainwashed by well-intended parents who selected scriptures that aligned with one strict way to grow up and live? Was it possible that Dad had gotten it wrong about what Jesus meant by love, obedience, and rearing children?

My mind bubbled like boiling water with questions, while the answers stayed immersed in its hot steam. I didn't have an ounce of certainty, but I had enough instinct to believe something was incubating—a shift on the horizon that included me.

ANTICIPATION

Dad still had his way of showing up as our father, but somehow he had managed to tame the monster. His behavior no longer included wild tirades of anger toward me or anyone else. Instead, he took his time eating, or reading the paper while teasing my brother about girlfriends, being a bookworm, carving wooden objects, and squeaking his saxophone. He coddled my sister's every whim; we'd all gotten used to her being the real boss.

I had studied Dad's moods and knew timing was everything. After mowing the lawn, weeding his roses, and washing both cars, he didn't much like being bothered after 2:00 on Saturday. That's when he seemed to move into a holy place with God. By 7:30 the next morning he'd be gone, off to see about his precious souls. Sometimes, he'd preach so hard I thought he was going to pass out. Those were the times he'd belt out a song, then cry his eyes out like a baby. People would flock to the front and cry right along with him, until Dad jumped up and down with joy, praising the Lord. I came to wonder about his hard tears, sensing maybe the wound of disgrace lingered in his heart like it did in mine. But no matter, it always brought folks to Christ.

On those Sundays he seemed just a little more mellow, and after reading the Sunday papers he would gather us around him for the week's news. Saving souls worked on him like that. I had picked such a day to pop my question.

Living under Dad's roof with an early curfew made it more difficult for me to see how he'd say "yes" to staying out unsupervised for seven days when I went to Quincy's graduation. My knees turned numb from praying for I strongly believed that Quincy held the key to saving me from the mess I'd made of my life. I didn't see it at the time, but it was just like my feelings for Victor. I would come to know that you can't depend on another person to correct your life. But I wouldn't have believed it then.

"Dad, Quincy invited me to his graduation in May."

"You really are taken with that young man, aren't you?"

"Dad, I've never met anybody like him. He's so smart, going to be a doctor like his father. You know I'm almost 21, got to start thinking about getting serious soon. You married Mom when she was 22. I'm not saying we're getting married, I mean he hasn't asked me. We haven't even talked about marriage. It's way too soon, we're still getting to know each other. But I'd like to go to his graduation as his special girl."

"Where would you stay? Are his parents going? You know it wouldn't look good for you to be unchaperoned."

"His parents will be there and I'll stay in the hotel with them. You know Dr. Fullerton, he wouldn't let anything happen to me."

"How long would this be for? You have your church responsibilities."

"Yes, I know, but this would be like a vacation. You and the family went to New York last year, but I couldn't go. This would be my vacation and I've got the money for the airline ticket and the hotel."

"You're going to stay in a hotel for a whole week?"

"No, Dad, we're going back to Shreveport right after graduation. I can stay with Ann or the pastor's daughter, Yolanda, at The Temple. She and Quincy are good friends. He asked her and she said okay. You know Yolanda's father. You can call him if you want."

Dad looked out the bay window, while I practiced my rebuttal in anticipation of his "No." "Okay, I guess you can go, but you must take responsibility for yourself, young lady. You know how you've been raised. You know how to act. Don't let me hear anything that I'd be ashamed of back in Shreveport."

I grabbed his neck tightly as a shockwave went through me. Looking back, I think Dad knew, Quincy was my sweet North Star.

⟨SOUL MATE⟩

It was my second plane ride and I couldn't tell if it was the turbulence or my excitement that had me gripping the seat all the way to New Orleans. The hot, muggy air hit me in the face as soon as I stepped down the stairs. Suddenly, Quincy's smile and outstretched arms stood out in the crowd. In front of everyone, he kissed me passionately, even better than I remembered, and if my heart had stopped beating in that moment, I would have died believing I knew the meaning of complete happiness.

We had spent hours on the phone talking about spending every possible moment together. I had lied to Dad about staying at the hotel with his parents, feeling slightly pressured to seal our relationship with more than a kiss.

"Are you still all right with our plan?"

"Yes, spending the night together is all I've thought about."

It was true, and I knew what it meant. I couldn't wait to feel his heart next to mine, but kept wondering, *Does he think I'm a virgin?* We had never talked about it before, and I assumed he knew he wasn't the first, but I started getting more nervous the closer we got to the motel. I wondered how many girls he had slept with and about orgasm. I had yet to experience one while having intercourse. All I knew was that I loved him and wanted to please him, and I didn't care much about my own pleasure.

The colored lightbulbs flashed on and off on the sign "Big Little Motel," but as far as I was concerned, it was the Ritz-Carlton. He jingled the keys and ran next door to the liquor store for a pint of brandy. I felt like a scared rabbit. We had taken our time for a year— sharing, dreaming, questioning—and now here we were alone. I sat on the bed as he poured a sip of brandy in the white paper cups.

"Turn around, girl, let me get a good look at you." I twirled shyly and obediently as the liquor took effect. Then he leaned in and we both fell across the mattress.

The cozy room was quiet except for the hum of the fan that echoed in my ear as he began to kiss me. Time had no boundaries, shape, or form. My mind went blank and my heart burst open, tumbling in an endless swirl of bliss and sweet promises. We took short naps in between, until sleep was all that was left to us. I opened my eyes to the reality of the next morning, and stayed still while I watched his chest move gently up and down. My bladder was full. I worried about my breath, sleep in my eyes and my ruffled hair. One eye opened and then the other and he grabbed me, pulled me close and kissed my nose. I sighed and relaxed.

All was well in the world.

On graduation day, he left early as I sat in the living room of his dorm, waiting for his father to pick me up. I had never met his parents. They were divorced, and Quincy didn't like sharing what had happened. I felt stiff as his father and I drove to the stadium, despite his attempts at social graces. "What college did you say you attended?" he asked. I hesitated, and then told him I was a music major but was taking a break. Once we arrived, we scrambled looking for seats up close, so his father could take pictures. With the humidity, I was already sweating in the two-piece green-and-pink silk dress and coat. I felt silly; Quincy didn't even wear a suit.

You'd have thought he won the Nobel Prize when they called his name. We cheered and he threw kisses! I saw an older woman with a man standing in the distance clapping and wondered, *Is that his mother*? After the caps flew in the air, we strained to find him in the crowd. It took a while, and then there he was. But he wasn't alone. A very attractive girl stood there smiling into his face, and he was smiling back—the smile he always gave to me. I hoped my face didn't give me away, because I wanted to tell her, "Back off, he's mine."

"Oh, she's just a pre-med girl in my study group who lives in New York. She wanted to say goodbye and good luck," he explained later.

"Nice to meet you," I said, as she walked away and turned around one more time, smiling. "See you." The hairs stood up on my skin. I decided she was a weasel.

There was nothing posh about his celebration, which surprised me. We ate at a chain restaurant and he became plain goofy, sitting between me and the woman I had noticed clapping earlier. She was remarried and, from what I could see, adored her son. I was embarrassed when I realized I hadn't purchased a graduation gift until he graciously saved me. "My sweetheart is my present." His father stood to make a toast and talked about his son following in his footsteps one day. That's when I knew Quincy hadn't shared our plans and the new footprints we were making together.

For the last few months, we had solidified our plans and the shellac had dried on my fairy tale once Quincy shared his final decision.

"I'm coming to live in California and be with you. I can stay with my aunt and uncle. I'll work in the family business until I get a job, save my money, and apply to med school."

"I'll save my money too, and help you with school. Then I'll get my degree and you can help me."

We had agreed, although embedded underneath my words was the presumption of matrimony.

Dr. Fullerton finished his toast and my mind took off on a marathon ride. Next morning, Quincy said goodbye to his roommates and we headed to Shreveport in his Volkswagen bug. It had been six years since we left. I was quiet, and unsure of my feelings about returning to the place where so much had happened.

Quincy noticed. "What are you thinking about?"

I didn't dare tell him. The beatings? Being good enough? Wondering if his parents approved of me? The girl with the smile? Our plans? I didn't dare tell the truth, fearful he might think I possessed a suspicious mind, especially about the girl, and get upset with me. It wasn't a good way to begin our *life* together.

"Oh nothing. It's been a long time since I was in Shreveport. I'm wondering how it's changed and hope I'll get to see some of the people I used to know."

By the time we pulled into his father's driveway, I had tucked my doubts away. Five days later, after staying in Quincy's home, he drove me to the Dallas airport, smothered me with kisses, and promised to be safe driving real fast to San Francisco.

He arrived two days later and within a week, the world was punched in the stomach once more.

After Dr. King's death it seemed the only hope we had left to claim our civil rights rested on the shoulders of Robert Kennedy. I had never been up close to a celebrity and grew excited when the singing group that I joined, in an effort to be involved in something important, was asked to open the rally in Oakland. I boasted to Quincy, believing that somehow my close proximity to someone important would make me important too. After we sang, I was touched by Kennedy's words about Dr. King and the hope that he had as the future president to end discrimination. I cheered when he won the presidential nomination on June 5 and then was shaken to my core as three shots were fired and he laid on the floor quivering.

The fragility of life—how one moment a man is eulogizing another, reaching out and consoling a wife, a family, a nation; a woman stretches her feet out on a plane anticipating a visit with her sister; a child runs playfully after a ball rolling in the street... and then death strikes. It hit me again. My senses of wrong and right were offended. Fear sent a chill through my bones and kept me repeating, *You could die before you live.* Lying awake each night, I pondered the thought, sure this quality of *living* was not something I had learned from church, my parents, school, or life lessons. I wanted to experience the feelings of *living*, caress it with my hands, moan from the silkiness of it prickling my skin as it ran down my spine, and hoped to hug the sensation with Quincy's love.

⌖ ROSE-COLORED GLASSES ⌖

I mmediately Quincy started working for the restaurant his aunt and uncle owned, and I found myself driving over the Bay Bridge every chance I got to sit with him behind the cash register. It was always crowded and the customers loved kidding around with him, especially the waitresses who flirted. He would flirt back, then grab my waist when I brooded.

"Now don't you go off and get jealous. I hate jealousy. I just like being friendly. It's good for business." He didn't know that kind of behavior was enough to really make me crazy. Sometimes I'd drive home dizzy from my locked box of repressed feelings, one too many cocktails, and a migraine.

My life settled into work, church, and waiting to see Quincy in reverse order. I walked around ready to make myself available at his every whim. I crafted Quincy into a kind of god and lived through his dreams, pushing him up and myself down, until the pedestal I placed him on had no room for me. He didn't waver from his stance about attending church, although I begged him, "Please, do it for me." Dad didn't understand, and frankly, I didn't either for I had come to believe his position about Christians. Yes, most were hypocrites, but you didn't go to church for other people, you went for your own personal relationship with God. When Quincy came over for visits and dinner, Dad would pick up his Holy Ghost hammer and start to pound, but the nail never penetrated.

We'd make out in his Volkswagen at the drive-in movies, laughing at scraped knees from being cramped in the back seat. I felt all the parts of my puzzle fit when I was in his arms and welcomed the infrequency of having sex. I didn't want to take birth control pills, but didn't worry, especially, after the doctor's recent examination. "It is very unlikely you will ever get pregnant." At first, the prognosis stunned me, and I didn't ask any questions about why, too scared to know the truth and the impact on my future with Quincy. And then I relaxed, thinking, *It's all for the best*, remembering I didn't want to wake my sleeping dragon. Quincy would understand.

I watched as Quincy's attire gradually shifted to mod leather coats, stylish boots, custom jeans, and two-piece outfits with lots of color. Everything he purchased looked expensive and even with his new eight-to-five job, I didn't understand how spending lots of money fit into our plan—wasn't he going to med school? But what stood out the most were his red eyes. I thought the Bay Area air had given him some kind of allergy.

One day I asked him, "Why do you always wear sunglasses and why are your eyes sometimes pink?"

He looked at me like a kid caught in a candy jar and then pulled over to the side of the road. He took out the strangest shaped yellow cigarette I'd ever seen. "This is why." I didn't get it. "Don't worry, just puff on it."

I thought, cigarettes again, but it must be okay if he's doing it. I coughed and almost choked and rolled down the window to get rid of the pungent smell. "I don't feel anything," I said as he started up the engine. Somewhere in my life, I had read a statement about "Not knowing when you don't know that you don't know," or something to that effect. That would describe my first marijuana experience. After about fifteen minutes of my mouth flapping, he laughed, "Yep, you're high."

I took to smoking grass like a duck to water. It gave me the illusion of courage; it left me feeling carefree and invincible. When high, my mouth either stuck together like glue or became a gun spitting bullets, right on the borderline of being disrespectful. But not in my father's house. I wasn't sure if Dad's backhand had become inoperative, even though he hadn't struck me since twelfth grade. On Sunday mornings, I heard the holy ghost with a clear mind, but by afternoon,

I'd often play the piano at church teas or fashion shows with the good sisters asking, "What you been crying about now, baby?"

Quincy came inside to socialize with my parents less and less, mostly because he didn't want to face Dad's questions about church or bringing me home at all times of the night. I knew a showdown was coming.

On Sunday mornings, Dad would start. "You're interrupting the flow and breaking the rules." I figured as long as I was in my place at church on Sunday service, what difference did it make when I came home? I started missing evening meals, the sacred time we all were together, and a couple of celebrations where I was expected to be with our larger family.

Dad said, "You're setting a bad example for Robert and Kelesha. You're the oldest, they look up to you." And then he'd end with his favorite saying, "Stop trying to vex me." It wasn't by design; I just couldn't say "no" to Quincy. But a showdown was coming!

HUH

God had shown favor to Dad after leaving the traditional church. So many people had joined that a large sanctuary had been purchased at 2100 Fifth Avenue in Oakland. On Sunday mornings, you'd have to park four or five blocks away and when the doors opened right after The Lord's Prayer, droves of twenty and thirty people would pile through the side doors and flow hastily into the balcony looking for a seat. I had to give Dad the invisible crown of visionary genius. The church bulletin stated, "The power to be free...the struggle to be faithful." I knew freedom was a powerful attractor, like bees to honey, but a packed church *every* Sunday surprised me. Any newcomer reading the first years of the church history would notice a rebellious nature, a sort of militancy almost. Dad made sure the church's turbulent history was known.

> "The Church of All Faiths is the outgrowth of a people—frustrated, disillusioned, and dissatisfied about a need for change in the spirit of Christ in making the church a progressive and more vital instrument in the individual and the world. We took a stand for what was right because we were distraught by the leaders regarding the mission. This church is God's answered prayer."

I'd read it over and over each Sunday while sitting in the choir stand like I was seeing the words for the first time. All those years in the Methodist church, I'd had no idea Dad had been "frustrated, disillusioned, and dissatisfied!"

I had to admit, when I finally understood the reason Dad was defrocked, I saw the irony. He simply broke the rules. I had to side with the bishop. He had no choice but to give Dad his whooping. If every pastor wanted his own house, the whole system would have fallen apart. But I wondered, *Whose idea was it to purchase a home, and so far away from our church in the first place*? Dad was steadfast in his beliefs about following the rules. I couldn't imagine his defiance. I wondered how Mom played into the scenario. I'd heard her speak to Dad many times about the instability that came from moving around, mostly how it affected our studies at school and with developing friendships. Maybe she really did care about her other two children moving around, but where was my consolation prize? As I looked back on the whole affair, what I truly believed was Mom felt she deserved the prestige of living in an upper-class neighborhood. And once she took off, gliding smoothly in the air with her career, she waited for the right time to land and found favorable conditions by writing the check for the down payment without asking Dad for a dime.

There was one more possibility. Dad knew exactly what he was doing and wanted to be free. He knew saying "yes" to Mom was his ticket home and his freedom to serve God without all the pomp and circumstance of the organized Methodist hierarchy. I didn't want to believe my father wanted to make up his own rules and be his own boss. It was opposite all his teachings about following Christ. But he was no fool, either, and no pushover.

It all had a strange effect on me. Had I been an oyster and you opened me up, you should have discovered a pearl. Instead, a jagged stone had formed years before in my heart and become more solid with each contradiction I witnessed. Dad had said, "Never gossip, always tell the truth, love everybody, don't break the law, respect your religious vows." I had heard Dad speak unfavorably about certain people, tell lies to me, speed, hate homosexuals and Jehovah's Witnesses, and break the vows he took to obey as a Methodist minister. And I was sure no place in the Bible talked about beating your child the way Dad had beaten me. Was that not contradiction in the first degree?

Either way, I now felt the bishop had done us a favor because Dad had changed. Not in his strong beliefs about Jesus as our savior. Not about heaven or hell, but his attitude about flowing with life. He was no longer like steel in his conservative views—his dress changed to relaxed blue-jeans outfits and three-piece fashionable suits. He grew out his hair into a natural, he allowed my brother, sister, and me to dance to any devil music we liked, and he even cut a rug himself sometimes.

I concluded that Dad was no dummy. He knew there would be repercussions for such a bold move as purchasing a home. Maybe he hadn't been as happy as he pretended—as happy as he was now, controlling his dark secret. That thought made me want to scream, *Have I been duped*?

Instilled in my character were the foundations of the Ten Commandments, the Golden Rule, turning the other cheek, obedience, repentance, and discipline. I had been taught these were basic good virtues for any human being and a requirement for individuals following our faith. I had no argument with that premise. But I had been led to believe that my faith would sustain and anchor me in times of uncertainty or darkness. Instead I felt unstable, like something was out of order—fuzzy, off-centered, like two legs on a three-legged stool. And I was left with a wooden sliver that from time to time would fester. I wondered, *Why were these teachings creating such a battle within me? Were they at war with my will?* Most times I felt directionless, a puppet drawn by the hands of others. Where was the confidence to deal with calamities in my life, the fortitude to be true to my own values, the sweet serenity of peace talked about in the Bible?

The more I noticed Dad's freedom emerging, the heavier the jagged stone grew—churning over and over in the shell that was me.

Dad wasn't the only one who had earned my disappointment and ire. Resentment toward Mom was at an all-time high. I watched her caring for my brother and sister, lingering in their rooms and making sure they had the right teachers, and subjects and attended the right social engagements. My brother brought light into her face, and she pampered him even though he didn't ask for it. My sister would sass her unrepentantly and never get disciplined. I thought about how Mom never spoke up on my behalf, never took my side, and never stopped Dad from taking out his frustrations on me. And her response to the mix up about my transcript was etched in my brain. I wanted to forgive, but was unable to do so without a sincere apology from her first. It never came. So my feelings toward her always felt unnatural, forced, almost contractual, like I had to love her because she was my mother.

On occasion the conversation between Mom and Dad would focus on us kids. She'd turn to him and say, "You set me up against the children. They like you better than me." She'd cover her face with her hands and take one piece of Kleenex as two drops of water rolled down her face. It was nothing like the tears that flowed from me when I was hurting, or like Dad when he got happy on Sunday mornings and cried on the shoulder of one of his trustees. Those were real tears. Hers were more like weeping on cue to get attention. Still, I'd feel sorry for her. I knew the feeling of being left out and seeing others being loved more, and I didn't wish that on anyone. But after seeing the exact two tears fall as she sat in the same chair, sniffling in exactly the same way, her performance no longer affected me. I was numbed by it and would side with Dad every time when asked to vote, "Who would you rather live with?"

I'd think about the years of tenderness that I longed for growing up, the times I'd wish she had sat on the bed and just listened to me like she did her students. But she had chosen to leave me in my father's hands, and I wouldn't allow myself to console her in her pain.

I had tried to make sense of my conflicted feelings for Dad. He had been the worst perpetrator of abuse and yet, when it was all over, he would become the father I loved with his caresses, jokes, laughter, and genuine interest in me. When he was angry, he was brutal—a giant monster reincarnated. But when he was calm, his love felt real. And that's when I understood why Mom was so blue. We did love Dad more.

 LEGAL

Dad's mellow mood didn't keep me from the litany of house rules and reminders about being the eldest. I started feeling like a pressure cooker about to explode, so I decided to hand over the baton to my brother and remove myself from our home. The want ad section of the paper became my primary reading material. My head would move across the page like a typewriter. I was flabbergasted at the cost of apartments, wondering how I would eat, pay for my car, and take care of myself. But I stayed focused, concentrating on freedom, and what it would be like living on my own. I was attracted to the nicely furnished one-bedroom apartments around the lake with a view of San Francisco. They were way out of my budget! But the cheap apartments in West or East Oakland smelled bad, had cracked linoleum floors and roaches. I'd make a dash to the door, hoping nothing crawled in my purse, and speed off down the road, shaking my head in disbelief that anyone could live in such filth.

And then one afternoon I saw the sign for two vacancies: "1 Bedroom and 1 Studio apartment." Not the lake, but not East Oakland either. Mrs. Adams, the property manager, was a nice lady about the same age as Mom. She grabbed the keys to the studio after introducing her husband and daughter and started in like a chatterbox.

"You can move in tomorrow if you like and we'll prorate you," she said.

The studio was the size of my parents' living room—beige carpet, built-in kitchen table, stove, refrigerator, pull-out couch, bathroom, and bay window that looked out at the belly of the apartment where I could see the sunset. I loved sunsets and felt it was a good omen. I held my breath.

"How much?"

"Ninety-five," she said, "including utilities."

Before she could change her mind I said, "I'll take it," already calculating the impact on my budget. I had never filled out an application and there were all these personal questions, like who to contact in case of an emergency and what credit cards did I use. I needed phone numbers and addresses and hoped my incomplete application would not disqualify me.

"Give me a twenty-five-dollar deposit and it's yours," Mrs. Adams assured me. "And don't forget, you can move in anytime." Shelling out the twenty-five dollars, I felt like I had just ridden the Matterhorn!

On the drive home, reality set in. A monologue sprang up in my head. *What can Dad do? I'm an adult, got my own job, my own car, and my own apartment. Well, you're still his daughter and never too big to slap around. Dad could stop speaking to you or turn away from you at church. Nah, he wouldn't do that—how would it look to the membership? He could take your car away, you know he co-signed. He could totally disown you, banish you from the family. You think he would do that? This is a bold move; you never know what Dad might do!*

My mouth turned to mush at dinner and after four days I phoned Mrs. Adams. "I need until the fifteenth of next month."

Meanwhile, I stood in front of the full-sized mirror in my room, practicing what I'd say. "Mom and Dad, it's time for me to be independent." No, no, too forward. "Mom and Dad, how would you feel if I got my own place for a while?" No, I don't need their permission. Finally, I settled on saying as few words as possible.

"Mom and Dad, I'm moving out." The words stuck in my throat. Their mouths dropped.

"What did you say? You can't move. It's dangerous out there. What do you know about living alone? We always dreamed of you marrying and then leaving home. I bet Quincy has something to do with this. What will people say?"

They went on for two hours. I listened, waited for the right pause, and then quietly unfolded the contract. Dad's eyes gobbled every word, while I waited in silence. "Well, I guess you've already made up your mind. I'm very disappointed."

ᏆFREEDOM'S BOUNTYᏏ

D ad was absent on moving day. My brother followed me back and forth as I loaded the car. "Where you moving to? Can I come see you? Can I move into your room? You mad at Dad? Why are you moving?"

I couldn't keep up. "I'm close, only five minutes from church. You can come see me anytime. Call me, I'll come pick you up if it's okay with Mom. I'm not planning on coming back, so my room is yours. I'm not mad, I'm just growing up. Anyway, Mom says the house isn't big enough for two women."

He looked at me strangely. "You're the big brother now. You've got to look after your sister, okay? I'll miss you." We hugged and I could feel he didn't really understand, he just knew I was no longer sleeping under the same roof.

After my last carload, I popped my head in the kitchen and found Mom in deep thought washing the breakfast dishes. "I'm loaded up, getting ready to go. Where's Dad?"

"He had a meeting," she responded. I didn't believe her, Dad never had meetings on Saturday morning. "I went through the cabinets. This will hold you over for a while."

I was appreciative of the used towels, sheets, bedding, and kitchenware and hugged her. "I made you a care package of food too," she said as I poked my head in one of the bags.

If Dad had been present, I would have told him, "Your dream of me marrying was my dream too." I wished Quincy had given me an engagement ring. I wished we had a wedding date and I wished I were leaving as a married women. But that act of the fairy tale had yet to come true. Besides, I had fulfilled my obligation of showing people how I loved Jesus. My assignment was done!

My hand had been forced; there was no other option. At least that's what I convinced myself as my car rolled up to the unsecured parking area of my new home. A short, old man in a white T-shirt and black silk robe hung over the railing smoking a cigarette as I unloaded the first round of boxes. He looked at me as if watching a brace of ducks waddling across a country road as I walked up and down the three flights of stairs. As I fumbled with the key on the last load, he shouted across the corridor, "Moving all by yourself?" Accustomed to being fearful of strange men I quickly closed the door, pulled the drapes, and sank into the single chair that furnished the room.

I don't know what I had been expecting—perhaps on one hand a showdown with Dad and on the other a helping hand with the move. What I did not expect was the silence that followed me up the stairs.

The first thing I did was hook up my stereo and pull out a joint. The room took on scant splendor. I emptied boxes, contemplating what small, colorful items would make me feel at home. I was on a budget—*one thing at a time*, I told myself. But by late afternoon logic had vaporized with the smoke and I was off on a spending spree. I walked through the department store, dizzy from the prices. By the time Quincy arrived, striped red-and-purple sheets, violet bathroom accessories, two grape leaf plants, and a bamboo rug added just the right touches as I lit the lavender candle, ready to fully inhabit my new space with him.

A few weeks after I moved in, I met a beautiful, brown-skinned girl named Lynnette. She and her new husband Devon were the main attraction of a motley group I'd seen congregating on weekends. Lynnette's father had been a Baptist preacher, but he had died her senior year and she no longer attended church. Their friends were just as pleasant—Antoine who wore blue scrubs and drove a green

Corvette; his brother, William, a telephone repair man; Fat Sam who sold insurance; seedy-eyed Charlie who I never saw without his navy-blue pea coat even after it got hot; Jude and his wife Allie, both teachers, and old Sandy with the cigarette, a retired army cook. All he did was stand outside all day and crack jokes at people as they came and went.

It was all new to me. Forty-five flavors of couples, singles, and families zipping up and down the stairs each day like one big clan. And then there was Xavier, the peacock in flashy jumpsuits of shiny material and jackets with fur who drove a white Cadillac with chrome wheels. I'd almost fall over the railing watching the promenade of girls piling out of his car dressed in every color—miniskirts, thick-heeled boots, scarves around large Afros, low-cut blouses, suede vests, long red fingernails. The way Xavier and those girls expressed themselves, I just knew I was living in the middle of a *Super Fly* movie.

Peeking out the window and socializing with Lynnette became a pastime as I adjusted to the rhythm of being with Quincy once a week and on weekends, whenever he didn't work at his aunt's. And there were weeks I didn't see him at all. But I never complained, enticed by the amusement of the building's inhabitants as I silently made up character stories about who they really were as if writing a screenplay. I adapted to a simple life of independence and freedom. I liked it! However, freedom came with a price. I'd talk to myself late at night as I looked at the meager furnishings surrounded by four walls. I missed the smell of coffee, saying "good morning," creaking stairs, and the chatter that accompanied meals. I missed knowing someone would respond if I spoke or simply made noise. I missed sitting on the porch gazing at the bridge, Dad's rosebushes and the status of saying "I live in the hills." And I missed my piano, duets with my brother, and a mattress that didn't sag or creak. In my quiet moments I talked to the silence, satisfied I had done the right thing. It was temporary—right? Quincy and I would be married soon.

I knew I had found the meaning of living on Saturday mornings, when the quiet apartment complex came alive at noon. The boom-boom beat of Michael Jackson, The Commodores, and Marvin Gaye blasted from Lynnette's open door. That was the signal for the fun to begin. By 2:00 Lynnette would clear the table and bring out the cards while one of the guys extracted seeds in the cigar box filled with marijuana. By late afternoon, we'd all have the munchies and would pool our money for pizza, Chinese food, and bottles of Ripple.

I was grateful to fit into an established community of people my own age where there was infectious humor, inflammatory language, and establishment renunciation—and no shame. The parties filled the alone times without Quincy and the silence that loomed. He was always invited and on occasion would join me, but I came to know Quincy as someone who wore his own shades of gray in the form of canceled dates, late-night knocks on the door, and sudden disappearances. I pretended not to mind, trusting we were marching toward the same rainbow. I dared not question his intentions. Better not to know, I thought, confident that the complexity of both Quincy and me was a necessary step to reconcile the two halves that made me whole.

Meanwhile, I busied myself dreaming of my future as a doctor's wife. I saw myself as a socialite—brunch at famous restaurants, shopping at expensive stores, entertaining other doctor's wives, and decided, *I'd better remove the gold caps off my signature front teeth.*

ᏣSHOWING OFFᏄ

F amily holidays were revered. By Easter, I was ready to show off my independence. It was a foolish notion given my apartment had such little space and dishes for only two. But I needed the family's approval and wanted to make a point of being fine, thank you very much. Planning the meal was easy. I was a good cook. Creating the ambience of comfort, flowers, dishes, and eating utensils was the challenge, especially with my financial resources. So I used my only option and talked myself into something that was fast becoming a habit with me—spending money I didn't have.

I was exhausted from the preparation and even more alarmed as the food bills started to mount. But I was too proud to accept the offer from Dad when he asked "Need a little cash?," not trusting that he wouldn't throw it back in my face at a later date.

Quincy helped me organize the borrowed card tables from Lynnette and, by the time the first knock sounded on the door, the place looked festive with pastel tablecloths, dishes, flatware, and little chocolate eggs. Entertaining was work—answering the door, watching the stove, paying attention to the conversation. I burned the flour gravy as smoke billowed from the black skillet. Dad blessed my home and even said some kind words about Quincy in his prayer as we settled into a traditional turkey dinner with all the trimmings. Mom and my aunts kept saying, "You've fixed it up real nice, Shaa," but I wasn't sure the words were meant to make me feel better. My feelings of triumph worked for a while until my uncle, who was always known to take a nap after eating, went into the bathroom and came out looking baffled.

"Where's the bedroom?" he asked.

His question caught me off-guard. "This is a studio, Uncle."

"Where do you sleep?"

"There, on the couch," I pointed.

He scratched his head as if contemplating a crossword puzzle. Aunt Zemma tried to smooth it over, "George, you sleep too much anyway."

I tried to regroup by batting the ball back with one of Dad's sayings, "Uncle, you've got to walk before you run," but the shiny penny was tarnishing right before my eyes.

Mom took the spotlight off me. "Anybody ready for dessert?" I could have kissed her. Uncle George took off his shoes, found a spot on the edge of the lumpy sofa and after ice cream, Mom's 7-Up cake, and coffee, nodded off. It was like old times—joking about the past, Nixon as president, the plight of black people, and the rising cost of gas, while Robert, Kelesha, and my two cousins debated over what to watch on my newly purchased television.

There was no trace I could detect of disappointment, pity, or regret as my family departed that evening. All I could feel was acceptance—genuine acceptance of the choice I had made toward standing on my own two feet. As I laid my head to rest all that was left was a pile of dirty pots and pans, a feeling of relief, the echo of Dad's blessing, and Quincy's body next to mine.

ᘓMOVING ON UPᘓ

Call it an unknown force or answered prayer but wouldn't you know it, just about the same time I was feeling the need for something better, Quincy took a step forward. I heard a knock on the door and found him standing with an overnight bag and a smile. I prepared our meals, he helped clean the dishes while we talked about our worlds—the wrong, right, suspicions, and unknowns about our life. Our chats took me back to our early days of honesty and truth. After a few weeks my faith in him was stronger than ever. It wasn't as much sexual as it was stretching to a level of risk without a net.

We never talked about it—I made him a key and he just gradually moved in. And after a couple of months of dangling feet over saggy springs, a cramped bathroom, and closet space, I'd had enough. We moved two doors from Lynnette and Devon to a one-bedroom. A month later, Quincy sold his Volkswagen bug and surprised me once more with a new baby-blue Firebird. I guessed medical school was indefinitely on hold, and I waited for him to pop the question.

By Fall we had moved to a modern apartment building on Dwight Way, right about the time school began on the UC Berkeley campus. There was no warning—only Quincy's fool-proof reasoning.

"I'm going to medical school at Berkeley. We'll already be settled. You'll like Troy and Florence who live downstairs. Living among college students has a vibe like jazz, we'll be in the middle of all the action. Smell the air, it's so fresh and clean and I'm closer to work." Except for my longer commute to work, I couldn't argue with any of his reasons. I knew I didn't like how he had made decisions for us—by opening the door and saying, "Surprise, I signed the lease, we're moving." I guess he knew I'd take to a modern building, shag carpets, paneled wood, and a large deck surrounded by beauty. Yes, we were paying more, but my need to appear successful blotted that out. Anyway, I had a raise coming in a month.

The only problem was my folks. I was comfortable pretending Quincy was visiting, the two times they stopped by unexpectedly. But with the switch to Berkeley, without my name on the lease, I suspected he wasn't going to hide out in his own apartment. *I'll deal with it when the times comes*, I kept telling myself.

We were three blocks from Telegraph—surrounded by chic bou-

tiques, rolling hills and landscaped meadows, Tower Records, restaurants serving global cuisine, and gathering places for some of the
finest minds in the world. We'd rise on weekends to the sound of every type of music imaginable from Poco to Mozart pouring through
the windows, accompanied by the constant smell of grass and in-
cense.

Troy and Florence were the quintessential hosts. It didn't matter if you were a four-year graduate or doctoral student; part-time
student, or drop-out; working, fired, or freeloader. You could be
black or white, black and white, fat and toothless, lean and shoe-
less, well-dressed or shabby, with or without children. You could be
from Berkeley, the Deep South, or my old apartment building—the
welcome mat greeted everyone. The only entry requirement was getting high, drinking, wit, and being able to hold your own. You could
even crash on the floor if you were too wasted to move and get blue-
berry pancakes and sausage the next morning for breakfast. It was
my first close-up of what Dad had called "Modern-day Sodom and
Gomorrah." Psychedelic music, strobe lights, breasts without bras,
water pipes, tie-dye, leather headbands, bare feet, free love, anti-war,
anti-Nixon, anti-establishment, and anti-religion. It came head-on,
spirited and full of passion with spit flying, finger-pointing and everyone shouting their views at the same time, followed by pats on the
back, "Hey, we still friends," and hard laughter that brought peren-
nial tears. Quincy slipped right into the gaiety like he had found his
tribe. And surprisingly, I did too!

❧DISAPPEARING ACT❧

There was no other place to be at 10:30 on Sunday mornings except sitting in the eighteenth pew. My end seat offered me a panoramic view, while placing me directly in Dad's line of vision. I liked looking in his eyes as he jostled back and forth like a boxer in the ring. As the last syllable of "Amen" left my lips, I'd search for my brother. We embraced each other like wide-eyed, giddy children approaching Santa with our toy lists. He looked taller each week in his blue usher's blazer and I was reminded once again, *You belong to a family.*

I'd jab him gently in his bony chest. "What girl's heart are you breaking now, you handsome thing?" causing his dimples to widen before his words sputtered forth like a car flooded from too much gas in the engine.

"When, when, when...are, are, are...you, you, you...coming... over?" He had stuttered for so many years that the quivering movement of his lips looked and sounded normal.

Sighing, I'd repeat what I'd said the previous Sunday, hell-bent on standing my ground. "Not until I'm invited."

Kelesha would charge toward me like a bull. "Did you hear my solo?"

I'd pat her soft, red-streaked hair. "You're getting better than me." She'd hunch her shoulders like a witch on a broom before taking off again, running. I'd shake my head. *What a difference ten years makes in showing your love for Jesus.*

Clusters of folks, mostly the good sisters, would block the aisles and repeat the same compliments about Dad that had clogged my ears year after year. I listened, unable to shake my training. Most Sundays, Dad's clothes were soaking wet, but he'd stand while people waited ten, twenty, thirty deep and draw them in like magnets. If Dad wasn't done shaking hands by the stroke of one, I headed to the family car to linger, wondering if Dad thought he had hit the ball out the park with his sermon. Most Sundays, his batting average was in the four-hundreds, but every now and then, he'd strike out. I'm not sure if anyone else noticed, or kept score, but I did. I had a lot of practice studying Dad's expressions. His face was a dead giveaway and set the mood for what came next—a warm embrace and kiss on my forehead or a quick tap on my back as he swung behind the steering wheel taking off in a hurry.

Each Sunday I felt like a traveler in the desert waiting for the water to moisten my parched lips with Mom's words, "Come to dinner," but they never came. If my brother or sister had moved, would she be so complacent and stoic? Did she have no sense of the real me? Did she *really* think I was doing okay without the family?

She told me years later that my being out in the world pierced her heart with worry. Perhaps at the time she couldn't allow herself to acknowledge her failure toward me as a mother—our failure as mother and daughter. She had shown more willingness to stand valiant on behalf of her students, rather than her own daughter. And yet she nodded with Dad's every word as he preached stories of forgiveness, kindness, family, and brotherly love. Was I not worthy of the same compassion extended to the parishioners who sat glued to his every word?

I always thought we emulated the wholesome, well-adjusted family. The Negro version of *Father Knows Best* and *Ozzie and Harriet*. But the good sisters and brothers didn't know; they only got a chance to stare into our fishbowl from the outside. There were Sundays I left with my heart broken and a gremlin laughing over my shoulder. *Maybe moving out was a mistake.*

In the beginning of our new life in Berkeley, Quincy and I dressed on Sunday mornings and went in opposite directions. For him, attending church was a non-issue. I didn't push. I had wounds too, much deeper than his, but I'd come to believe locking the door and throwing away keys from the past would force me to forget. What became more important was to keep pushing forward, believing and remembering stories from the Bible—Ruth the "kept" woman, Solomon sleeping with concubines, King David who killed to make Bathsheba his wife. So many stories of disobedience and yet, in time, all was forgiven.

Keeping up the front of living alone got harder to conceal each time I saw my parents. I felt a dirty grit building, leaving an emotional abrasion, and I couldn't distinguish what felt worse—telling the lie of my living arrangements or denying the flame of my love. After several months of grimacing in the steamed-up bathroom mirror and getting down on my knees at the church altar, I didn't want to do it anymore. I was too chicken to hear Dad's testimony about fire and brimstone, and what felt less painful at the time was to put one foot behind the other, back away slowly without a sound, while facing the wild new frontier of my existence. Once out of range, I took off running. Without a telephone number or address, I evaporated from my family, leaving not a trace of dust.

My disappearing act pulled me further and deeper into the cave with Quincy. I'd wake in a fog from the previous night's party, snuggled in his arms. What felt natural was to stay right where I was and allow myself to be wrapped in the moth's silk web. John Coltrane replaced the choir's processional song, "Holy, Holy, Holy," as hot grits popped, biscuits turned brown, and we laughed at comics in the Sunday funny papers. Whatever adventure fancied Quincy, fancied me—football, walks on Telegraph Avenue, rides on his motorcycle, watching movies in bed. Sometimes, we'd invite Troy and Florence for brunch, becoming referees about Vietnam, the meaning of democracy, or the usefulness of the police force. I enjoyed the distraction of playing hostess, feeling abandoned by my family. I missed them. *What if Mom or Dad were deadly sick? What if I died? Would they care?* But after several months of worrying and utter silence, I came to one conclusion. I didn't matter to them anymore! I had done it this time and I told myself, *Grow up, move on, stop looking back.*

INTEGRITY

Quincy's way of easing my estrangement began with an unexpected Tuesday evening ride to San Francisco. It was the week after Thanksgiving, the first holiday celebration away from extended family. We parked close to Market and Powell, passed red miniature Santas riding bicycles, elves hanging whimsically over counters, and the scent of Chanel mixed with cinnamon and pine flowing through the golden brass doors of Macy's. Cable-car and Salvation Army bells formed a competitive duet with tooting car horns, and the hum of the big city. The gravity of the crowds pushed us forward into wool coats, shopping bags of red bow-tied presents, curly-top babies in strollers, and the mist from the ocean.

My hand felt warm against his as I asked Quincy, "Where are we going?"

"You'll see" were the only words I could rouse.

The white, wrinkle-faced guard looked at our faces with suspicion before asking, "What floor?"

I felt like a six-year-old asking again, "Where are we going?" as Quincy responded. "Sixth floor."

The elevator stopped with a jolt and the guard buzzed us through the gold doors—a jewelry treasure chest. I suddenly felt warm, as a round-faced woman dressed in black with large, dangling white pearls greeted us. The sparkle in her eye reminded me of an Italian grandmother as she stretched out her arms to Quincy.

"I'm Bess, you're right on time. Your aunt told me you're looking for wedding rings."

My eyes would not stop batting. Round, pear, opal, marquise, and princess-cut rings formed a crescent around me. I'd hold my hand in the light to Bess's praise, before my eye slid to the next setting. For ninety minutes I became dazzled by the sparkle until seven rings shined majestically against black velvet cloth. But I felt something wasn't quite right, and my mind took off running.

Why am I sweating picking out my own ring?

You'll get what you want.

Well, what is the protocol?

The man purchases the ring and asks you to marry him.

That's old-fashioned.

Times are changing.

Sometimes, I like old-fashioned. I want to be surprised.

Finally, I gave up and turned to Quincy. His eyes and ears were only half on me, beguiled by trying on and selecting a diamond band for himself. I poked him gingerly in the ribs. "Hey, are you serious about this?" He grinned like a teenager caught putting the keys in the ignition after being told no.

When Quincy chose my favorite—a round, one-carat engagement ring resembling a flower when paired with the wedding ring— a euphonious chorus of songbirds harmonized inside of me. I was ready to prance through the doors with the ring on my finger, but Quincy stopped me. "Got to get it sized." All the way home I was the little girl in the swing, hollering "wheee."

My head was still in cumulus clouds as I dialed home. The six months of silence felt like years since we talked.

All Dad had to say was, "It's about time," before sticking it to me. "Tell that young man to get over here and ask my permission."

I hoped he wasn't serious; Quincy wasn't about to go through the formality, not after living together. But secretly, I too held a dream— four-star restaurant, violins, Quincy on one knee whispering, "Will you marry me," corks popping, people clapping, me smiling. Ah yes, what a beautiful dream. Meantime, I'd have to get used to the bootleg version.

Mom became a locomotive engine pulling the weight of my wedding train, which forced me to give up my privacy and my telephone number. I had been running a tally over the years, comparing myself to my brother and sister. Seemed to me my parents owed me. So I scribbled the amount of what they'd spent on my siblings since I moved out in a column and added it up, not wanting to be greedy—$5,000 on tuition; $1,500 for food and clothing; $500 for missed vacations. Pain and suffering. Um, that's a big number.

The figure helped me imagine the ceremony of "Ronita and Quincy's Wedding Day." The Hilton would do, the Marriott even, but when I keyed in on elegance, I saw a more beautiful ballroom of grandeur and style—the Claremont in the Berkeley hills. I'd be the one people were trying to see behind the dark, tinted windows of our extra-long, black, stretch limousine. Contour white-silk, beaded bridal gown with a twelve-inch train, six bridesmaids, four junior bridesmaids, champagne, five-course sit-down dinner, seven-tiered cake, and a partridge in a pear tree. Yes, I deserved every opportunity to be the breathtaking, enchanted princess happily captured by zooming lenses.

"Not so fast," Mom said, pulling the already developed pictures out of my imagination quicker than I could pop a bubble. "I don't know what you're planning but weddings cost money. The ceremony and reception will be in the sanctuary and the church hall! I'll gather the women to help with the cooking and decorations. We'll pay for your dress, flowers, and food, you pay for the invitations."

Inside, I screamed *No, no, no, no. I'm marrying Quincy. His father is a doctor. He's going to be a doctor. I'm going to be a doctor's wife, not a chicken farmer's wife. And no, please, not the church reception hall! It's all wrong, wrong, wrong!*

I had attended more wedding receptions in our church hall than I cared to remember. All were decorated with ribbons and bows by the Progressive Women's Guild, a group of snappy dressers if ever there was one. They'd use the same decoration over and over again, adding a new ribbon depending on the bride's choice of color, and plastic flowers. My wedding had to be the final scene of *Cinderella*, a castle filled with fine people bowing and curtsying. But once I came down from the clouds what could I say? Not once had I thought about the consequences of moving out. I had no extra money, no credit cards or a for-real fairy godmother. My brother was graduating, my sister needed braces, Dad was attending graduate school, and Mom held the purse strings. My parents had said "Yes" to supporting the most important day of my life, but on their terms. I had to take what they offered and be grateful.

We settled on the first weekend in April. The time for red-tailed hawks diving in acrobatic flight, doves preparing to nest, the smell of soil and grass mixed with an earthy aroma, honeybees darting in and out of freshly bloomed tulips, sleeveless days, sweater nights, and daylight saving. A perfect time for new beginnings.

ᏚᎬROARING RAPIDSᏙᎧ

Love driven by desperation is like the exchange of hot humid air mixing and intensifying with cold, unstable air as it moves across warmer waters. Under the right conditions of resentment, separation, judgment, guilt, and fear the air bursts forth with gale-force winds and heavy rain until everything in its path is destroyed. The only way to save yourself is to get out. The problem was I refused to listen to the voice telling me to look closer at the instability of my container with Quincy. All the red signs were blinking "warning, warning" but by then, I had closed my eyes and hunkered down, believing my love for him could withstand any storm.

I had tasted the terror of those blinking lights right at the beginning of our relationship, once we had become intimate. It was our second motel rendezvous after graduation. He was my man and I wanted ultimate intimacy—his mouth all over me kissing, licking, nibbling, making me moist, moving me to endless sensations of gratification and pleasure like I had imagined from the movies. Just at the right moment, I wasn't afraid to ask for something specific. Quincy dislodged himself swiftly with a mouthful of venomous insults that cut me like a razor and reminded me of Dad's tirades. I became a snail covered in salt. On the drive home, he turned away. The next morning he spoke only to his father and when I tried to touch him, he pulled his hand away. My world crashed around me. Two days later, all was forgotten; he rallied in my corner and we never spoke again of what he felt was an *inappropriate* request. I should have known that you can't sweep those kinds of emotions under a rug forever. They just fester, inflame, and spill over, causing a more critical condition to erupt.

Those same warning lights showed up a year later after Quincy moved in with me for the first time. One evening he walked in with his white obi tied around his waist. I wasn't even aware he was taking karate. He grabbed me off the bed, threw me down, and held me too tightly, while I struggled. After I shouted, "You're hurting me," he released his grip around my neck and laughed. "I'm practicing for my next level." I sulked and told myself, *He's cruel and mean. How could I ever love him*? But I shooed the feeling away like a fly.

At the Monterey Jazz Festival I blamed our first experience with LSD for the painful cigarette burn on my hand. Next day he claimed not to remember smoking a cigarette. *Was it possible he temporarily lost his mind*? I didn't want to know, but the warning signs were flashing on and off.

After moving to Berkeley, two more blinking lights glared in my face. A four-hour lockout in the cold on our balcony while I beat on the glass doors. "Quincy, please, please let me in." He looked at me, while a friend settled on our living-room couch, drinking wine. The last blink occurred right after Christmas when he sat on me in a body lock and watched me cry and plead. Each time those warning lights turned off, he apologized, denied it, blamed it on tension and marijuana.

Fear smoldered, but I was determined to put out the embers it was trying to ignite, for he made me legitimate and I was sure he loved me. I had come to learn from Dad that being loved and loving sometimes comes with unexplained hurt and pain. With confidence, I told myself he would never harm me again, now that we were engaged.

ᐰSLOW DEATHᐰ

We had six weeks and counting marked by the beginning of Mardi Gras in New Orleans. I had just checked off the last set of wedding items when Quincy arrived home late on Friday. His voice sounded like all the life had been sucked out of him as he spoke his first words, "I'm going home tomorrow to see my father."

"What?" I questioned, concerned. "Is he all right? Is he still coming to our wedding? Is there anything I can do?"

"Dad's fine," he said solemnly. "I need to go home."

I was baffled, not so much that he was going home, but by the absolute lack of a hint or pre-warning that this was coming. And then, just like that, our discussion was over. The wolves chased me that night.

The next morning, it took all of thirty minutes for him to throw clothes in an overnight bag, peck me on the lips, and close the door. He must have arrived at the airport on a magic carpet because he refused a ride from me. Immediately, I felt a chilly breeze come over me as Quincy walked out the door. I tried to talk myself out of the sensation, but had to admit a toxic silence had seeped under the door, beating my head like a drum and wondered, *What is this all about*?

Monday passed slowly. Wednesday lasted forever. By Friday, my fingernails were bitten off and my prescription for migraines needed refilling.

The Quincy I had grown to accept and love never returned. His 6'1" lean frame walked through the door one week later with a faraway look. At first I tried to remain calm.

"Did someone die? Is your dad ill? Your mother? Are you sick? What's wrong?"

Resting with his head folded over his arms on the bed, not one word did he utter, his lips fused together like petrified fossils. I became more alarmed, unable to imagine the mysterious secret known only to him. Nothing loosened his tongue. Boxes of invitations sat stamped in the corner. I wrung my hands, pushed salad from one side of my plate to the other, took the phone off the hook, tiptoed, threw my arms against his cold back, waited for his ice to thaw. One week and one day later, his mouth moved and his body rose.

"Let's go for a walk." It was Sunday!

Witness to each other's solitude, we walked the cracked side-walks, kicking imaginary cans, his fingers laced between mine. It was a cold, gray day and my gut told me, *Something awful is coming your way.* A squirrel bobbed and weaved across the street as my thoughts rose up high, flipped, and tumbled again like a kite. By the time we arrived at our favorite hamburger joint several blocks away, I want-ed it over and looked deep into his face. Seven words met my ears, changing me forever. "I want to call off the wedding." He offered no excuse or apology. It felt like a sumo wrestler had grabbed me from behind and held me in a vise until I nearly passed out.

Walking home, I didn't grovel or flinch. I simply went on automat-ic pilot and put one foot in front of the other. *What had happened? Had my natural way of being gotten me in trouble again? What had I done wrong?* Basking in the sunlight of loving him, I pulled grapes from the vine of undying affection, coddled, cooked, cleaned, zipped my mouth from curious questions, even blinded my eyes from those blinking red signs. Quincy's words had torn through my flesh like shark's teeth.

In a haze I dialed my parents' home and hung up before anyone picked up. On the fifth attempt, words somehow formed. "Mom, I've got something to tell you." From that moment on, my body switched to its own life support, keeping me breathing and my organs func-tioning. I felt nothing except a blade dissecting every chamber of my heart.

Quincy's darkness seemed to drain down the sink with our evening meal dishes. That night I closed the door, crawled into bed, and wished that I would never awaken. It seemed as though sometime during the night, I bought a one-way ticket to the museum of withdrawal and empty spaces. My automatic pilot bathed me, dressed me, drove me to work as my heart bled. My head split with pain, worrying about what other people would think. There were no stars, moon, or radiant sunset light. All that was left was the darkest darkness. *Where will I live? What will I say? Who will love me now? What about our rings? My dress? Save me somebody, please save me*, I screamed, but heard no response.

With the lease in Quincy's name, the choice was simple; I would move out, the sooner the better. But he wanted me to stay and tried to simplify our situation.

"The wedding was too much of a production. I wanted something small. I love you. We'll still get married; not now, but maybe we'll go to Reno."

Desperate for answers, I called his mother. She was generous with apologies but couldn't shed any light on Quincy's mood. Our friends reached out with their own theories, trying to calm me down and give me hope. "He'll change his mind. It's nerves. Just don't push." But our perfect, warm, sunny day in April came and went.

Call me a fool, but the possibility of a simple answer never entered my thoughts.

Months before our wedding, Quincy had introduced a new couple into our lives. They weren't my kind of people and for the life of me, I couldn't understand Quincy's fascination with them, least of all his laughter at their sordid jokes and simple stories. I said nothing to weekend movies or Sunday dinners, but they bothered me like an allergic itch. Alone with Maggie one evening after our canceled wedding, she noticed my grieving. "Girl, you need to get yourself together, because Quincy is seeing somebody else. Somebody from his college days. She's been living here for three months." I didn't want to believe her, but something inside told me, It's true. By the time the guys returned from the store, my mind had moved to the factory, assembling all the pieces leading up to Quincy's announcement. *Someone from his college days. Another woman. But why wouldn't he want me to move out?*

Days floated from one to the next, while I drifted in and out of reality. On good days, I made myself believe he would change his mind and come back to his senses. I had not forgotten how my credibility depended on our marriage and clung to the belief our continued cohabitation was a sign from God that the fruit on our love tree needed just a little more time to ripen. I had no choice but to continue the masquerade and was grateful to be waking up to his face each morning, knowing I was nothing without him! But at the same time, I could feel something dark and ugly stirring inside as I stared at his back at night; a sickening feeling that scared me when I thought about it erupting. I wore a halo for Quincy's benefit, but angrily ripped days off the calendar wondering, *Is this the final act?*

On the Fourth of July weekend, Quincy awoke bouncier than he'd been in weeks. "I'm going to Los Angeles to visit my grandmother."

I waited for the rest of his sentence, before asking with a childlike plea, "Are you taking me?"

He turned away. "No, I want to go alone, I need a couple of days to think." His words sliced me in two, but I carefully concealed my face. *What the hell does he need to think about; I'm the one who's being jilted.*

Dreaming during the night, all I heard were voices: *Cancel our wedding, woman from college, I'm going out, don't wait up, I want to be alone.* I woke up in a sweat, jolted by what felt like a 7.5 earthquake, sat up and looked straight at the clock. It was 2:43 a.m. Every nerve ending fired. I didn't want to face my decision, but I knew what had to be done.

I stumbled downstairs to Troy and Florence once the sun came up. "Quincy went to L.A. I've decided I'm moving, enough is enough." As soon as the words tumbled out, I asked God for strength and spoke the words again three times. *You're leaving Quincy!*

My friend Claudia greeted my phone call like I was a lost puppy. "Oh sugar, I'm so sorry. You come over whenever you're packed and stay as long as you like on the couch."

As my hands trembled, I hoped Quincy would walk in to stop me from filling boxes so I could shake my head indignantly and say, "No, I'm moving unless you marry me now." By early afternoon, Troy had picked up the last box. I feebly sorted through the 45's looking for the right record to leave on the turntable, and found these words by Aretha. "I love you and I love you and I love you. My dearest darling, I know we've got to part. But, I'm keeping you in my heart. Will you call me, 'cause I love you." It said everything I couldn't—a message of confusion and conflict. In the moment I meant every word of it—but maybe because there wasn't a record called "Kill Him."

Troy knocked softly. "Let me know when you're ready," as I turned for one last scent of memory, smothering my head in Quincy's pillow.

After three days on Claudia's couch and no word from Quincy, I picked up the phone and sucked in my pride.

"Mom, may I come home?"

Moving into my old room snapped me back to reality. *What am I doing? Quincy is my everything, the only way to complete me.* I persuaded myself life was not worth living without him and prepared myself to beg for his forgiveness. On Saturday, I drove to Dwight Way and parked, waiting for my adrenaline rush to settle down. I was almost ready to slam my car door when the garage opened and his baby-blue car pulled out. Brown skin and long hair occupied the passenger's seat. Shaking, I tried to settle myself. *Maybe she's a friend? Was she there all night? Where are they going? Should I follow? Is he thinking of me?* The blade in my heart pressed deeper. I was terrified of what I might do next, certain I couldn't survive a face-to-face showdown.

I was a glutton for punishment because the next morning, I parked around the corner again. I refused to believe the evidence and kept telling myself, *There is a logical explanation.* But when the garage door went up, I got a good look. The girl sat proudly admiring him—the way she did that college graduation day.

My worst fears were confirmed. Finally understanding, I fell right through a gaping black hole to the place I'd heard about in Dad's sermons—the place of pitchforks and hollow eyes.

ℛUNBEARABLE ACHE✍

I wanted to twist my head off my body and begged the invisible winds, *Please God, make this go away!* What good was pain, anyway, except to leave you withering on some forsaken battlefield within yourself, hoping, begging, praying someone or something would strike with such a force, that all traces of misery would implode and vanish. But God was off attending Vacation Bible School. I got used to puffy eyes and was sure they would stay that way permanently. At work, the gas station, ordering a burger, I saw pity in people's eyes, whether I knew them or not. Feeling totally abandoned, I returned to church, the only place I could hide in peace where my scars wouldn't matter. At the altar praying, I would have sold my soul to the devil to get Quincy back. He was mine!

After living with my parents for two months, I was suffocating. Although they never talked to me about my situation, I was sure Mom and Dad were whispering about my dilemma. And Dad reminded me in his new, gentle way there was still a curfew and I had a responsibility to show even more respect as the grown daughter. It all made for more unhappiness. I needed space for my own self-pity to flourish without feeling guilty, disgraced, or obligated.

There was only one thought that pressed against my cerebrum. *How do you love and hate someone at the same time*? Oh, how I wanted to be near Quincy, as if the sight of him would organically fuel me to the moon, but at the same time, I knew if I saw him walking across the street, I would try to run him over.

The one-bedroom vacancy sign on Alcatraz Avenue was right on the city limits between Oakland and Berkeley. The old property manager reminded me of Ichabod Crane in *Sleepy Hollow* as his bony fingers unlatched the glass door. The walls needed painting, the bathroom fixtures were green from mildew, deep scratches cut into the hardwood floors, and shredded drapes covered broken windows that rattled. The worst offense by far, however, was the smell of dried urine hitting me in the face. But it was cheap and the landlord didn't hassle me with details on the application, once I said, "I'll pay you today in cash." I moved in immediately, settling into my self-proclaimed jail of doom. Two weeks later, I invited my folks for a visit. The next day Mom called. "Your dad cried all the way home."

At work I robotically performed my duties well enough to keep the supervisors off my back. At night, the tears kept rolling. Marijuana and cheap wine became my breakfast, dinner, and friend, encouraging thoughts of suicide. I cut my hair into a boyish, unattractive natural and wore heavy black makeup in hopes of avoiding male attention. And at the same time, I drew stares and whistles from passing cars of men, after trading my Toyota for a red TR6 convertible with no down payment. Once in a while I'd drag myself to a party, but I'd sit in a trance loathing the kissing couples who swayed to the slow beat of Smokey Robinson, The Ohio Players, and Gladys Knight, my head nearly collapsing from too much booze. Dressed in tie-dye, peasant skirts, and low cut blouses exposing breasts hanging freely, sometimes, I became the third wheel with Troy and Florence—Taj Mahal, Santana, Blood Sweat and Tears, Jefferson Airplane, Grateful Dead; we saw them all. As long as I dulled my senses, kept moving, danced to wild music, and drove dangerously fast, I was fine. But in the quiet long days and nights, I found myself in a well with no bottom.

To ease my suffering, I opened the doors of my apartment, inviting in whoever looked like they needed a place to crash. I entertained with chili or tuna casserole, spending everything but my last few dollars. I stapled a stack of book covers I found in a dumpster on my walls, creating a psychedelic entrance, bought a cheap, king-sized water bed for the living room, strobe lights and a red bulb for the kitchen. By the time I was finished, my dump created the perfect atmosphere for anything-goes conversation, smoking fat reefers, dancing to Chaka Khan, and drinking rum and coke. Sometimes, in the middle of the night, I'd open my eyes wondering *Who is this person on top of me*? And then remember—oh, you are the man with the rap telling me how interesting, smart, beautiful, hip, and sexy I am. All I felt about myself was contempt and revulsion; the taste of disgust coated my teeth each morning. Self-loathing ran freely through my veins.

Strangely, my brother tuned into me like a homing device. He knew exactly when I needed a visit. Making his way as a high-school senior, he didn't need or want anything from me—nothing except his big, silly sister. I made light of the dump I lived in, boasting about my freedom, hoping he couldn't see the sadness behind my eye sockets. Sometimes he brought friends from school, kids I would never have guessed would hang out with my proper brother; a few even smoked marijuana. I didn't want them getting in trouble in the streets and offered my place anytime they wanted. I'm pretty sure my free lifestyle helped my brother's peers to see him in a different light. He started out quiet and somewhat estranged from the group, but won the last term of vice-presidency of his senior class as a crowd-pleaser.

Every visit from my brother ended with a big hug and the special words "I love you" that meant more to me than I was willing to admit at the time. But once the door was shut, I returned to the dark side of myself that was always lurking. And I still couldn't stop crying.

A younger man in my building started knocking on my door, hanging around, showing attention and admiring me. He reminded me of myself, lost and filled with sadness. For my birthday, he bought me a puppy, a black and white poodle I named Mister. I thanked him with my body. All the unfulfilled expressions of failure and abandoned love poured into Mister as he cocked his head to one side like he understood my burdens and brokenness until the day I came home and found him chewing up my shoes—the ones from Quincy. I screamed, yelled, and beat the walls, sending Mister scurrying under the sofa. A week later, it happened again, but this time lava spilled from my volcano. I popped Mister with a newspaper, until I saw blood trickle from his nose. I dropped the newspaper like a red-hot poker, shaking with shame, "No, no, no! I'm sorry, I love you," as a sickening feeling rose like vomit. I had released the dragon. The truth knocked me over. I was Dad—a Jekyll and Hyde, a beater, a dangerous threat who could turn deadly in a flash.

Right then and there I made a promise to honor until my death. I would place my hands around the throat of rage, press my fingers tightly against its flesh, squeeze and squeeze while it choked and spit until it lay collapsed, and lifeless. Dad's kind of abuse intertwined with my deep feelings of self-hatred would never be passed to another. No matter what I had to do, I could never be trusted to give birth to another human being. I would never parent a person like myself—a neurotic person.

The realization that, *I have become what I most detested* forced me to look at myself, even though my eyes wished to be blinded. One morning after a stranger left I asked myself, "Who have you become? Do you see the reflection of the person you used to be?" My eyes sagged; my face was gray; I trembled. "You're a nobody, a dropout, a bum. You tried to fool Quincy, but he saw right through you." I tore at my face, screaming, "Daddy can't save you, nobody can. Even Jesus has forsaken you. You got what you deserved." Faced with the truth, I reached for the aspirin bottle as the only way to bring me sweet peace. Lying resolved on the bed, I grabbed paper and pen. *Got to leave a note.*

> Mom and Dad,
>
> I can't stop the pain and it hurts too bad to go on. I'm nothing without Quincy. I'm sorry I was such a disappointment. Give my stereo to Robert. Kiss Kelesha and Aunt Bea.
>
> I'm sorry. I love you. Please take care of Mister.
>
> Ro

I didn't know who would find me, but I hoped it wouldn't take days, like the man I had read about who got eaten by his dog after suffering a heart attack. Quincy would receive the news, cry, and hang his head low and feel terrible, carrying my death to his grave. I left everything neat the way Mom had taught me, so when I was found she wouldn't be embarrassed. I put on my favorite silk, melon-colored pajamas and sat on the bed. Steadying my right wrist with my left hand, I threw the pills in my mouth and washed them down with brandy. Thoughts of my green evening dress passed by, along with Mom's red V-neck sweater, Marilyn, piano sonatas, and Little Princess. I thought of waltzing as a debutante and Howard University, and wondered where I'd be if I had been able to fulfill what had been promised. Death scared me, but living scared me more.

I don't know how long I was out, but when my eyes opened dizziness, disorientation, and heart palpitations came with it. I barely reached the scummy toilet bowl, gagging and heaving until nothing was left. I lay crumpled on the floor and the scruffy linoleum collected hot tears. I was disappointed. *Not enough pills.*

Hours later, I drowsily opened my eyes, weaving unsteadily, and stumbled to my knees, mouth dry with tiny muffles of moaning, "Thank you, God, for saving me." I kept repeating it over and over again, strangling on my words, not sure why I was thankful—the heavy pain was pounding in my chest. But I couldn't question God's decision to leave me breathing and didn't want to think. My head was throbbing. I pulled at my hair trying not to remember, *You tried to kill yourself.* As I breathed in the darkness of the night, I knew God had given me another chance. But where could I turn to find the help and the strength to push past my own self-destruction?

SHAME

Dr. Marcus Foster, the first black superintendent of Oakland Schools, lay dead, murdered by the Symbionese Liberation Army. Our family felt a particular sadness as Robert was dating his only daughter. As I saw the anguish on her face, a tender new root sprouted and I pledged to heal old wounds with Dad.

After almost a year of wearing hot pants and long suede boots, arguing venomously with men and trying to act tough, my loneliness caught up with me. The streets were hard, and the free lifestyle of a non-committed hippie wasn't my way. I was too weak to be a full-fledged rebel. And at heart, I was really still a soft-spoken gentle girl. Once more, I asked my parents if I could move home. I had listened to Dad preach the story of the prodigal son wasting his fortune and being welcomed back by his father many times. I was the prodigal daughter. The only consideration was my poodle Mister. Dad said, "You are welcomed, but that dog's got to go." I cried my eyes out leaving him at the SPCA, but it was either him or me. Both my parents treated me with kindness and never once threw my past in my face. There was much they didn't know, but I could tell they sensed the battle scars as I sat quietly in thought, often crying as I watched movies. Having shelter, wholesome food, and clean living eased my mind, preparing me for whatever was next—the unknown.

Quiet moments were spent reflecting, comparing, as feelings of jealousy rose up in my throat choking me. Peers from church and school were graduating, marrying, securing successful careers, purchasing homes, having families, traveling. *Those were my dreams too!* I still didn't understand what went wrong, why I had stumbled and felt I had taken the fool's path. Had my own will betrayed me? I wanted integrity, responsibility, and truth. Truth about myself, my friendships, my intimate relationships. I wanted real communication—factual, straight-shooting, open, forthright, honest. I wanted the truth, even though I knew sometimes it would hurt my feelings. I knew I'd have to work hard to get it and keep it, but it was the only door to choose to feel sane again.

No eraser was large enough to wipe away the past. I had to wake up from the television-inspired story of happiness flapping in my lap. I had to shake things up. I had to realize circumstances in my life would not change just because I wished them to, even as I also thought, if I had a magic wand I could use it! In order to change my life, I needed to quit my job, give up my sports car, stop smoking grass, go back to college, and remove the people surrounding me. The demon on both shoulders toyed with my mind. *It sounds easy. Give it all up. Turn your life around. Who are you fooling? You will never amount to nothing!* And as I rattled through my archives of Dad's lessons, I recalled, "Words are empty without action."

My faith was shaky, but it was all I had to give me strength to face a bad-ass, seedy world. I could have stayed with my parents, but it was important to take every next step on my own. I was feeling worthless and it took every fiber of discipline not to spend money on frivolous things to make me temporarily feel better. After a few months of saving every dime, I found an apartment within walking distance from our church; allowed my car to be repossessed, which humiliated me further; and submitted my resignation at work. I was like a newly released prisoner with no idea how to support myself, eat, or get from one location to the next. But the thought of almost dying forced me to remember, *There is a reason you survived!*

Dad taught Black Studies at my new college, and picked me up three days a week. It was a humbling experience—like learning how to walk again. I applied for financial aid and received just enough to take care of myself by counting every penny. It was difficult; I still coveted the prosperity of others.

It had been over six years since my college days and I felt old looking around at the bright faces of eighteen-year-olds, worried my time of learning had passed. On the first day of registration, Oregon insecurities flooded over me when the registrant couldn't locate my packet. It was misfiled.

In school, I dived in timidly, asking myself, *What brings you joy? What comes naturally? What do you want to do in life?* You may think after all I had experienced, the answers would come easily. They didn't. In fact, it would take many, many years before I came to a place of peace about why I was born. But one thing was for sure; nobody could cancel me out again for not having my education. Especially me.

ᗒWET WINGSᗔ

Dad's face was the same. His voice was the same and he still stood six feet, with a tiny paunch. His hair had begun to bald in the middle, but he camouflaged that spot with ingenious maneuvering and hair spray. But as I slipped into the front seat, I was looking at a new man—from his stylish slacks and sweaters, platform shoes, colorful sport jackets, and sideburns to his maroon Mustang. While I was off getting kicked around by the world, he had morphed. He sure wasn't the Dad I had known! I guessed being liberated from presiding elders, bishops, competing pastors, and the threat of being shipped off allowed him to become a peacock. In all ways, his faith was stronger; being knocked off his throne appeared to have been an eye-opener. But by pursuing his Master's and doctoral degrees, his once-hard doctrine of loving Jesus had softened. He seemed more human—more empathetic, and connected to spirit in his soul. No subject was off limits, from drugs to homosexuality. Talking with him became natural, easy, and peaceful, like snuggling up to a warm fire. I'd find myself laughing with him at the silly things. With a new sense of safety I had never felt before in our relationship, I fell in love with him all over again.

Dad became my deep-sea depth-finder and my anchor as I kept to myself at college, afraid I might self-destruct again with the distraction of friendship. I had to buckle down through statistics and dissecting rats, choosing psychology and Black Studies as areas of concentration. I was proud when students came up to me in the two classes I took from Dad and asked, "Are you Dr. Thomas's daughter?" If I could have made it on his reputation, I would have been home free. But Dad gave tough examinations, and expected me to ace his classes. I did. But numbers and formulas kept me up nights as two years dragged by slowly.

After graduation in 1975, I put on the happy face, but within was no closer to finding my own niche. Confusion and emptiness followed me around like a lost puppy. Wasn't a college education designed to prepare me for the rest of my life? Where was the passion? I sure didn't feel it filling out applications and reading want ads. I had bills to pay and no more financial aid. After three months I was flat-out discouraged. Dad rode in like the cavalry. "Show up at the Community Action Agency at 11:00 on Tuesday for an interview." I didn't want to be indebted, but rent was due.

The director was controlled and suave, opening the interview with a monologue. He liked hearing himself talk and bragged—about knowing Dad, going to a Southern college, and marching with Martin Luther King, Jr. I looked him straight in the eye.

It was twenty minutes before he asked me a question. "What do you like? What subjects interested you in college?" I wondered, *When are the tough questions coming?* "Describe your experience? Give me an example of how you would handle this situation? Here's a scenario—solve the problem using customer service and teamwork." I had heard them all before and concluded, *This isn't going very well.*

Sweat rolled down my white blouse, dampening the back of my one navy-blue pinstriped suit.

"You like people?" He quickly answered his own question. "Of course you do, or you wouldn't be here."

His secretary knocked on the door to remind him of a lunch engagement, and he stood after fifty-five minutes. I felt dejected as his put out his hand until he smiled. "Be here Monday at 8:00." You should have seen my eyes; I looked like Lightnin' *from Amos and Andy.*" Couldn't tell you my job title or my salary. All I knew was I was an employee of the City of Oakland; a working girl.

That Sunday morning I threw my head back, singing and clapping until my hands turned pink. I shuffled around so long on my knees during altar call that the usher had to signal me to get up. "Amen, Amen," I said so loudly that people in front of me turned around to see who was praising the Lord. From the pulpit, I caught Dad smiling directly at me. It felt so good!

IN THE RIVER'S FLOW

Life took on a structured, new rhythm as I learned more about my job as an outreach worker. I was shy when it came to small talk, but quite comfortable speaking in front of the predominantly black staff. After several weeks, I still wasn't completely sure what I was supposed to be doing, but I flipped through the papers on my desk each day trying to look important. Assigned to work in East Oakland, I was bewildered by my supervisor who spent hours gossiping on the phone, leaving for mystery appointments, and eating greasy food at her desk right in front of our customers. It wasn't hard work, just frustrating trying to match people with jobs, and provide food, temporary housing, and safety for battered women and children.

I attended church dutifully, choosing to hang out whenever I could with Dad. I'd meet him for lunch as he proudly recited all the latest hip expressions, "What it is? You looo-king gooood! How's the gig? Far out, right on, can you dig it? Catch you on the flip side." Stopping for soup and salad or hamburgers and fries, I'd listen to how he talked cheerfully without boundaries, my heart warmed by this new man—one who would never have forsaken promises, treated me cruelly, or closed his eyes to his rage. Dad was hanging out, cracking jokes, and even taking a little nip of wine at special occasions. I still shook my head. *Not the Dad I knew.*

For a while, I had Mom and Dad to myself. After graduating from

UC Davis, my brother left me his car while he joined the Peace Corps and headed straight to Kenya. Kelesha was three hours away, attending Chico State, balancing studies with partying. We spent every Sunday enjoying dinner, laughing about Flip Wilson dressed like a woman, the bigotry on *All in the Family, Good Times* and the foul mouth of Richard Pryor. With a job, my own apartment, and a sense of accomplishment I figured I could finally rest!

Feeling rooted for the first time in a long while, I chose to celebrate with a small gathering. Nothing special. Old friends, except for one, but no boyfriend. My heart still belonged to Quincy, even though I put up a very good front. The one guy I didn't know kept catching my eye. He reminded me of a 200-pound linebacker as he leaned against the wall in his beige sweater and slacks. He stayed on the fringes, laughing at the stories, but just enough not to seem snobbish. As the crowd thinned, I halfway expected him to corner me. He didn't; just held out his hand. "Nice party. Very nice to meet you. Hope to see you again." Over the next two months, Matthew managed to be with my friend Dena whenever she dropped by unannounced. Their visits were short, enough for one drink and a quick catch-up on gossip. After three visits, my curiosity got the best of me.

"Girl, are you sure he's not your man?"

"No, but he really likes you."

"What? Didn't notice, you know I'm not interested in no man," I quickly responded. It wasn't true.

Dena and Matthew found me tangled in stereo wires on their next visit. "You know music is my savior, my best friend, and I got to have it!" I snapped.

"Mind if I take a look?" Matthew asked.

"Are you mechanical? Do you know what you're doing?" I didn't want anybody messing up my new equipment.

He just began inspecting the mess I had made, pulling and tugging until an hour later, he had totally rewired my system.

"Who hooked this up?," he asked. "I'm surprised it worked at all."

"A friend," I lied. "Let me pay you," I offered.

"No, I don't want your money. But how about going out with me for dinner?" One date turned into two and before I knew it, we were a couple.

Matthew attended the police academy, attracted by the pay. Abandoned by his mother, he loved his eighth-grade-educated great-aunt and-uncle who raised him.

From our first conversations, I could tell he wanted the American dream, but his desires seemed practical without a lot of drama. Lots of quiet space fell between our sharing with a slow, easy pace reminding me of light rain on a Southern country morning. As Winter set, I felt safer than I had for a long time, uncompromised by his calmness. My heart wasn't throbbing, but he was respectful and undemanding. I felt, *Maybe I can care again.*

One night during dinner at our favorite Mexican restaurant, he surprised me. "We both want a home: we could save money if you moved in with me." I hesitated, pulled by the memory of living with Quincy and what I would tell Dad. But by the time I downed my second margarita I had made up my mind, impressed by Matthew's spacious two-bedroom lake apartment with the romantic fireplace and contemporary burnt orange and beige furniture. On the surface, he appeared to be one of the good guys and gave me his undivided attention. I thought, *What harm will it do to live with him. I can save my money.* Honestly, I didn't know what I wanted in a boyfriend or what I wanted at all, but the need to be with someone—anyone—was still a vibrant flame that engulfed my heart. I had tried being alone. I wasn't enough for me! Hanging with Matthew felt like a good way to fill in the spaces, and I didn't see any harm in pairing up with a person with the same dreams.

❦CHILLIN'❧

Matthew reminded me of my meticulous mom. He was constantly picking up after himself, and every article had its proper place. Most days when I got home from work, I'd find him in the second bedroom listening to meditation tapes. I couldn't figure out what he got out of sitting in silence with his eyes closed going "Ommmm." Cooking for two, holding hands, watching movies, and having the same arms caress me in the dark felt satisfying. I compared my sensations each time he held me, waiting for the hot coals to ignite. After a while, I gave up and resigned myself. *A burning heart isn't necessary to be happy.*

My luggage didn't have one cobweb when the doorbell rang one sunny afternoon. An attractive woman with fire in her eyes stood glaring at me through the screen door.

"Where's Matthew?" she snapped.

"Just a minute," I said, not quite sure of the look on her face.

As he turned the corner all I could hear from her was, "Who is this bitch?" She burst through the screen door and headed straight for the kitchen, grabbed a black skillet, and came after me.

I ran around the table, covering my head. *Who is this crazy person?* She clawed at me like a wild animal, screaming obscenities, as Matthew pushed her out the door.

"Who's she?" I demanded, panting heavily and scared out of my wits.

"My old girlfriend, Gwynne. We broke up way before I met you," he kept saying, reaching out to touch me. The bells in my head went off. *I can't go through this again, I'm out of here....*

As I thought about what to do next, I stopped, realizing I had never told Matthew the truth about my past. I poured out the story of my brokenness, locked away like a forbidden treasure as he held my hand. When I finished, he said, "Now I understand. I won't hurt you. I promise." Lying in his arms I said to myself *I've got to start trusting sometime,* hopeful Matthew was the right choice.

ᕲᒃBALANCING ACTᔆᕕ

By the Summer of 1976, a pattern had developed; silence on the end of the receiver and late nights once a week without an explanation from Matthew. I was old enough to know, *This is not a good sign.* But what words would I use to say what I was thinking? How would I position my body—hold my hands? Would I raise my voice, point my finger, accuse, swallow hard then blurt out something inflammatory? Would I stand still, stomp, or pace? Would I pierce his eyes, look away? Be guarded like a mommy robin bird watching her nest? Should I allow warm tears to roll down my face and settle in little splotches of wetness staining my paisley blouse? Should I be stoic, bite my lip—wipe the blood from my wounded knee and go back up the hill? I didn't think of myself as brave or courageous enough to express the words, "This is what inspires me to be in a relationship." I didn't know what inspired me, except the thought of rejection. I didn't want rejection attacking my soul like a rabid dog. As I thought back, the only real conversation I'd ever had with Matthew was the story of brokenness. And when I thought about it more, I wondered, had I ever had a real conversation with anyone, afraid if I allowed myself to breathe for one moment the truth soaring in my heart, Dad's belt or backhand would catch me in mid-sentence. Love would evaporate. I needed to be loved.

All around me men and, surprisingly women were cheating on

each other. The women would say, "Girl, what's good for the goose is good for the gander." I acknowledged these words of unfaithfulness as a cheap coping mechanism of "get back." In the end, the only person hurt was the one doing the cheating. I wanted to believe another alternative beckoned to me. Faith. Truth. Dedication. What if I had the patience to pick up my shovel, bend over, put some sweat into it and dig, dig, dig like the couples I knew from my parents' generation? I'd hit the bottom, find redemption, and cultivate our love from the roots. I was sure if I tried—if we both tried—we could grow into a strong tree. Why couldn't I say these words to Matthew—let's really try to tell the truth, have faith and dedicate ourselves to each other? Why couldn't I believe that I was a candidate for redemption?

What came easier was to numb myself by swearing to an allegiance of illusion. *It will work itself out*, I told myself. The truth was staring me right in the face, but honesty's price was too high for me to pay. Frustrated, I ended up at a party with Dena one night, pouring out my troubles, looking to become a gander. She was sure my imagination was playing tricks on me.

"He loves you, I know he does because he tells me all the time how much you mean to him. How fortunate he is to have you. Call him, and go on home before you strike back without cause."

By the third time I dialed our number and got a busy signal, I was worried. I broke city limits speeding home, wondering if Matthew was okay.

As I slipped my key in the chamber, the door slightly opened, held securely by the chain lock. Wanting to believe it was locked in error, I pressed my thumb against the doorbell repeatedly, listening through the tiny opening for any signs of movement. My knuckles ached as I knocked and knocked. Nothing but silence. *Maybe he's in the shower.* I waited, pressed the doorbell and knocked again and again before calling him from the corner store. Still busy. The serpent of fear and anger I knew too well began to awake. *What if he's hurt? Why am I locked out?*

I paced back and forth against the railing as the serpent swam in circles, until my brown platform shoe landed solid in the center of the door, sending a hard jolt through my body. I kicked again and again until the hinges gave way, hoping I wasn't too late for 911. All I heard was my breath entering the cold darkness as I braced myself for the worst.

I discovered Matthew spread out like he was shooting a center-fold, eyes closed, talking on the phone with his hands moving under his leopard caftan. He was in such deep lust with whoever was on the other end of the line that he didn't even hear me. Disgusted, I slowly removed my clothes and went to sleep. The next morning, he was the one pacing, back and forth like a caged animal shouting hysterically.

"What happened to the door? What happened to the door?"

I was cool and calm; rather proud of myself for the strength I had been able to muster. "You locked me out, so I kicked it in."

I purchased an imaginary magnifying glass, hoping I could read the fine print that would show me the way through whatever was next for my life. Was I so desperate I was unable to see the obvious? Or had I chosen a situation and a man that would help me hide from myself? My fears? My path of finding me? Was I even interested in pursuing the conversations required to build a strong tree? Or was I all mouth, avoiding and pretending? I was no longer sure of anything other than the fact that everything had gone wrong in my life. When was I going to shake hands with the past? Call it a fair fight. Replace the bitter with the sweet. Why couldn't I move on and mend? For-give myself for the choices I'd made and the choices that had been made for me. When would the words respect and confidence burst through my four-chambered heart and flood me with serenity?

I wasn't sure what scared me more—hearing his true confessions or confessing to myself, "I will no longer be a victim."

Moving out wasn't easy. But I was determined to be the conductor. No more second string for me. At least when it came to another woman. My only choice was to put myself before Matthew.

Within weeks Matthew was calling, apologizing and making promises I wanted to believe. At night I'd spread my hands across the right side of the unmade bed and weep, remembering his warm body next to mine, convinced I needed him. Parties and social activities took on the color of gray as rejection's perfume dabbed itself behind my ears and between my breasts. The familiar voices engaged in battle, *Better take what you can get; you're spoiled goods. Nobody wants you. You're dead wrong. I'm a good person, a deceit human being. I deserve better.*

Months passed. Flowers bloomed, wilted, and died as Fall's first frost settled on leaves of gold and rust. I leaned in a little closer each time Matthew made a promise—"You're the only girl for me"—until snap, I was right back in the same trap with nothing within me to believe, *You can do this alone.*

I told myself, This time would be different. No more dishonesty. No more façade. Living life as a lie, pretending things were okay when they weren't, didn't work. I needed every ounce of my true self to navigate where I was going. I was thirsty for an answer, any answer, as the idea of redemption continued to make tiny noises in the attic of my mind, scurrying around in the light before disappearing into dark corners. I knew it would take strength and fortitude for simple everyday decisions, but wasn't I a grown-up? Yet, each day had me second-guessing myself. One moment I'd be beating up myself over my mistakes, obsessing over the fairy-tale dream, and thinking about Quincy. *If only* became my tormenting theme. *Why am I thinking about Quincy when Matthew is here?* And then I'd be strong, filled with the faith of David as he slew Goliath. I too had powerful pebbles to hurl. All I needed was to hold on to faith.

Doubt in myself and my relationship persuaded me that I had to somehow regain the strength to swim steadily and strongly against the tide that held me back from being me. I couldn't understand why all my efforts felt fixated on one idea—to simply exist. Didn't I have dreams, hopes, imagination, creativity? Wasn't I going to make something of myself, be of service to others, help make life better because of some contribution? Funny and sad, how easily I had lost my way and forgotten!

I knew my father held the magic key, or so I told myself, as *If only* continued to chime like a cathedral bell in my ears. I had little distinction of what was real or false. All I knew was it felt good to blame my father for his unforgiving sin—the beating and broken promises that fueled me like a coal engine. But I resolved to spend time with him having grown-up conversations where we sometimes could disagree without regressing into an all-out fight. It drew me closer to him... closer to believing that I could one day ask him point-blank, "Why did you raise me this way? Why were you so brutal? Why did you try to kill my spirit?" I would earnestly listen to his responses with an open mind. I hoped it would lead me to a deeper understanding of myself, and why my life turned out the way it did. I was certain that the deeper I understood this, the closer I would come to redemption. For now, the hardest work would continue to be trying to erase the flashbacks of defeat by accepting me in all the ways I was... for me.

I would soon learn that the hardest work was yet to come, shattering me with the force of an apocalypse.

ᝰTWO BIRDS – ONE STONEᝰ

I t didn't take Dad long after Matthew moved in to share his truth. "I'm not happy. How can I preach to the congregation about the Bible when my daughter is living in sin? Why don't you get married?"

I couldn't help but think, *I don't care a hoot about the congregation. What if the good, holy people knew your secret—knew how you beat me?* I wasn't out for revenge, I was taking a stand.

"I love you, Dad, but you can't tell me what to do anymore."

Ironically, my feelings toward Matthew plagued me. I wasn't sure how much he meant to me. An older woman gave me some good advice. "Don't worry," she told me. "Most of us have one true love in our life. We suck on the red lollipop and remember the sweet taste on our tongue. But when that true love disappears, deserts us, we move on. So, marry whoever comes to you next, because it will never be like your first love." It made sense when I thought about Quincy. But I was twenty-nine. Jealous of the girls I knew that had married and were having children. And sensitive to jabs about my unmarried state from my relatives. Sometimes families say cruel things.

I wanted to show my new Victorian apartment off to my family, confident this time I would make a good impression. My brother had graduated on schedule and traveled to Africa; he represented success in my eyes. Never feeling quite good enough in front of my sister and cousins all in college, I wanted to impress them, too, and invited everyone for another Easter dinner.

As I prepared, Dad kept pestering me. "When are you going to marry? You can't keep living in sin!" Matthew and I had talked about the idea, but I wasn't sure he wanted it, either. There wasn't a feeling of uncontrollable desire or *I can't live without him* that had been prevalent in my feelings toward Quincy, an ingredient I foolishly thought was essential for marriage. Yet Matthew had a few desirable qualities of his own—he was pleasant, he never tried to control me, he wanted a home, he held a steady job, and not once had he mentioned fathering children. Maybe I could justify getting married. At least once.

As the weeks passed, Dad's old saying, "You can kill two birds with one stone," took on new meaning. I kept allowing the feeling to percolate, *I think I love him. Yes, I know I like him. Maybe, liking someone is better than love. Won't hurt so much if we don't last.* With a mind made up to try marriage, Matthew and I had pledged fidelity. My heart beat wildly as if holding the mane of a stallion; I hoped I would be brave enough to speak the words "Yes" when the time came. A feeling of déjà vu swirled around me as we crossed the Golden Gate Bridge to Sausalito to purchase matching gold bands with the assurance they would be sized for our April 10 wedding. What was it about me marrying during the month of April?

Although I still wasn't absolutely sold, I pulled Dad aside the next day after church. "Everybody is coming over for Easter anyway. Will you perform the ceremony?" The smile on his face made the leap I was about to take worth the effort.

I wore a baby-blue linen sheath with matching pants. When Dad found out I had no wedding bouquet, his florist friend made an arrangement of white lilies and red roses. There were no violins, bridesmaids, flower girls, or soloist singing The Lord's Prayer. No oohs and aahs as I passed with my face hidden behind lace or throwing of rice. I didn't even order a cake. Troy and Florence joined my family as witnesses to observe our simple ceremony. I hung tight to Dad's neck after he pronounced us man and wife, trying to submerge the feeling, *We won't last*, and spoke softly in his ear. "I hope you're happy now."

❧BRITTLE SUCCESS❧

M y work responsibilities as a community liaison shifted when I was promoted to a management position. I welcomed the pay raise and was proud of the title, even though I wasn't quite sure how I had moved past my colleagues with more experience. Managing the federally funded weatherization program threw me into a political quagmire—fighting for funds, backbiting, collusion, trickery, lying, and invitations to sleep with men in high places. An introduction to Business 101. *Who can I trust?* became my sixty-four-thousand-dollar question. The clinical psychology classes I took in college were of little use, and I was green with a budget of over half a million. I needed help and leaned on Dad to navigate the treacherous waters.

The energy contract came with a mandatory board that met every month comprised of community representatives, the utility, and the Department of Energy. Sometimes, I would shake my head at the ridiculous suggestions, capers, and childlike tantrums the community folks would engage in. I had to give it to them, though; these people were ingenious. Wise to the system, they knew how to play the game to get what they wanted. I was bothered by the unethical practice of greasing palms and the influence of power on people's lives and for the first time understood how money seemed to bring out the best and the worst in people.

I quoted statistics and sounded fluent when interviewed about the program services by reporters from the newspaper or television; I was a quick study with a natural affinity for what people wanted to hear. It was the only conclusion that made sense to me, for suddenly I was transformed into a capable, dependable, confident person. "You're political," a colleague told me. I agreed, that must be it, all the time wondering, *What does that mean?*

I was tasked with supervising crews of unskilled, undisciplined youngsters who weatherized the homes. Most of them were only six or seven years younger than me and were street-smart and slick. I'd drive up in my car and they'd move into action like ants, grabbing caulking guns and weather stripping, looking for glue and nails. "How you doing, Boss?" At first, I stuck out my chest, *Yes I'm in charge*, remembering Dad's demand for results as the head of our house and the leader of our congregation, until I realized the work stopped when I turned the corner. Materials disappeared, budgets ran over; nobody was watching. I didn't know diddly about creating a vision, leading, or motivating people, but pride kept me ignorant and conceited. When it was all said and done, the utility bills got paid and the houses received insulation. At meetings I'd stand and smile proudly, as the applause filled my ears, and for the first time in my adult life I believed, *I'm a successful woman...professionally anyway.*

ᏻOLD WOUNDᏻ

Four months after our marriage ceremony my parents took a three-week vacation to visit family in Louisiana and invited me along. It was the summer of 1977. I was looking forward to ending the rhetoric from folks back home, "How old are you, girl? Ain't married yet? Going to be old and gray with your first child."

Our drive from town to town brought back childhood memories of segregation and harassment. But there were also sights I never would have imagined seeing in this part of America in my life—black and white people mingling as they went about their daily business. As we passed the outskirts of Tucson, Arizona, I saw a lady in front of a convenience store with a red V-neck sweater. That vibrant color took me way back to the circumstances leading up to my beating. I'd never figured out who sent the mysterious letter. The beating held a piece of the puzzle I needed to understand and from time to time the episode would rise up in my consciousness, haunting me. I knew something had cracked open in me that morning, a crack that had never quite sealed, leaving me broken and leaking of spirit. I wondered many times how the beating had affected my self-esteem, my issues with trust and the way I allowed myself to be treated in relationships with men.

Heat rose from the cracked dirt and wind blew the tumbleweeds as we rode through the Arizona desert. My thoughts swirled together, as I sat in silence remembering. I felt pressure on my temples. My head began to ache as if a neon sign were pressing my membrane. To ease the pain I closed my eyes and dozed off. The blinding sun woke me. In the distance, I could see the rays of heat rising across the crusty dried soil. But wait, there was more. Was I dreaming? Out in the distance I saw words marching, marching across the soil like solders keeping up with the speed of our car. The message was unmistakable, *Forgiveness. You must come to a place of forgiveness*. Was it a mirage?

Suddenly the question burst out.

"Dad, remember the letter? The letter from that lady whose daughter was pregnant?" I had angled myself in the back seat to detect the slightest facial expression behind his tortoiseshell sunglasses. He was motionless and silent. "I never told anybody about what happened with Murphy and all these years have tried to figure out how she knew."

Dad repositioned himself in the driver's seat before turning to look at Mom. My heart speeded up. He cleared his throat, swallowed, and paused before responding with an alarming truth. "There was no lady. We were regularly snooping around in your room, going through your drawers, your closet, your desk. You were so young, so vulnerable, and we loved you, our firstborn girl. We wanted to protect you from the outside world, wanted to make sure you didn't get caught unaware like some of the other girls. I found the letter you wrote to Murphy in your diary. You know you almost got raped? We didn't know what to do, so I wrote the letter and mailed it to myself."

I felt a tidal wave move through my senses. I was speechless for several moments before leaning forward, touching Mom's shoulder to draw her into the conversation. They had to know, THIS was serious and I was holding them both accountable. Looking straight into Dad's face, struggling to make sense of his confession, I blurted out, "Dad, how could you? All these years I've believed I was a terrible person. How could you?"

He kept repeating, "We loved you, we loved you."

"Oh, that gave you permission to lie? Dad, you made up a lie. A lie. You didn't trust me? You set me up to justify beating me. What you did was much worse. I'm so disappointed. All these years of deceit. All these years of hating myself." Tears began to stream down my face for all the wasted years of self-persecution—all the lost moments of contentment and peace.

Dad, Mom, and I rode in silence. In that moment words from the mirage lost their meaning. Betrayal, exploitation, and abuse bled together.

Closing my eyes once more, the grainy picture I carried of that time became clear and it explained the unreadable handwriting and my lack of success in finding one pregnant girl at school. Memories of the pain washed through me as if I were back in that moment. I waited for an apology. The gesture would have been the smallest sign of remorse I deserved. Dad said nothing. I remained quiet and slouched against the stitched leather, almost defeated, remembering the words, *Forgiveness, you must come to forgiveness.* Between the spaces in the light I told myself, *You're strong. You will get over this. Eventually, you will forgive him.* At the same time I screamed inside, How could I possibly forgive him? The wound from long ago was so deep, so sharp, so raw, that forgiveness felt far off in my future, untouchable; and if it came at all, it would come in wobbly baby steps.

⃟DEVIL ON EARTH⃟

I'll never know if the wound poisoning my system served as a neon sign for more trouble. All I know is I met the "sho 'nuff'" devil at the beginning of 1978. He was intelligent, a Berkeley graduate, dark-brown skin, 5' 9", and wore a brown tweed sweater the first time I saw him. You could hear a pin drop as city commission members threw question after question at him, asking for interpretation of our government contract. He never raised his voice, preferring to ponder before speaking, as if he were a Supreme Court judge. I left before he finished.

A month later, I drove to Fresno for the quarterly meeting of the Community Action Agencies. He was speaking, directing everyone to page 23, paragraph 7, Article 4, as I entered. He looked up, adjusting the bridge of the thick, black bifocal glasses with his middle finger. *He sure knows his details.* During lunch, he slithered like a snake next to the vacant seat in front of me and reached out his hand. "Hello, I'm Reese Harvest from the Department of Energy. You're one of my subcontractors." I met his handshake and introduced myself, noticing how his stare made me feel a little uncomfortable.

The oldest of fourteen children from an illiterate mother, he had a Master's degree from USF and a GS15 salary. He epitomized the saying "pulling yourself up by your own bootstraps." He was single with a ten-year-old son, loved music, asking questions, and listening. Ambitious to excel by climbing up the ladder, I saw an opportunity to become a savvy investor in my own success. He became my mentor.

Ten months had passed since Matthew and I spoke the words "I do," but I was suspicious. Early evening disappearances, no appetite for dinner, a sudden click after answering the phone, the smell of perfume, turning away in bed. *Does he think I don't notice?* But the hurt didn't penetrate my heart like it did with Quincy. Still, I was baffled by how childish men act and started talking with Reese to try to understand. "What do men think, we're stupid? I don't wear that kind of perfume. Why did he get married if he wanted to sleep with other women? Men want cake and ice cream together, all the time."

It was an old story with a predictable ending—all of Reese's empathetic listening landed me in his bed.

Having learned to fake orgasm, I was stunned by the explosion of our first sexual experience, caught off-guard by what my body was capable of receiving. Old worries of being frigid faded. Like a thirsty dog, I became greedy, lapping up our intimacy, clear I did not want his love. I became the Christmas circus clown on a unicycle, juggling balls—finding excuses between orgasms, feeling satisfied while feeling guilty. I tried showing Matthew what Reese was doing. But you can't show a man, especially a black man, who just knows that he knows what he knows, what to do. So I talked myself into believing my indulgence was reasonable...even deserved. *Why should I be deprived? He's getting his; I want mine.* I knew from previous experience that playing with matches could begin a raging wild fire, but I was willing to stand in the center of the heat, sure I could juggle my way through the smoldering woods without getting burned.

With my mental reasoning set, marriage to Matthew became dangerously tolerable.

❧ EXPLOSIONS ❧

I was on a slippery teeter-totter, riding up with my husband, down with my lover, then up with my lover and down with my husband. Neither allowed my feet to touch ground as I ceremoniously complained to Reese about Matthew's infidelity, while justifying my own. He took my side. "That man's a fool and if you were my wife, I'd love you to pieces."

Other than work and spending a couple of hours a month with his son, Reese had plenty of time on his hands. He began to question me about how I spent my time away from him. I hated his inquisitions. *Who does he think he is, my husband, my daddy, my brother's keeper, my bodyguard?* I was living on the edge, constantly looking over my shoulder, working overtime to keep my lies straight, maneuvering—sighing with relief as I laid my head on the pillow at night. I wondered, *How long can I keep up the masquerade?* The longer it lasted, the harder it became to break free of the lie I had created.

The fire burned out of control one day after a San Francisco rendezvous. We were at a bar when Reese's eyes got really tiny. "You're fucking with my mind, trying to drive me crazy. You know what they call women like you?" I didn't know what he was talking about, but the way he spoke sent chills up my spine. He kept saying the same thing over and over, slurring his words as I tried to quiet him. "Don't you shush me; I'll say whatever damn thing I please." He ordered his seventh scotch. "I should tell everybody who you are right here and now. Tell the people you work with. Tell Matthew. Hey, you know what she did to me?" he yelled out at the bar. Everyone turned away, which only seemed to anger him more. By his ninth drink, the bartender cut him off and I persuaded him to leave. I hoped we could ride the public transportation in silence, but as the train pulled out, he started in again. Riders looked at him, then me, asking him to respect the older people and children on the train. He spat out more derogatory words. "Mind your fucking business, you bastard. Don't you dare lay a hand on me." Helplessness washed through me once again.

As we disembarked the rapid transit, I wanted to leave him in the parking lot and run to the safety of my home, but he continued to threaten. "I'm going to tell your husband all about us if you don't come home with me." A shockwave went through me. I didn't want to believe him, but I couldn't take a chance, either. He forced himself on me as I sobbed quietly and entered a sort of twilight zone. Reese had transformed into a psychopath right in front of my eyes. Of course he was sorry afterwards; flowers and presents arrived at work, accompanied by words of love. Frightened, I gave in, figuring that's what people do. Make excuses, pretend it didn't happen, try to forget.

Over the next few weeks, his drunken behavior continued while I grew more afraid, tormented by his threats of disclosure. Driving from my house to his, the question that kept shrieking in my head was one I knew too well: *How did I get to this place of loathing myself again?* My acceptance of putting up with his loathsome threats and emotional abuse made one thing clear: I believed mistreatment was what I deserved. The mixture of feelings for Reese rolled through me like thunder—hate, resentment, fear, tenderness, sorrow, as the days turned into months leading up to my two-year anniversary with Matthew.

We were mulling over where we would celebrate the next day when we heard a knock. Reese, clearly drunk, was at the front door. My stomach dropped inside my socks. He asked Matthew, "Hey man, can I talk with you?"

I was sure Matthew would slam the door, but he invited him

in like they were old army buddies. I retreated to the bedroom and closed the door, caught like a moth in a spiders web. For two hours Reese calmly told Matthew about our affair as they emptied a bottle of brandy. Matthew owned a gun and my mind filled with stories of lovers' quarrels. None of them had happy endings. At first, I paced back and forth, weighing my options, and would have escaped through the window, but the screen was stuck. Without tools, I couldn't shake it loose. So I rocked back and forth, drowning out the monotone of voices as fear riddled my body like bullets. When I was sure my mind would explode, the bedroom door suddenly opened. Reese was gone.

There was nothing to say. "I'm sorry" seemed weak, even though I kept repeating it. I didn't want to blame Matthew for my actions, but I used the old line, "You screwed other women, so I decided to screw another man." But still, no woman had come to our house, sat down, and told me to my face about having an affair with my husband. With my eyes closed, I saw myself creeping up to Reese's window and shooting him twice in the head with Matthew's gun.

The remorse I felt weighed on me like two tons of steel. *How had I let this affair get out of hand?*

We both sat pushing food around on the plates at our anniversary dinner, our minds drifting to places known only to ourselves. By the end of the month, I had moved out to a lovely apartment by the water. I felt shame for my behavior, but couldn't help wonder if I had unconsciously used Reese as the key to set me free.

ℭFOOL'S PARADISE℧

Separated and with a false sense of security, I began to venture out alone. Oddly enough, I liked going anywhere I pleased without having to be accountable to Reese or Matthew. But after several weeks, I became uneasy and wasn't sure why until one day, I realized Reese was stalking me.

I would look up and find him standing there, pleading. "Please forgive me. I'll make it up to you. You were miserable. He didn't deserve you."

I noticed his clear eyes, his unslurred speech, and his sensibility. Small items of antique furniture appeared outside my apartment; messages came through our mutual acquaintances. "Can we please talk? Can we be friends?"

I was so angry, so very, very angry, and I wanted to punish him. And he was persistent. I backpedaled. I allowed one chaperoned conversation then another and another. He poured out his heart, promised he would go to AA, asked me to consider starting over slow being friends if he sobered up forever. I can't say my heart wasn't affected by his plea; I knew the pain of lopsided love. But could I trust him? My mind said, *No. Stand on your own. You don't need this anymore.* At the same time, I wanted to believe maybe I could help him to quit drinking, maybe something good could come out of the mess I had created.

Every time we were together I checked for the slightest hint of Wild Turkey or Christian Brothers on his breath. Little by little, I began to trust him again. I felt met in our intellectual conversations as we analyzed concerts, museum art, cuisine in off-the-beaten-track restaurants. I drank good wine. He ordered Coca-Cola. At night, I pondered the question of going back to my marriage, although Matthew and I weren't speaking and there was no hint of reconciliation. After several months had passed, and no signs of Reese taking a drink, I began to believe we were on the road toward intimacy someday. But when the time came, my body rejected his touch.

Alcohol breath greeted me the next time we were together at his apartment. I kept banging my hand against my head, *Why did I walk through the door?* as my "No" to demands for sex snapped him like a twig. He pulled me toward the bedroom by my collar and threw me across the bed.

"Who are you sleeping with, I know you're sleeping with someone."

"I'm not sleeping with anyone. Honest, I'm not." There was no one, but my denial fell on deaf ears. Slamming sounds came from the kitchen as I shuddered. When I looked up he was holding a ten-inch kitchen knife in each hand. He laid them on the bed and started talking calmly.

"Tell you what, why don't we end it now? You take your best stab at me, and I'll take my best stab at you."

I started moaning and screaming, "NO, NO, NO, I DON'T WANT TO TAKE A STAB AT YOU," my shrill voice growing louder as he slashed the knives back and forth in the air. He looked crazed, delusional, like a psychotic monster. He raped me.

Afterwards, he revealed his plan. "You're walking on thin ice. If you don't have sex with me next time, I'm going to your parents, then your job and your church. I'll be watching every move you make."

I was being blackmailed! The thought of Reese talking with my father or roaming down the church aisle turned me white. I was in grave danger, nearly comatose with fear. *What to do? What to do? He's going to tell Dad, I know he is. How could I be so stupid? How do I get out of this mess?*

Once again I turned to my ugly past to explain away why I was being punished. *You can't erase the bad choices you made. Flunking out of school, loose sex, moving out of the house, being sneaky, telling lies, smoking grass, disappearing from the word of God, spending instead of tithing, displaying ungratefulness instead of grace, running around with all kinds of people, lying to yourself.* God had saved me from suicide once. Now, I was sorry he hadn't let me die. Embarrassed to call out for help, I kept the terror of Reese's threats private. I had an image and Dad's reputation to protect. The rapes continued.

Reese verbally taunted me with threats and I made up stories to explain my swollen face—an eye infection, insect bites, allergic reactions. The management in his apartment and mine beat on the doors when they heard my screams, but the police never responded as I cried hysterically from his verbal and sexual attacks. "Stop, please don't, please don't," until screaming turned to whimpers. I was never sure if any day would be my last.

I was looking out at the boats sailing in the evening light from my window, wishing I could sail away with them, when knocks sounded at the door. I jumped. Reese's pattern was familiar—pleasant, warm politeness turning into sarcastic rage. "Let's take a ride."

Reluctantly, I got in the car. The smell of alcohol was stronger than usual. He shifted gears, straining the motor of his MG coupe. A sinister look appeared across his face. "Doesn't the freight train come through here about 5:45?"

I heard a whistle in the distance as I glanced at the clock on the console. It read 5:43. He sped up the car and revved the engine. "I wonder if we can beat the train...you think we can beat the train?" The train whistle grew closer; the knuckles of my hands grabbed the dashboard tighter. I could feel my body tense as a runaway thumping took over in my chest.

"What if we got stuck on the train tracks?" he continued. The transmission made a gravelly sound as he switched gears again. I thought I was going to be sick. I could see the rail crossing, hear the "ding, ding, ding, ding." He chuckled, "Think we'll make it, think we'll make it, THINK WE'LL MAKE IT?"

I closed my eyes. Disappointing Dad flashed through my mind.

The car wheels crashed over the tracks, bouncing us up and down before landing with a hard thud seconds before the train passed by. I could feel the train's velocity blowing on us as I trembled. The conductor acknowledged our idiocy with a long pull on the horn as we sped toward downtown Oakland. All I could remember was my promise: *God, if you get me out of this, I'll become a nun!*

We stopped on Lakeshore Boulevard and entered a bar. Men were hugging and kissing. He ordered doubles for both of us. "Wow, what a rush. We'll have to do that again, maybe on our way back. Now tell me, how was the fuck with that guy?" I didn't know what he was talking about. "You're no better than a prostitute, a streetwalker, a whore. Yes, you're a whore! Hey, this woman is a whore," he bellowed. I covered my ears, knowing his words were all lies. When the brandy arrived, he threw it in my face. "Say something, bitch." I sat trembling as tears streamed down my face. Reese barked, "Another round, make it the same."

The bartender tried to intervene. "Hey man, why are you treating her like that?"

Reese lurched, "If you know what's good for you, you'll mind your fucking business, you faggot."

A woman eased up next to me. "Baby, you need some help with this bully?" she asked. Her face was kind like an angel, and my eyes said everything. It was my only chance to muster up the courage I needed. Two guys were standing at the bar and the bartender looked at me with compassion. "Will somebody please hold him down?" The two guys held Reese as he struggled to get loose, and I motioned to the bartender, "May I use your phone to call my father?"

"Bitch, you'd better watch what you're doing. You're going to regret this."

I had no alternate plan. Only hope, as my finger dialed and Reese shouted.

Please, Dad, be home.

⟪BREATHE AGAIN⟫

Twenty minutes later Dad drove up. He wrapped his arms around me like I was a papoose and led me away. Mom ran a warm tub of water. I slipped between the bubbles, wishing I could submerge the terrible memories of Reese. Why was I such a bad judge of character? I was dreaming of the color pink when the phone rang. Dad's voice had a cold anger and I flashed back on Murphy; no wonder he never spoke to me again.

"She doesn't live here. Don't ever call this house again, or I'll have the police after you."

Food tasted like chalk at breakfast when I poured out the whole story from beginning to end. Dad sat with a grim look on his face, saying nothing to condemn me. Mom cared about how it looked. "How could you do such a thing, act like some cheap person off the street without the right upbringing?"

Jesus could not have talked me into going back across the train tracks alone to my apartment. Faith was gone. "I'll take care of everything," Dad assured me. One call to my building management and one to the police station was all it took. We followed two policemen with drawn guns through my front door. Within three hours my apartment was stripped clean. Before leaving I ripped the letter Reese had left under the door to pieces and flushed it down the toilet.

Three days later as I was sitting like a mummy in my parents' backyard, a hummingbird appeared, mesmerizing me.

Yes, you met the devil.

That's what it took for your hard head to get it.

There are consequences in life.

You're born at least twice. The first time you lived through extreme conditions.

But there is hope. This time, redefine your life through the eyes of love as freedom.

Love yourself. LOVE YOURSELF.

Just open your mouth and ask for what you want.

Believe in you.

God still loves you.

But first you must learn to forgive!

Oh, how I wanted to believe it was possible and that it could become true.

A few weeks had passed when Matthew rang the doorbell one Saturday afternoon without notice. I had a hunch Dad called him. He hung his head and frowned listening to my ordeal. In some ways, it would have been easy to turn the page and fold back into the safety of his arms. But I realized, *My wounds go so deep, they sabotage any chance I have of living a normal life.* I needed help and lots of soul-searching before considering such a bold move as returning to a broken marriage. This time, I wasn't about to turn the message I thought I had heard from the hummingbird into another misfortune without getting professional help. I couldn't trust myself to make sensible decisions anymore.

❦OUT OF NOWHERE❧

By the Fall of 1979 I was reconciled to rebirthing and rebuilding my life slowly, authentically, without leaning on needy love. It had been four months since Dad had rescued me, and I was regularly going to therapy. My brother had recently returned from Boston after separating from his wife and we rented a house together in North Oakland. Matthew and I were casually dating, but still unable to ask each other the hard questions or share our deepest desires for cultivating a strong marriage. Honesty and trust. Kindness and devotion. Joy. Respect. And yes, forgiveness. Staying true to our identity while mutually growing our tree. I was breathing deeply through the spaces of uncertainty, hopeful over time I was going to be all right.

Dad and I were talking after dinner in the front seat of his car one chilly Fall night in late October. "I pulled a muscle cleaning your Mom's walls. My right hand's weak, shaking, and I drop things too. Either that or your dad's getting old with arthritis. You know, I'm not a spring chicken anymore," he chuckled. I looked at his leather-gloved hands gripping the steering wheel, but I didn't think anything of it.

By January, the shaking had turned to more frequent and noticeable tremors. A CAT scan revealed the culprit—a brain tumor the size of a pinhead. "No big deal," the doctor reported, showing us the tiny spot on the X-ray. "We'll go in, take it out, and he'll be good as new." On the morning of his surgery, he looked up and smiled as I bent down to kiss his forehead. "You know, I don't care if they have to cut this arm off, I just want to live." I waved good-bye as they rolled his gurney through the doors, thinking, *That was a strange thing to say*.

We paced for six and a half hours until the doctor came out at

1:30 to give us an update. "The tumor is in a delicate place. We've got to go slow and try to preserve as much as possible." I thought, *Preserve as much as possible? Wasn't it a simple benign tumor?*

Our pacing continued until 4:00. It had been ten hours. The doctor's blue eyes looked serious. "Everything went fine; he's in recovery and is doing very well, but..." *Who invented that word*? "We found tumors in the lymph nodes we didn't expect and cleaned them out. We're sending them to the lab; it will take a few days. Don't worry, everything went fine."

That Easter was the first time Dad wouldn't host the seven last words of Christ or the 5:00 a.m. sunrise service. It was Dad's favorite time of year: resurrection—the foundation of our faith. I kept reflecting on when I was a little girl, climbing hand in hand with Dad up Mount Davidson to pray in front of the giant cross.

We celebrated dinner in Dad's room, giving thankful grace. But my uneasiness wouldn't go away. Wednesday, Thursday, and Friday had passed with no results. It had been over a week, and I became more uneasy. By Sunday, I was agitated and complained to the head nurse. She must have heard the anguish in my voice because within an hour she whispered in my ear, "Dr. Smith will meet you in his office at 5:00." I braced myself as he opened the file. "The results are not what we hoped for. Your Dad has a meningioma. It's cancerous and stage three." Surprisingly, the words floated over me as if they were meant for someone else. Some other father's daughter. I spoke with calmness.

"How much time?" I asked.

He looked away for a moment before speaking. "Six months. Maybe a year." The force of his words knocked the wind out of me. I held a vision of growing old together.

"I've known for five days, but wanted you to celebrate in peace as a family. It wasn't going to change anything. I'm really sorry. I'll come up tomorrow to tell your dad and mom."

I pleaded with him. "Dad's not the kind of person who will do well with this kind of news. He's a solution kind of person, a problem-solver, a visionary. You've got to give him some hope, something to fight for. Mom needs it too."

We were at cross-purposes. "I can't speak what is not true."

"Please, please," I pleaded. "You don't know how long for sure, do you? Only God really knows."

The next day, Dr. Smith had just left as I arrived in Dad's room.

Mom spoke matter-of-factly, "Your father has a cancerous brain tumor, but they don't know how long—two, three, maybe five years with radiation and chemotherapy." I looked into Dad's face and heard what I expected. "I'm going to beat this thing. Miracles happen all the time." Same old Dad I knew. He'd ride the storm until the very end.

I never saw Dr. Smith again, but that night in my prayers I thanked him for his generous gift of hope.

A few weeks later, I sat down with Matthew. "It's going to be tough; I'll need your strength to lean on. Can you do that for me?"

I wanted to believe wherever the journey would take us with Dad's condition, the two of us would brave it together, and use the adversity as an opportunity to grow into each other's arms. I wanted to believe, I could be losing my father, but gaining my best friend.

❧SEASONS CHANGE❧

Life changes when you know death is knocking at your father's door. Instantly, all that was before ceases to exist. Colors are dimmer, air is thinner, flickers of light pass over the sky like falling stars.

There is no time to practice how to react. No time to distinguish what feels real or what is make-believe. As soon as my eyes opened each morning, Dad's health omen greeted me, "6 to 12 months, he's going to die." The dismal prognosis followed me around like a child dragging a Raggedy Ann. Within, ghosts of the past swirled around me as guilt grew a thorn that prickled my heart. I asked myself if there was *anything* I had done to contribute to Dad's death sentence. Had God heard my insincere request from long ago?

I didn't want to be angry with God, but I couldn't figure it out. Dad's predicted early death felt like a dirty trick. He was just coming in for a smooth landing with his doctorate completed, a tenured faculty position, the church membership exploding, and his elected position as President of the National Council of Community churches. He had settled into a good place of being—long weekends every fifth Sunday taking Mom to Monterey, active in the ministerial alliance, and community involvement in the city of Oakland. He appeared happy, at peace, seemingly exorcised from his anger and ready to tackle the next portion of his ambitious life with gusto. *Why now?* I kept asking myself. There had been far too little time to enjoy the fruits of his labor.

My constant questioning took me in and out of denial as I quarreled with the unfairness of Dad's bitter cup. The only thing I could fathom was karma. The scripture, "Reap what you sow," kept humming in my ear. Had Dad's past transgressions caught up with him? Had he orchestrated his fate? I had always been a person that prayed, but became more devoted to how I talked with God. "I forgive him. Please heal him or at least give him more time" became my mantra.

I had stopped by the house one day after chemo when Dad patted the bed. He was weak, but persistent. "Sit down, let's talk. What's happening with you and Matthew?"

"Oh Dad," I blushed, "let's just focus on you."

"I'm going to be fine, but you need to really think about going back to Matthew. He loves you, and I think you both learned your lesson. Besides, I worry about you." A momentary sadness came over me. I didn't dare tell Dad—I was worried about me too, but for the present eased his mind when I shared, "We're back together, Dad."

I didn't know if Matthew and I had the ingredients to make our marriage work in the long run. All I knew was I wanted to be held at night after visiting Dad's sickbed, and I didn't want to walk down the aisle behind Dad's casket alone.

By July, Dad was looking like his old self. Mom was juicing, reading about wheatgrass, and buying organic food. He returned to church steady as ever—singing, cracking jokes, preaching and planning for the New Year. The surgery had left him looking like Yul Brynner. We liked it, but he wanted his sideburns back and sent away for fake hair like Elvis. I watched him like a little kid getting his first baseball glove as he glued the hair to the side of his face. Tears rolled down our cheeks with laughter when he tried to get them off. The glue stuck like cement, and we had to cut his fake sideburns off with scissors.

It was important to bring as much laughter back into our family as possible and I began teasing Dad whenever I could about his twitching right arm. I'd put on his overcoat and his jazzy feathered hat, make a lopsided monster face, and cover my right hand with his black gloves. I'd stagger around, dragging my foot and snarling, calling myself the one-armed bandit while my family cracked up, especially Dad. My act became a main course each time I came to visit, like dessert to finish a tasty meal. I think it brought the reality of Dad's cancer closer to the surface. Years later, I came to believe somewhere within himself he knew time was precious and laughter was like exotic, rare fruit. But we never spoke a word about the future.

Dad contracted shingles in August and blood clots in his legs by late Fall. Mom wrapped his body in warm towels trying to relieve the pain and each time he returned home from doctor visits or un-expected hospital stays I noticed his body was deteriorating. I was beginning to believe that God might be testing Dad with Satan like he did Job, raining affliction after affliction on his broken body. Some mornings I'd wake right before dawn, close my eyes, and see Dad's body healed from a miracle or our family awakened from the dream I wished would disappear. Dad seldom complained, choosing instead to hear Aunt Bea, a church member, Mom, or me read his favorite scripture. Psalm 139 read like a confession—God is present every-where and knows about everything we've ever done. When we feel worthless, feel we have done terrible things, hate ourselves or hate others, we can ask God for direction to help us recognize our short-comings. God will open our hearts, show us the way and forgive us.

There it was again, that word, forgiveness woven almost inno-cently into the complexity of my life, like a stitch in a hem. Was it a coincidence that my father's favorite scripture was all about the heal-ing that wanted to take root and sprout in me? I thought not, but had no time to concentrate on the meaning, believing forgiveness was a task to be put on a list and checked off casually.

TYRANNY OF DEATH

The medical forecast had been right—more like six months to a year. I could hear the distant foghorns of death getting closer as the cold days of 1981 folded into themselves. On February 18, without notice, Dad slipped into a coma. I was unprepared, still reel-ing from Quincy's surprise visit. He had come to town for a medical convention and found me through a mutual friend. I couldn't believe almost ten years had passed since our breakup. He had married the girl from college, but was cotton-mouthed about their life together. I told him nothing of how his actions had affected me, and how I still felt like I could bash his head in with a brick at the same time that I could fold right back into his arms. Some things were just better left unsaid.

In the hospital we took turns talking to Dad, watching him breathe, holding his hand as hospice prepared us for the final days. When we were sure we were down to the last hours, he woke up. "Can I have some water?" We were stunned, happy to look in his glazed eyes and hear his voice. Over the next four days, Dad talked with each family member and said good-bye in his own special way. He gave me the thumbs-up after listening to a one-hour radio interview about my energy program. Oh, how his approval did me good! I wanted him to know he didn't have to worry; I'd be fine. And for the first time, I heard Mom expressing herself with a wailing cry without any regard for how it looked. It surprised me because in the thirty-three years of watching my mother, I had come to know her as a woman made of stone.

A little before sunset on March 6, 1981, surrounded by family, church members, and friends, Dad's soul left his body. He looked peaceful as he stopped breathing. An eerie quietness filled the room as I looked at his face and whispered, "I'm going to miss you, buddy." Dad had given everything to serve God and I believed soon he would be soaring like an eagle in heaven. Hours later, walking in the chilly night, I looked up at a million stars, and saw one shining brilliantly. A slight grin spread across my solemn face, for I knew that Dad had arrived home safely.

Every seat in the sanctuary, from the main floor and balcony to the overflow, was filled at Dad's funeral. Petals of pink, red, violet, and orange flowers fused together in one sweet aroma as they rested crowdedly against each other. Mom and Dad's old friends, the Jacksons, were present, along with her sisters and brothers from Louisiana and Maryland. I knew Dad would have liked the attention; he loved people and big turnouts. The choir sang Dad's favorite songs. The mayor spoke. Robert read a farewell testimonial. Proclamations were spoken as I stared at the mahogany casket. So many people talked about Dad's exemplary life; by the time he was to be formally eulogized, there was nothing more to say.

You'd have thought a movie star or famous politician had died when you saw the lights in the processional. It was a true testimony of an extraordinary journey by a man who lived and died believing in right and wrong and the power of God.

I went tearfully to the mausoleum almost every day stopping at the corner florist to purchase Dad's favorite flower—Birds of Paradise. The folding chair and the cold touch of granite were waiting for me with the muttering that stumbled from my lips. *How can you be gone at fifty-eight?* Like a missing limb, the vacancy he left could never be replaced by anything artificial.

I can't explain why or how, but whenever I looked up I felt comforted. Any time a leaf or unexpected raindrop fell, I'd say to myself, *That's Dad, saying I'm fine up here and hello.* The hard part was I kept asking him and myself the same question: *What now?*

Experiencing Dad's death brought me face to face with my own mortality—if nothing else, I had to make peace with my home life. I couldn't keep stalling the inevitable, for Matthew had struck out. If he couldn't support me emotionally through Dad's ordeal, how could he support us in the roller-coaster ride of marriage? It was the only reason I had gone back. But Matthew wasn't entirely to blame for our failure—we just didn't sync up anymore. With my eyes more open than ever, I longed to find the peace I believed existed. No more Cinderella stories or white picket fences.

Six weeks after Dad's burial, I walked away. This time, I didn't turn back.

ᴄ⍚STILLNESS⍚ᴄ

Once again, I was alone. Snapshots of life passed me like images on a kaleidoscope. Quietness impaled me. It was hard looking at the truth. I was weary, blushing with deprivation and did not yet fully understand the phrase "life is a journey." After leaving Matthew, I began to hear whispers in the quietness of the mausoleum, as if Dad and thousands of souls were cradling me, cheering me on, and creating a sacred womb for me to face myself. They kept poking at me in the soft spot of my heart with a razor's edge. *"Wake up! Don't you want to be free of guilt and shame? Wake up! Isn't it time to come out from behind the blue curtain and stand securely on your own two feet? Aren't you tired of feeling pitiful? W-A-K-E UP! Life can be beautiful!"*

Sitting in the mausoleum forced me into stillness and stillness forced me to see the chasm, the places where I had cracked open. I didn't want to admit it, but my wounds still pierced through me like shattered glass, swallowing up all the positive seeds waiting to explode into fullness. I'd find myself at the will of an invisible force whipping me this way and that, creating the illusion of solid footing before dropping me down, down into the darkness of my being. I loved my father, and had blamed him for my misery. Now he was dead. Who else to blame—Mom? Myself? God? Was it too late to forgive?

The questions never stopped jogging through my mind, and I had almost resigned myself to believe that, the golden light I witnessed beaming on everyone else's life had burned out when it glowed toward me. And yet, in the many months that would follow, what I would come to know was that angels had been watching over me every moment for 12,000 days. Now, they were congregating, contemplating, eagerly inviting me to see beyond my sight. *Stop putting up smoke screens. You become the seeker. You become the believer. Trust in yourself. There are clues to a life of joy and peace, but you will only find them within by becoming satisfied with being you.*

Being me? But could I do it, could I really become me? Was I ready? Hmmmm! That's when I realized how wonderful the truth is when you realize it's the truth, because it slides down your throat like a warm, buttered cinnamon bun and lands sweetly in your tummy. I had been still enough to ask myself the right question and was getting closer to understanding the meaning of my life—why my path had been so crooked. But another test stood before me, the most difficult test I would ever face.

I had to face up to the feelings of unworthiness. Parts of me felt soiled, trampled, contemptuous about my behavior from years of reading the Bible and Dad's sermons of hell. Who was I to believe I deserved to have a beautiful life outside of what I had been taught as a Christian? Every act on earth was only for the purpose of going to heaven to be with GOD, wasn't it? The afterlife?

But what if there was another possibility? What if THIS was a part of heaven? What if every act on earth was real, not preparation for anything except for NOW? What if I was present and walking with GOD every second of the day—through the good and the bad? What if God had forgiven me long ago for all my transgressions and my repentance was complete? I realized that the very thought of this notion was against everything I had been taught, but it made more sense to me than anything I had ever contemplated about God before. Perhaps, if any parts of my thinking were right, all that had happened in my life was to bring me to this epiphany. If this new awareness was true, I had to dig deep into my wounded soul; make every effort to heal by releasing the self-pity, remorse, fear, resistance that I carried and all the rejection and wrong that was ever done to me in my life. It weighted on me like bushels of hay.

Over time, I would come to know this as my *work—my spiritual work*, the only path to pure love and the expression of the divine in me. A path with many seekers, a journey that never ends...

ENOUGH

Reflecting on my deep desire to feel worthy and my new understanding of what it would take to be a different, truer, and worthier me, it became clearer that a big part of my *work* in finding me was to stop feeling like a victim and learn the true meaning of love—that is coming to forgiveness. Forgive my father, my mother, my circumstances, my past, and most importantly myself. Forgiveness without conditional ifs, buts, excuses, or buckets of blame. In the process I hoped to evoke a new story of inspiration finding the best in me while simultaneously fulfilling Dad's last request that I whispered back to him in promise, "Don't worry, I'll always take care of her." One last time, I moved back to Melvin Road, but this time my purpose was as clear as a flawless diamond—develop a relationship with my mother, save money to purchase my own home, and hide out from the external pressures of life long enough to build muscle to face the world as me.

I was thirty-five years old, but had no idea what it meant to do my *work*; and when I asked Mom, she looked at me like I just escaped from a mental ward. Were there books, an organization, a process, a community to guide me? Was I crazy to nurture the belief, *One day you'll feel worthy?*

Over the next few years, I timidly and awkwardly searched for evidence, any evidence that resembled doing my *work*. Often I felt neurotic, bashful, and foolish, as I met people I labeled as sophisticated because they spoke words I couldn't pronounce and shared philosophies that were foreign to me. I stumbled into churches and temples of different faiths searching for a replacement for my father and tried to make sense of my Myers-Briggs personality type. I was learning the world was way bigger than I ever imagined, more complicated and filled with a plethora of teachings about love, compassion, and forgiveness from Gandhi to Buddha. I read *Roots*, *The Autobiography of Malcolm X*, and Dr. King searching for similarities of racial struggle within my own life.

I tossed and turned at night assessing and reassessing the kaleidoscope of pebbles and rocks I'd walked upon. And then one day while thumbing through Dad's library, I came upon a book that would change my life. At the time, it felt hidden, seemingly thrown haphazardly behind Dad's theological books. But as I read the first sentence, "Life is difficult" and felt my body release a breath like never before, I realized the book had been there all along, waiting for me. I had simply not been ready. I couldn't lift my eyes from the words on the pages of *The Road Less Traveled*. I had been beating myself up for decades, searching for solace, and there between the pages, I found answers and found myself.

&ILLUMINATION&

Tilden Park became my place of reflection. There, high in the Berkeley hills, it seemed millions of lights would twinkle across the suspension cables of the Bay Bridge as the deep orange and gold of the sun would paint itself down into the twilight of another day. Often, I sat chilled by the evening air, and would hug myself thinking about the path of my life. It was there I stopped asking about the purpose of suffering. I came to understand the question as moot, realizing suffering is a part of living. It teachers us about Life.

Perched on the hood of my car, I'd dance through the chapters of my life. As far back as I could remember, I had been caught up in being the perfect preacher's daughter. That part of my life felt as if I was forever treading water, my foot barely able to reach and hold on to a rock or seaweed to keep from being dragged in the undertow. 3D images of those times showed me caught in the rapids, trashed about, split open, nearly drowning.

And then, every once in a long while, there had been moments that seemingly came out of nowhere—golden as the sunset before me—when everything inside me was normal and natural and life was good. That part felt like my body had been catapulted out from the dark watery depths below by some invisible force and I was free... free to be me. Life became a blissful flow of me exploring every-thing, asking the questions of my heart, a confident swimmer diving with abandonment and spontaneity into the mysterious depths, and coming up shining, giggling, and laughing at all kinds of life's hidden treasures I'd discovered. I hugged myself once again, in recognition that, after a long, long struggle, the scales were finally tipping and that hurt little girl in the dark throes of trying to become someone else's perfect child was disappearing—this time forever. In her place a strong, confident, wise and compassionate woman stood able to dance with the rhythms of life.

She would learn to apologize graciously and with humble dignity. She would learn to forgive. Forgive without illusion, reason, or justi-fication. Forgive generously and sincerely. Forgive with great respect and compassion for others. Forgive with love for herself and for all of humanity. She would learn forgiveness is priceless and costs noth-ing except a willingness to be whole. She would learn forgiveness as the only way—the starting place, the finish line, and everything in between. And overtime she would grow into the words of Gandhi, believing that "The weak can never forgive. Forgiveness is the attribute of the strong."

❧EPILOGUE☙

It's been over forty-nine years since that fateful night when, writhing in pain, I looked up at the stars and knew I would write my story one day. What I didn't know, was how I would be required to rid myself of bitterness and revenge before I could put one word to paper. I had enough sense to understand that another angry story served no benefit to human kind. But as the years tumbled forward, I let go. My forgiveness *work* and the beautiful life that I had always longed for revealed itself like a treasured fossil buried in the sand.

I met my husband-to-be in 1986. I had changed—no longer believing I was half a person searching for someone else to make me whole. I had been alone, but was no longer lonely. With him I learned to accept and appreciate simplicity. The feeling inside of me was not the way I'd felt with Quincy; in fact, it was not like anything I had ever felt before. It was transparent, mature, and real.

On February 14, 1987, John and I exchanged wedding vows in Maui, Hawaii. An elderly Chinese couple wreathed in smiles served as witnesses in the little Methodist chapel in Lahaina. I couldn't shake the feeling of floating and wondered, *Am I dreaming?* as we stood at the altar dressed in ivory with traditional Hawaiian flowers—a haku lei for me and maile lei around John's neck. Light rain and dark clouds shrouded us as we said, "I do." As the church doors opened a spray of burnt orange, pink, gold, and maroon burst through the western skies—a perfect sunset of colors that had brought me through the storms of my life.

I continued my personal work with race, thrusting myself into conversations with white people, mostly women, where my wounds were opened over and over again. We spoke of history, hurt, pain— advocating, agonizing, wailing, collapsing, consoling, apologizing. And then one day, synchronicity happened. I was invited to a women's circle—a safe place for telling my truth and being witnessed over and over again until there was nothing left but silence. Silence and an incredible outpouring of love and self-acceptance. I emerged a living testament of what my circle elder called "The birthplace of the new human."

These days are dedicated to the practice of women's circles, a sacred place that holds the portal to my soft spot—my place of authenticity, listening, wisdom, courage, beauty, and joy. My place of exploration, shedding, discovering truth, and transforming with a sense of spirit-consciousness.

I've learned that each day is a choice to live without borders—exploring and expanding, releasing and replenishing, believing I can do anything. I've learned that parasitic love—whether for my husband, my family, my friends, an item—is not love at all. Love is a feeling of freedom and interconnectedness simultaneously. I've learned to live each day with intention and discipline—daily meditation, deep breaths, nourishing friendships, and gratitude for the unique gift of life that comes in every shape and form my way. I've learned that material things are wonderful, but don't bring lasting happiness and can only fill a teacup of abundance without love, hope, and faith— the true prosperity.

My professional and personal relationships opened many doors and lead me into fields I would never have imagined possible—walking among 30,000 at the Beijing Women's Conference; jumping with the Maasai in Kenya; singing in St. Oran's chapel in Iona, Scotland; standing before the Taj Mahal; riding camelback around the Pyramids in Egypt; convening with my Millionth Circle sisters at the Parliament of World Religions in Barcelona, Spain.

It would be many years before I felt at home in a congregation to worship. But when I did, I realized that God had walked within me hand in hand—guiding me, consoling me on this path of spiritual awakening.

I have learned the biggest tribute I can give to my father is to be kind and gentle to myself. From that waterfall, sparkling lights of love thrash against the rocks of life and flow freely into the pool of wellness before surfacing bright and glowing in the clear stream of beauty, worthiness, and acceptance.

From that place, forgiveness comes easy...

I used to ask about the purpose of suffering
It feels unimportant now
I've come to the realization we all suffer, but yours will never look or feel the same as mine
Seasons come and go and I continue to discover the chrysalis of my soul, molting soft, and vulnerable
As for my becoming, I cringe to think what I would be, if the uphill battles hadn't prepared me, for the great mystery
The vine of faith found my feet, curled itself around my waist, until head to toe my whole self wrapped, awakened me to grace
Surrender, let go, accept life where you are
We each have a story; reframe it and find joy
Take the good with the good, in truth there is no other
Some days won't be easy, boxing life's blows and blunders
Before we know it the years have passed by, we'll look backwards and stare hard lessons in the eye
We'll wonder...what was all the fuss and noise?
And then sigh contently, knowing with poise
Acceptance, forgiveness, gratitude for each day; where the things that came freely, rained love our way
Nothing will ground us more than twenty minutes of daily silence. It's a practice we cultivate, connecting with God's wonder.
One day we look up, a big smile across our face
We've gained wisdom and dissonance has been replaced
Fingers pop, we get in the groove
Loving self was all that mattered,
Now I say, "Yes, I approve!"

THE END

ᏉACKNOWLEDGMENTSᏒ

I would never have come to write *Coming to Forgiveness* without a host of incredible and beautiful people in my life. I would like to thank everyone who helped me complete this promise to myself.

I want to thank my Chakra circle for fourteen years of listening me into myself, and providing a sacred community of nourishment, wisdom, joy, laughter, teachings, and magical mystery. Without your unconditional love, I would never have had the courage to reveal my story with such truth, empathy, and compassion: Our wise elder, Anne Dosher; Sarita Chawla; Stephanie Ryan; Teresa Ruelas; Linda Booth-Sweeney; Peggy Sebera; Andrea Dyer; Kristin Cobble; and Gisela Wendling. We've ridden the waves together—marriages, births, death, divorces, work-life shifts, planting of pomegranate seeds, watching whales, sitting in silence, drinking bed tea, and listening, then listening deeper until something transformed. You have been sisters, holding me gently in the transitions of life.

I want to thank my Writers Circle for tireless support and encouragement: Diane Woods and Cheri Allison for reminding me who I was and keeping it real; Teresa Ruelas for the nitty-gritty nuance editing from beginning to end; Stephanie Ryan for meticulous editing the first few years; and Linda Booth-Sweeney for lifting my spirits on those hard days. Your guidance on the manuscript offered incredible insights, and your moral support pushed me steadily toward my dream.

Robin Calderon, who opened her home for the first days of putting thoughts to paper and encouraged me on the long path to completion.

Mary Jane Ryan for gifting me with the first edit.

Deborah Stevenson, who has had my back and been there for me since 1963.

All the circle sisters in Shona, Dancing Hearts, and The Millionth Circle.

Friday's Writers for your editing and words of encouragement.

The family and friends focus groups.

I have eternal gratitude for Linda Williams, my editor, for your willingness to read and reread my manuscript over and over again through all my rewrites, jumbled metaphors, and inconsistencies. Our coming together was pure joy because you kept me true to myself. Your patience, thoughtfulness, and open heart are eternally etched within me.

To Terri Hinte, my copyeditor. I put my trust into your expertise with confidence and faith. Working with you was a pleasure, and a gift as the last i and t was crossed on this journey. Thank you.

To Suzanne Nason, my book designer, thank you for your intuition, insight, and patience. What a time we had growing into each other's ways and into friendship. Your soft, and wise direction revealed itself in a most incredible creative process of collaboration and partnership.

To my husband John, my best friend, my glue. Your unconditional faith, support, and belief in me brought me to a new understanding of what it means to be loved. You told me long ago, I could do anything I wanted. Thank you for your patience and for loving me just as I am.

To my daughter Genji, you taught me the meaning of unselfish love in ways I could never have imagined. You inspire me to be a better human being.

To my mother, Juanita Thomas; my brother Robert Jerome Thomas; and my sister, Kelesha Thomas Martin, thank you for loving me all these years. I know that sometimes it wasn't easy.

To Fagen, my companion and recently deceased miniature schnauzer. You sat with me each day as the words and sentences poured from me. Your spirit will live within me forever.

I thank God, my ancestors, and the wise ones—both seen and unseen—for walking with me on the path.

To anyone I hurt along the way, please forgive me.

Dad, I know your spirit watches over me.

Made in the USA
Charleston, SC
24 August 2012